Death and the regeneration of life

Death and the regeneration of life

Edited by

MAURICE BLOCH

Reader in Anthropology
London School of Economics

and

JONATHAN PARRY

Lecturer in Anthropology
London School of Economics

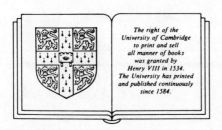

The right of the
University of Cambridge
to print and sell
all manner of books
was granted by
Henry VIII in 1534.
The University has printed
and published continuously
since 1584.

CAMBRIDGE UNIVERSITY PRESS

Cambridge
New York   Port Chester
Melbourne   Sydney

Published by the Press Syndicate of the University of Cambridge
The Pitt Building, Trumpington Street, Cambridge CB2 1RP
40 West 20th Street, New York, NY 10011, USA
10 Stamford Road, Oakleigh, Melbourne 3166, Australia

First published 1982
Reprinted 1986, 1987, 1989

Printed in the United States of America

Library of Congress catalogue card number: 82-9467
British Library cataloguing in publication data
Death and the regeneration of life.
1. Death
I. Bloch, Maurice   II. Parry, Jonathan
304 6'3 (expanded)   GN485.5

ISBN 0 521 24875 2 hard covers
ISBN 0 521 27037 5 paperback

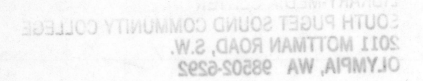

036638

Contents

Preface

Apart from the Introduction, all of the chapters in this book were originally presented as papers at an Intercollegiate seminar at the London School of Economics in the summer of 1980. In soliciting contributions we were aiming at a wide ethnographic spread; but we decided to confine ourselves to our London colleagues so that all the contributors would be able to attend regularly and discuss each other's papers. (Only one of the papers delivered at the seminar – that by Dr S. Humphreys – could unfortunately not be included in the present volume as it was already committed elsewhere.) Our collaboration was continued at a one-day meeting which brought the contributors together before they submitted their final drafts. Though this does not mean that we all share a single point of view, it does mean that all the papers were revised with the others in mind and with the benefit of comments and suggestions from fellow contributors. We hope that as a result this volume will display a unity not always found in collected works of this sort.

MAURICE BLOCH
JONATHAN PARRY

Notes on contributors

MAURICE BLOCH was born in 1939 in France. He took his BA at the London School of Economics and his PhD at Cambridge. He is currently Reader in Anthropology at the London School of Economics. He is the author of *Placing the dead* (1971) and the editor of *Political language and oratory in traditional societies* (1975), and *Marxist analyses in social anthropology* (1975).

OLIVIA HARRIS was born in 1948 in the UK. She studied at Oxford (MA) and the London School of Economics. She is currently Lecturer in Anthropology at Goldsmith's College, University of London. She is the author of various articles on the Laymi of Bolivia.

JOHN MIDDLETON was born in 1921 in the UK. He studied at the University of London (BA) and Oxford (DPhil). He was previously Professor of Anthropology at the School of Oriental and Asian Studies, University of London, and is currently Professor of Anthropology at Yale University. His numerous publications include *Tribes without rulers* (editor) (1958), *Lugbara religion* (1960), and *The Lugbara of Uganda* (1965).

JONATHAN PARRY was born in 1943 in the UK. He took his BA and PhD at the University of Cambridge. He is currently Lecturer in Anthropology at the London School of Economics. He is the author of *Caste and kinship in Kangra* (1979) and various articles on Indian society.

ANDREW STRATHERN was born in 1939 in the UK. He took his BA and PhD at the University of Cambridge. He is currently Professor of Anthropology at University College, London. His many publications include *The Rope of Moka* (1971) and *One father, one blood* (1972).

JAMES L. WATSON was born in 1943 in the USA. He received his PhD from the University of California, Berkeley. He is currently Lecturer in Asian Anthropology at the School of Oriental and African Studies, University of London. He is the author of *Emigration and the Chinese lineage* (1975), and the editor of *Between two cultures: migrants and minorities in Britain* (1977) and *Asian and African systems of slavery* (1980).

JAMES WOODBURN was born in 1934 in the UK. He took his MA and PhD at the University of Cambridge. He is currently Senior Lecturer in Social Anthropology at the London School of Economics. He is the author of various articles on the Hadza of Tanzania.

1 Introduction: death and the regeneration of life

MAURICE BLOCH and JONATHAN PARRY

Introduction

This volume focuses on the significance of symbols of fertility and rebirth in funeral rituals, though all the contributors have found it impossible to exclude consideration of many other aspects of the treatment of death which are related to this central theme.

While it would take us too far from our central concerns to embark on a systematic historical review of the various ways in which our problem has been approached in the literature of anthropology and related disciplines, a few preliminary remarks may help to place the collection in relation to some of its direct predecessors.

The observation that notions of fertility and sexuality often have a considerable prominence in funeral practices excited the attention of anthropologists and their public from the very beginning of the discipline. The Swiss anthropologist Bachofen was one of the first to pay any systematic attention to the topic in his *Versuch über Graber-symbolik der Alten* which was published in 1859 and parts of which have been translated into English under the title 'An essay on ancient mortuary symbolism' (in *Myth, religion and mother right*, Bachofen, 1967). His study was principally concerned with Greek and Roman symbolism, particularly as manifested in the Dionysian and Orphic mystery cults, and its starting point was the significance of eggs as symbols of fertility and femininity in some Roman tombs and in funerary games. The eggs were painted half-black and half-white, representing the passage of night and day and the rebirth of life after death. 'The funeral rite', Bachofen concludes, 'glorifies nature as a whole, with its twofold life and death giving principle . . . That is why the symbols of life are so frequent in the tomb . . . ' (p.39)

The theme was picked up by a number of subsequent writers. It became, for example, a central preoccupation of Frazer's *The golden bough* (1890) which more ponderously reviews the material on the ancient mystery cults considered by Bachofen. The key question here

1

is how killing can be a rite of fertility and renewal, and in particular how the killing of divine kings regenerates the fertility of the community. Although Frazer ranges widely, the extent to which his central ideas derive from classical examples is striking. What appears to be the fruit of cross-cultural comparison was in fact little more than an excursus on the ideas which inspired the Dionysian cults.

A comparable use of similar sources is to be found in Jane Harrison's influential *Themis* (1912), where the logic by which the mystery cults transformed death into birth is pursued much further, and where she goes beyond Frazer in discussing the significance of such symbolism as a way of linking the social order with the natural order. The combined impact of the works of Frazer and Harrison on literary circles in the first part of this century was considerable, as is well illustrated by the use made of the death and rebirth theme by Robert Graves in *The white goddess* and T. S. Eliot in *The waste land*. The irony is that – quite contrary to the spirit of Frazer and Harrison – Eliot used their work as justification for an antirationalist mystical point of view.

A discipline anxious to establish its academic respectability may well have been disposed to distance itself from the over-enthusiastic way in which its findings were sometimes used. But it was no doubt more directly because, by the 1940s, the central preoccupations of most anthropologists had moved away from a concern with systems of belief towards an emphasis on social morphology, that they subsequently seem to have shied away from any systematic consideration of the place of fertility in funerary symbolism. An exception here – more in tune with the spirit of an earlier generation – was Lord Raglan, on whom the influence of Hocart was formative and who was still preoccupied with the theme of the life-giving death of the divine king in a work published in 1945. Of course, specific ethnographic studies such as Evans-Pritchard's (1948) discussion of Shilluk kingship and G. Wilson's (1939) article on 'Nyakyusa conventions of burial' have a direct bearing on the issue, but it is no longer handled in the wide comparative manner characteristic of the earlier authors.

A quite different tradition concerned with the symbolism of death stems from Durkheim's pupil, Robert Hertz, whose 'Contribution to the study of the collective representation of death' was published in the 1905–6 volume of the *Année Sociologique* (English translation, 1960). Hertz knew of Frazer's work, and Harrison knew Hertz's essay. But neither seems to have been particularly influenced by the theories of their predecessor, to whose work they merely appeal for confirmation of the striking parallels between funerary and initiation rituals. The difference between Hertz's study and those of Bachofen and Frazer is both theoretical and ethnographic. Unlike these earlier writers, Hertz does not turn to Greece and Rome for his sources, but primarily to funerary cults of Malayo-Polynesian-speaking peoples. Although beliefs concerning the soul provide a key element in Hertz's argument, at the time it was written the informed reader – familiar with the works of other anthropologists like Tylor and Frazer and with those of folklorists and theologians – would probably have been struck by his comparative lack of attention to them. Nor was the link-up between death and sexuality given the same prominence as this was largely absent from his sources. The major symbolic themes on which Hertz elaborates are rather the characteristic South-East Asian contrast between the bones and the flesh, the pattern of double obsequies, and the parallels he discovers between the state of the corpse, the fate of the soul and the ritual condition of the mourners. It might in fact be argued that much the same criticism as we have made of Frazer would also apply to Hertz: that is, his general model was somewhat over narrowly related to the particular ethnographic material with which he started.

The central theoretical purpose of Hertz's essay is clear enough if we put it into the intellectual context in which it was written. The argument of the essay parallels his teacher Durkheim's famous study of *Suicide* (Durkheim, 1952; first published in 1897). Durkheim's main point was that although we think of suicide as a supremely individual and personal act, it also has a social and non-individual aspect; as is shown by the fact that different types of society produce different rates of suicide. This social aspect, argues Durkheim, can be studied in its own terms and suicide cannot be seen as a purely individual phenomenon. Hertz similarly chooses a topic which in the thought of his time was seen as peculiarly private and individual – the emotions aroused at the time of death. But 'death has not always been represented and felt as it is in our society' (Hertz, 1960:28); and following Durkheim's example, Hertz set out to show that these emotions – as well as the conception of death (for us occurring in an instant but for others a lengthy process) and the practices surrounding it – are in fact social and can be studied as sociological facts. Thus the detailed attention to the sequence of mortuary rites is intended to show how these rituals organise and orchestrate private emotions, a point which is illustrated with the example of weeping which, Hertz argues, is both institutionally governed and the manifestation of an emotion which appears falsely internal. As in the case of suicide, what had at first appeared as supremely individual, turns out to be the product of socially-constructed emotions and beliefs.

More than this, Hertz was concerned to emphasise that the problem

3

which has to be met at death stems from the fact that the deceased was not only a biological individual but a 'social being grafted upon the physical individual' whose 'destruction is tantamount to a sacrilege' against the social order (1960:77). 'Society' had to meet this threat by recuperating from the deceased what it had given of itself and regrafting it on to another host. There are thus two phases to the mortuary rituals: a phase of disaggregation (represented by the temporary disposal of the corpse) followed by a phase of reinstallation (represented by the secondary burial) from which the collectivity emerges triumphant over death. This dual process is mirrored in beliefs about the fate of the soul and the ritual condition of the mourners. It takes time for the collectivity to readjust to the death of one of its members, and this finds expression in the idea of a dangerous period when the departed soul is potentially malevolent and socially uncontrolled, and in the separation of the mourners from everyday life. The final ceremony, however, involves the reassertion of society manifested by the end of mourning and by the belief that the soul has been incorporated into the society of the dead and has settled down – in the same way as the collective consciousness of the living has been resettled by the funerary rituals. It is not, then, a matter of the fate of the soul determining the treatment of the corpse, but rather of the nature of society and the state of the collective conscience determining both the treatment of the corpse and the supposed condition of the soul.

The transfer of the soul from one social order to another (albeit imaginary) order is, however, invoked to explain the parallels between the symbolism of mortuary ceremonies, initiation rites and marriages; each of these involves a transfer in which a new social identity is grafted onto the individual. It is for this reason, Hertz argues, that funerals are double, not only overtly in the Indonesian and Malagasy examples considered, but also covertly in other cases. There are two jobs to be done: on the one hand a disaggregation of the individual from the collectivity, and on the other the re-establishment of society requiring a reallocation of the roles the deceased once occupied. Consistent with such an analysis, 'the death of a stranger, a slave, or a child will go almost unnoticed; it will arouse no emotion, occasion no ritual' (Hertz, 1960:76). Such individuals have not been fully incorporated into the social order, which therefore remains largely unmoved by their deaths for it is 'not as the extinction of animal life that death occasions social beliefs, sentiments and rites. . . . Since society has not yet given anything of itself to the (new-born) child, it is not affected by its disappearance and remains indifferent' (1960:76, 84) – thus illustrating once more the socially-determined nature of the emotional and ritual reactions to death.

Hertz's emphasis on the problem of reallocation necessitated by death led to much important work, such as Goody's (1962) analysis of the way in which the roles and property of a deceased LoDagaa are redistributed. But this focus has tended to take the discussion away from the relation between death and fertility symbolism, although Goody's own ethnographic evidence contains some intriguing information on the topic which might, we think, be worth a closer analysis.

The parallels which Hertz noted between death and other rites of passage were, of course, to be emphatically restated by Van Gennep (1909), though his analysis of funeral rituals was far less interesting. It is in relation to these parallels that Hertz's concerns briefly converge with those of Bachofen and Frazer. Every life-cycle ritual 'implies the passage from one group to another: an exclusion, i.e. a death, and a new integration, i.e. a rebirth' (Hertz, 1960:81). The rebirth which occurs at death is not only a denial of individual extinction but also a reassertion of society and a renewal of life and creative power – a position which is easily reconcilable with Frazer's.

The interests of both Frazer and Hertz are taken up in a recent book by Huntington and Metcalf (1979), though no new analytical framework is proposed and their intention is seemingly rather to stress what is valuable in a number of earlier contributions. Since they make no real attempt at a synthesis between the quite disparate theoretical approaches they draw upon, and do not consider the extent to which they are compatible with each other, the result is somewhat eclectic.

Both authors have worked in societies which display the classic Hertzian theme of the double funeral (Huntington in South Madagascar and Metcalf in Borneo), and it is for Hertz's analysis that they reserve their most fulsome praise. What is striking, however, is that their discussion of his essay almost totally ignores his central preoccupations with the social construction of emotion and with the relationship between the biological individual and the social collectivity. What they approvingly stress is rather the point of method he makes in emphasising the need to pay close attention to the treatment of the corpse, and the parallels he discovers between the state of the corpse and the fate of the soul. The particular example with which they choose to illustrate this last argument – the example of the Berawan of Borneo – is however shown to be rather equivocal; and we suspect that this might also be the case for other material on which Hertz relies. But while the matter was certainly important for Hertz, it is only a part of a much wider and more general thesis concerned with the non-individual nature of reactions to death.

More in line with the Frazer–Bachofen tradition, another central theme of Huntington and Metcalf's book is the way in which 'the life values of sexuality and fertility (often) dominate the symbolism of funerals'. The centre-piece of their discussion of this issue is provided by a fascinating and elegant analysis of the funerals of the Bara of southern Madagascar, and we shall return to their interpretation of this case later on. Their more general views on the connection between death and fertility are, however, less fully elaborated and seem to amount to little more than the observation – reminiscent of Frazer – that such symbolism is a reassertion of life in the face of death.

Sociological, symbolical and psychoanalytical interests all come together in Morin, 1970 (first edition 1951), and more recently in Thomas (1975); but both of these studies are intended as a critique of western ways of dealing with death and as a result are of a very different character to this book. Nonetheless several of the points which Thomas makes are re-echoed in our introduction, although for different ends.

The present collection follows Huntington and Metcalf in trying to combine the concerns of the two rather disparate traditions we have outlined. Like Frazer and Bachofen we are primarily interested in the way in which the symbolism of sexuality and fertility is used in the mortuary rituals; but with Hertz we share a concern with the social implications of mortuary practices, though not his view of society as an entity acting for itself. If we can speak of a reassertion of the social order at the time of death, this social order is a *product* of rituals of the kind we consider rather than their cause. In other words, it is not so much a question of Hertz's reified 'society' responding to the 'sacrilege' of death, as of the mortuary rituals themselves being an occasion for *creating* that 'society' as an apparently external force. It is therefore particularly important for us to consider cases, like the four hunter–gatherer societies discussed by Woodburn, where at best this ritual recreation of the social order occurs only in the most attenuated form.

We have tried to combine the two strands deriving from Frazer and Hertz in that to a greater or lesser extent each of our authors is interested not only in the cultural logic of the kind of symbolism which preoccupied Frazer, but also (and here we are more in step with the sociological orientation of Hertz) in seeing this symbolism in relation to the organisational aspects of the society in which it occurs. For us, sociological analysis and symbolical analysis are not alternatives but need to be combined – and this we attempt to do in the present essay.

While all the contributors to this volume have attempted to ground their analysis firmly in a specific cultural context, several of the papers are explicitly comparative – though in rather different ways. Thus we have comparisons between the death-related practices of different categories of people within the same society (Parry; chapter 3), between different societies of the same economic type (Woodburn; chapter 7) or of the same cultural region (Strathern; chapter 4), as well as a discussion of the logic behind the variability between mortuary symbolism in different types of social system (Bloch; chapter 8). But further than this, we would claim that our papers are sufficiently closely related as to be mutually illuminating and to invite parallels and a continual cross-referencing. In however cursory and inadequate a way, we shall endeavour in the rest of this introduction to direct the reader's attention to at least some of the general considerations which might emerge from such an exercise.

'Fertility' and the vision of life as a 'limited good'

At the outset we should make it clear that we do not use the term 'fertility' in any restricted or technical way, but in the dictionary sense of 'fecundity' or 'productiveness'. If death is often associated with a renewal of fertility, that which is renewed may either be the fecundity of people, or of animals and crops, or of all three. In most cases what would seem to be revitalised in funerary practices is that resource which is *culturally conceived* to be most essential to the reproduction of the social order.

The mortuary rituals of the four hunter–gatherer societies considered by Woodburn display little concern with ensuring the continuity of the human group itself, or the replacement of its personnel. The emphasis is rather on the group's ability to appropriate nature – an ability which is put in jeopardy by the birth, sexuality and death of humans and which is restored by such rituals as the *molimo* of the Mbuti and the *epeme* dances of the Hadza. Harris stresses that in Laymi ideology the value of land is paramount, while large families are disapproved of because they upset the balance between people and land. Consistent with this, it is agricultural rather than human fertility which is the primary value and which is elaborated upon in the mortuary rituals. The Merina world, by contrast, is premised on a total identification between specific groups of people and specific areas of land, and the fertility which is ensured by the proper combination of ancestral corpses and ancestral land is the generalised fertility of both

7

the group and its material means. In Strathern's Gimi example it is more a matter of reproducing the clan (which requires the mediation of the forest and the cannibalistic necrophagy of women). In the Hindu case discussed in this book, by contrast, we seem to be dealing in part with a more general notion which symbolically equates the funerary rites with the mystical regeneration, not of specific groups, nor merely of the deceased himself, but ultimately of the entire cosmos – a regeneration brought about by the 'sacrifice' that occurs on the cremation pyre.

The logic of Hindu sacrifice rests on the implicit assumption that a life must be relinquished if life is to be attained, and this in turn suggests that – from one point of view at least – life is seen as a 'limited good'. The papers by Bloch and Parry draw explicit attention to such a world view, which is also clearly implicit in several of Strathern's examples. Another obvious illustration is provided by Malinowski's (1948) discussion of Trobriand beliefs – according to which there would appear to be a given stock of souls in each sub-clan which is absolutely constant. On death the soul of a sub-clan member goes to Tuma, the island of the dead, where it settles down amongst its kin for another lifetime as a ghost. When it returns again to the land of the living it will find its way into the womb of a woman of its own sub-clan. Each sub-clan thus has a given quantum of soul-substance, some of which is contained in the living on Kiriwina while the rest is with the dead on Tuma.

It is not difficult to see – as Bloch points out – that this basic theme of life as a limited resource lends itself to various permutations. A more belligerent variant is to attempt to deny your enemies of their corpses in order to prevent them from recuperating the life-essence they contain (Bloch's 'negative predation'); while a further escalation would be a system of 'positive predation' in which you endeavour to appropriate to yourself the life-essence of others by killing them. The purpose of this may either be to enhance the vitality of the killers themselves (as in the Jivaro case) or the vitality of the non-human resources on which they depend, as is suggested by Barth's report (1975:151) that the killing of a Baktaman enemy promotes the growth of the taro.

It is clear that such conceptions imply that death is a source of life. Every death makes available a new potentiality for life, and one creature's loss is another's gain. The corollary, that the regeneration of life is a cause of death, is illustrated by our Hindu and New Guinea examples, where sexual relations (especially for the male) are seen as entailing a depletion of life-essence. But in the Daribi case (Strathern's paper) both sexes suffer. The man loses his 'juice' in ejaculation while a woman loses hers by breast-feeding; and this loss must be made good by eating meat, including the consumption of human flesh which is a 'way of supplementing one's vital juices' – (an example of 'positive predation' requiring an actual ingestion of the victim). The Etero provide a transformation on the same general theme: since sexual relations imply a transfer of life-essence, and since wives are disruptive outsiders, heterosexual intercourse is viewed as a somewhat prodigal activity. Male homosexual relations within the lineage on the other hand are approved, for they keep substance within the group and help young boys to grow. At this stage, however, the more general point we wish to stress is that there is a logical connection between the conception of life as a limited good and the idea that death and reproduction are inextricably related.

Given a world view of this kind it is therefore obvious why the rituals surrounding death should be so thoroughly permeated by the symbolism of rebirth. But such symbolism is, of course, by no means always associated with such a view of life, and at the most general level may be related to the fact that almost everywhere religious thought consistently denies the irreversible and terminal nature of death by proclaiming it a new beginning. Conception and birth are the most striking and obvious symbols available for asserting such a dogma. What complicates the matter, however, is that while the overwhelming majority of cultures deny that death is an individual extinction, the extent to which they use the symbolism of procreation to do so seems highly variable, and this variation needs to be accounted for. Moreover, biological reproduction – as we argue below – is a highly ambiguous symbol, and is often dramatically acted out in the mortuary rituals more as representative of something to be overcome than as an affirmation of regeneration.

Neither that which is regenerated nor the symbolic means by which the regeneration occurs can therefore be taken as self-evident. This must be examined in each case, and the answers must be seen in relation to the wider social and cultural context. It is only then that we can begin to account for the variation.

Death and the denial of duration

Leach (1961) has outlined what is essentially a sophistication of the argument about the way in which religious ideology uses the promise of rebirth to negate the finality of death. He suggests that our inherently ambiguous concept of time facilitates the assertion that birth comes after death as day comes after night. The category 'time' covers two quite different kinds of experience: time as repetitive and time as irreversible duration. By merging both kinds of experience within the same category we manage, Leach argues, to muddle them up and to avoid recognising irreversibility by assimilating it to repetition. As a result birth appears to follow death, just as death follows birth. ' . . . If it were not for religion we should not attempt to embrace the two aspects of time under one category at all. Repetitive and non-repetitive acts are not, after all, logically the same.' In the paired essay, Leach discusses the way in which time is created by festivals which act as the boundary-markers by which duration is divided. 'We talk of measuring time, as if time were a concrete thing waiting to be measured; but in fact we *create time* by creating intervals in social life' (1961:135). The relationship between Leach's theory of taboo (Leach, 1966*a*) and the idea that festivals serve to carve up the naturally continuous world into discontinuous chunks is obviously close.

In one way or another this interest in the relationship between concepts of time and death recurs throughout this volume. In the Laymi case it is the festivals of the dead which mark out the agricultural cycle and divide the year between a period of household production and a period of communal consumption. While people toil the ancestors are on holiday in the world of the living. But after the First Fruits ceremony, when their descendants are liberated from their labours for a period of leisure and conviviality, the dead must return to the cultivation of red chillis in the inverted world of Tacna over the sea. Death itself is unpredictable (its unpredictability being symbolised by the games of chance played during the final preparations for the interment) and this aspect is stressed in order to represent the irreversibility of time. The spirits of the recently dead are similarly unpredictable. But these capricious spirits are tamed by a series of rituals, so that at the festival of All Saints, which initiates the agricultural year, they can – as it were – be socialised into a source of potential recurrent fertility. While death as an event may defy all regularity, the dead are eventually incorporated into the predictable cycle of the year and are harnessed (however imperfectly) to the reproduction of social life. In this way – as Leach's argument would imply and as Harris suggests – the discontinuous is ultimately merged with the cyclic; and death is consequently transformed into a process which is essential for the continuation of life.

For Leach the problem with duration is that it implies the irreversibility of individual death, and is therefore psychologically unpalatable.

By contrast, the emphasis in Bloch's contribution to this volume is rather that duration and the contingency of events (as manifested pre-eminently in death) present a problem – not of individual psychology – but of an essentially political nature to do with the legitimation of traditional authority. In such systems positions of authority are conceptualised as belonging to an eternal and unchanging order, and their inviolability is therefore premised on a denial of history. It is thus that things have always been and must always remain. But individuality and the flow of events pose a problem for this theoretically static world and a threat to its continuity in that different role holders are patently different and the social order is not eternal. Both must consequently be negated. As one might expect, the funeral is one of the principal means by which this negation occurs (Thomas, 1975:178). The mechanism involved consists in a radical devaluation of the deceased's individuality by identifying this with putrescence and pollution 'which are elaborately constructed because once constructed they can be expelled'. But the mortuary rituals do not leave it at that. Having as far as possible erased individuality, they reassert continuity by equating death with birth into the de-personalised collectivity of ancestors which is the source of the continuing fertility of the living. The denial of ideologically threatening duration is thus accomplished by a denial 'of the main discontinuous processes in the social group, i.e. death'. Where we find the classic Hertzian pattern of double obsequies, the first disposal is associated with the time-bound individual and the polluting aspects of death, and the second with the regenerative aspects which re-create the permanent order on which traditional authority is based.

Middleton's paper also relates the themes of death, time and the legitimation of the social order. A central opposition in Lugbara thought is that between the 'home' (the domain of controlled fertility, presided over by male authority represented by the symbol of ordered speech) and the wild 'bushland' (the domain of uncontrolled sexuality and power, identified with barren female eroticism). Death comes in from the wilderness. Associated with this dichotomy are two different kinds of time. In Middleton's terminology, 'duration' governs the world of the home. 'Order, hierarchy and authority are associated with and sanctioned by differences in genealogical generation and by age', and thus depend on the passing of time. But the wild exists in a timeless vacuum in which there is no duration, change or growth, and which lacks order, fertility and hierarchical authority (as opposed to uncontrolled power). With the passing of generations the dead will eventually move into the timelessness of the wild and cease to exercise authority. But in the meantime the main concern of funerary rituals – of important men at least – is to hang on to the 'soul' which is the durational authoritative aspect of the person and which is installed in a shrine at the very centre of the home, while getting rid of the 'spirit' which is the 'timeless' wild aspect.

At first sight this situation might appear to be quite at odds with the line of argument which Bloch develops. While Bloch stresses the theoretically 'timeless' character of the Merina descent group and sees 'duration' as a threat to legitimate authority, Middleton seems to be describing a situation in which the 'durational' time of the home and the shrine is at the heart of authority, while the 'timelessness' of the wild is associated with the lack of it. The difference, however, is more apparent than real. What underlies the Lugbara concept of 'duration' is the idea of seniority, which legitimates the authority of the elders and thus maintains the continuity of the lineage. By contrast, the 'timeless-ness' which the Lugbara associate with the wild implies a lack of continuity and hence the absence of properly constituted authority – which is precisely what lies behind the Merinas' determined denial of discontinuity. The two cases are therefore more analogous than they might appear, the illusion of dissimilarity being largely the product of the ethnographers' discrepant use of English words. The essential point is that in both instances legitimate authority is founded on the orderly and faithful replication of the pattern ordained by the ances-tors. What lies outside this orderly world, but threatens to engulf it, is unrestrained and insubordinate individuality – which the Merina identify with biological birth and death, and which the Lugbara identify with the non-procreative sexuality of women as opposed to their controlled fertility under the proper supervision of responsible men.

In one way or another the funerary rituals of each of the three societies we have considered so far in this section attempt to negate the unpredictability of death, for – as we would see it – an uncontrolled event of such centrality puts in question the extent to which the social order can really govern the lives of its members. The most threatening quality of death commonly appears to be its aleatory character (a sentiment from which we ourselves are to some extent distanced by the fact that we live in an environment where – for the first time in human history – survival to old age has become the norm). The symbolic negation of the apparent arbitrariness of death is, however, often accomplished by a rhetorical emphasis on what is being denied – as, for example in the case of Laymi gambling.

This endeavour to control the contingency of death is highlighted by

the commonly encountered discrepancy between the event of physical death and the social recognition of it. After the Lugbara has said his last words to his heir, the latter emerges from the hut in which they have been closeted and calls out the *cere* – the personal chant – of the dying man, an appropriation which would be unthinkably evil at other times. This marks the moment of succession; and even if the patient lingers on after it, he is socially dead and his mortuary rites are performed as if he were dead. In the case of the rain-maker, the discontinuity between physical and socially-recognised death is likely to be very much more pronounced. He undergoes death – including a symbolic burial – at the time of his initiation, and when he is physically dead his corpse is interred at night and in silence, in a manner which is quite different from normal burial and which seems to approximate to the mere disposal of a carcass. An even more extreme example is provided by the Dogon (Paulme, 1940) where in some cases funerary rites are performed for people who are presumed to be, but in fact are not, dead. When this occurs, and the 'dead' man returns, not even his closest kin will recognise him and he is forced to remain a nameless beggar until his physiological death.

All this is strikingly paralleled by the Indian case. The Hindu *ascetic*, who performs his own funerary rites at the time of his initiation, henceforth exists in the world as a wandering ghost, and his corpse is not cremated but simply immersed in the Ganges. The effigy of a missing person who is presumed dead will be cremated, and his subsequent mortuary rituals performed. If he then reappears, he does so as an intrusive ghost who has no place in the world of the living, and (in theory) nobody at all will eat with him. In all these examples the social recognition of death precedes the physical event. But in the case of the Hindu *householder* this order is (with the exception just noted) reversed. The message encoded in the cremation rituals of one who has died 'properly' is that death 'really' occurs mid-way through the cremation when the chief mourner cracks open the deceased's skull with a bamboo stave in order to release the 'vital breath' from the body, and it is at this point that death pollution is commonly said to begin. The same sequence recurs in the case of those who have died a 'bad' or 'untimely' death. Here too an effigy of the deceased is constructed; a piece of lighted camphor is placed in its navel, and it is only when the flame burns itself out that the deceased is regarded as truly dead. Again this ritual performance discounts the actual physiological death and re-runs the event so that it conforms to the ideal of a controlled release of life.

The conquest of time is – on Parry's analysis – a central concern of both the mortuary rituals of the Hindu householder and the practices of the Aghori ascetic, though the two cases deny duration in rather different ways. The ideal Aghori lives on the cremation ground, consumes his food from a human skull, eats excrement and the putrid flesh of corpses, consorts with menstruating prostitutes, and in other respects too inverts the proper order. Parry argues that all this represents a systematic attempt to escape from time, and hence from death. By systematically combining opposites the Aghori recaptures a primordial and static condition of non-duality, and identifies himself with Lord Siva, who transcends time. Like the Lugbara prophet, he does not die; he attains *samadhi*, a perpetual state of deep meditation or suspended animation in which he is immune from the normal consequences of death.

In the case of the Aghori ascetic, time is – as it were – halted. The ideal death of the householder in the sacred city of Benares suggests, however, a different kind of victory over events. Firstly, the person who has gone to Benares before his death has *chosen* to die in a particular place at a particular time, unlike those who are caught unaware by untimely death. Secondly, the symbolism of cremation aligns death with a perpetual cyclic renewal of time; for every cremation in Benares may be seen as an act of self-sacrifice which re-enacts the original cosmogonic sacrifice, and rekindles the fires of creation at the very spot where creation began. Consistent with this, Benares is seen as immune to the ravages of time and exists perpetually in the Golden Age of origins, while the rest of the world has progressively run down into the Black Age of the *Kali Yuga* (Parry, 1981).

To the non-Indianist such concepts may at first perhaps appear arcane and culturally specific. But our own cultural background provides us with a parallel which is not after all so remote. The cremation ground at Manikarnika *ghāt*, which is the navel of the cosmos and the scene of its original creation, may be likened to Golgotha, which has often been represented not only as the site of Christ's crucifixion, but also as the centre of the world where Adam was created and buried. The blood of the Saviour falls on the skull of Adam interred at the foot of the Cross, and redeems him and mankind (Eliade, 1965:14).

> We thinke that Paradise and Calvarie,
> Christs Crosse, and Adams tree, stood in one place;
> Looke Lord, and finde both Adams met in me;
> As the first Adams sweat surrounds my face,
> May the last Adams blood my soule embrace.
>
> (John Donne, Hyme to God my God, in my sickness)

Here again, then, death becomes an act of universal regeneration, which renews time and which is performed at the centre of the world, the place of original cosmogony (Parry, 1981) – a death that is regularly re-enacted in the ritual of the Mass.

It is evident, then, that individuality and unrepeatable time are problems which must be overcome if the social order is to be represented as eternal. Both are characteristically denied by the mortuary rituals which, by representing death as part of a cyclical process of renewal, become one of the most important occasions for asserting this eternal order. But in contemporary western cultures the individual is given a transcendental value, the ideological stress is on his unique and *unrepeatable* biography, and he is conceived of in opposition to society and his death is therefore not a challenge to its continuity. Moreover, while man's nature may be seen as immutable, the existing social order is not. It is therefore not surprising that in this context the symbolic connection between death and fertility should be far more weakly stressed than it is in the cases we have considered here. Other aspects of the ideology preclude any such elaboration, or render it superfluous.

'Good' and 'bad' death

Both the impulse to determine the time and place of death, and the dissociation of social death from the termination of bodily function, clearly represent an attempt to control the unpredictable nature of biological death and hence dramatise the victory of order over biology. The specificity and contingency of the event itself is suppressed so that death can be represented as part of a repetitive cyclical order. The 'good' death is thus the one which suggests some degree of mastery over the arbitrariness of the biological occurrence by replicating a prototype to which all such deaths conform, and which can therefore be seen as an instance of a general pattern necessary for the reproduction of life. By contrast, in nearly all of our examples, those deaths which most clearly demonstrate the absence of control are those which are represented as 'bad' deaths and which do not result in regeneration (Thomas, 1975:192).

For the Merina there is no worse nightmare than that one's body will be lost so that it cannot enter into the communal tomb, since the secondary burial of the corpse not only recharges the fertility of the descent group and its land, but also rescues the deceased himself from complete obliteration. Without this reburial not only is a potential source of regeneration lost to the group, but the death of the individual is truly terminal.

15

Maurice Bloch and Jonathan Parry

In the Lugbara case the 'good' death is that which occurs in the home, the place of the shrines of the ancestors and of legitimate authority represented by the symbol of speech. The dying man must speak clearly to his heir, who then marks his orderly succession by taking over the personal chant of the moribund. In this way the proper order of the lineage is maintained in the locality where the lineage is anchored and continuity is guaranteed by the smooth transfer of authority. 'Bad' death on the other hand occurs at the wrong place, away from the ancestral shrines to which the deceased's soul cannot therefore easily return; and at the wrong time so that the orderly succession of speech cannot occur. The regenerating element of the dead man is lost in its antithesis, the disorganised wild.

Again, for the pious Hindu the 'good' death is that of the man who, having fulfilled his duties on this earth, renounces his body (as the ascetic has earlier renounced his) by dying at the right place and the right time, and by making of it a sacrifice to the gods. 'Bad' death, by contrast, is the death of the person who is caught short, his body still full of excrement, and his duties unfinished. It is the death of one whose youthfulness belies the likelihood of a conscious and voluntary renunciation of life, or of one whose body is contaminated by a disease which makes it unfit as a life-creating sacrifice.

In all these examples the 'good' death not only promises a rebirth for the individual but also a renewal of the world of the living; while the 'bad' death represents the loss of regenerative potential. But in some cases a 'bad' death is not merely a lost potential for, but is an actual threat to, fertility. The Laymi can harness an ordinary death to the agricultural cycle, but the death of an unbaptised infant is positively harmful for the crops. The point is particularly well illustrated by the famous case of the Dinka Spearmaster (Lienhardt, 1961). The 'proper' death of the Spearmaster – at which he presides over his own burial alive – robs death of its contingency, and is an occasion for joy at which there must be no mourning. Such a death enhances the fertility and prosperity of the community of which he is the embodiment. On the other hand famine results if he is taken by death rather than his taking it.

This last example brings us to a consideration of what in a great many cultures is the supreme example of 'bad' death – the suicide, whose self-destruction is regarded with such incomparable horror that the soul may forever be excluded from the society of the dead and must wander the earth as a lonely and malignant ghost, while the corpse may not be accorded the normal rites of disposal (as in Christian cultures where it could not traditionally be buried in consecrated

16

ground). This total rejection of the self-inflicted death might at first sight appear to represent a marked contrast to those cases – like that of the Dinka Spearmaster or the pious Hindu – where death must appear to have been chosen. However, the apparent difference is superficial and it is quite possible for both conceptions to coexist. In the Hindu case, for example, suicide is also the bad death *par excellence*, and is conceptualised as something quite different from the voluntary renunciation of life which is the 'good' death. While the one is a surrender to the disappointed desires of life and thus evinces an acute involvement with the material world, the other stems from *absence* of desire for life and a calm indifference to mundane existence. The 'good' death – whether we consider the Hindu case or that of the Merina or Lugbara – is a kind of handing over of a vitality which can then be recycled. In this way it recalls the supreme altruistic gift of the Christian martyr, or even of Christ himself, by whose death life is supposedly renewed. By contrast, the suicide acts for himself alone, and loses for others his regenerative power.

In spite of this clear ideological difference between suicide and self-sacrifice, the categorisation of any particular instance is not always unambiguous. While from one point of view the hunger-striker sacrifices himself for the cause, the authorities present his death as suicide. Indeed we would suggest that what feeds the horror with which suicide is so often regarded is that it is an act which, by its apparent similarity, almost parodies the death which is the ultimate manifestation of altruistic self-abnegation.

A further ambiguity may arise over whether any given death was 'good' or 'bad'. Even though in principle the distinction between them may be sharply drawn, in practice it is not always possible to be entirely confident about the case in hand. Despite the most fastidious endeavours, a mistake of ritual detail may have nullified the efficacy of the rites by which the rebirth of the deceased is guaranteed; while the mourners' actual experience is likely to tell them that the death they mourn fell some way short of the perfect case represented in the ideology. In almost every instance there remains a place for the suspicion that the victory over discontinuity which is acted out in the mortuary rites is an illusory one, and that death has not been successfully harnessed to the cycle of regeneration.

The uncertainty which surrounds death is also manifest in the existence of a number of beliefs which are different and even contradictory to the central ones – (for example, the belief in ghosts in Christian Europe). Such beliefs are usually less elaborated and less emphatic, but their occurrence is extremely common and is illustrated

17

Maurice Bloch and Jonathan Parry

by the Hindu, Chinese, Laymi, Merina and !Kung examples in the book. This inconsistency stems in part, we suggest, from the way in which death is transformed into regeneration by acting out a victory over (and thus giving recognition to) the finality and uncontrollability of death. The 'good' regenerative death can only be constructed in antithesis to an image of 'bad' death, which it therefore implies. It requires and must even emphasise what it denies, and cannot obliterate that on which it feeds. We have already alluded to this antithetical process in our discussion of time, and it will emerge much more clearly in the sections which follow. All we wish to propose here is that since the dominant ideological representation is created out of its contrary, the negative aspects of death are accorded a prominence which it is hard to entirely erase. As a result, that which is asserted by the central ideology is unlikely to appear as a complete cosmology, and thus allows space for the elaboration of all sorts of subsidiary beliefs which are inconsistent with it.

Fertility and female sexuality

We have noted above that sexuality in general – and female sexuality in particular – is often seen as the cause of death; and also that the fertility which is regenerated by the mortuary rites may be either human or natural (or both). In order to push the analysis further we need to examine some of the ways in which these various elements – death, female sexuality, human reproduction and natural fertility – may be combined. More specifically, we must examine the fact that female sexuality is often associated with death only to be *opposed* to the 'real' fount of human and natural creativity; and that sexuality may be seen as the source of death and human procreation, which stands in opposition to non-human fertility.

The Judaeo–Christian tradition provides an example of this second possibility. In this tradition, it is the temptation of Eve which brings death into the world and results in the expulsion from Paradise, where the bounty of God's creation had provisioned the primeval couple without any significant effort on their part. But when they sinned against God's ordinance, God cursed Eve: 'I will greatly multiply thy sorrow and thy conception; in sorrow thou shalt bring forth children ...' (Genesis 3:16). Adam's punishment, however, was that the ground was cursed so that it brought forth thorns and thistles, and 'in the sweat of the face shalt thou eat bread'. He was then banished 'to till the ground from whence he was taken' (Genesis 3:17–23). Although sexuality (initiated by woman) results in human fertility, this contrasts with the divine asexual fertility of Eden, is intrinsically flawed and is accompanied by death and a decline of natural fertility. Human and natural fertility are thus opposed to each other.

Much the same idea seems to be present in two of Woodburn's examples. For the Hadza, female reproduction is mystically incompatible with hunting big game: if the hunter's wife is menstruating the poison of his arrows loses its efficacy, and if she is pregnant a wounded animal will recover from its wounds. Again, for the Baka a pregnancy or death amongst the clanspeople of the same camp will ruin the hunt, until – intriguingly – the identity of the pregnant woman or dead person is known. Here again, then, human fertility is in some way antithetical to man's appropriation of nature.

In other instances the biological fact that human reproduction is the consequence of human sexuality is suppressed, or even denied, by the way in which creativity is ritually represented. So while Huntington and Metcalf – like Frazer before them – take commonsense as their guide and assume that the sexuality which is enacted in the mortuary rites must be a symbolic regeneration of life, we would perversely suggest that sexuality may be ritually elaborated as something to be overcome as antithetical to fertility. By this we do not intend to resurrect the old controversy over whether all peoples are aware of the connection between copulation and conception. Our point is rather the one suggested by Leach's (1966b) discussion of 'Virgin birth'; symbolic representations may totally transform what is perceived in other contexts. That is, the dissociation of fertility from sexuality is dramatically established by ritual in a way which denies what we and they know of biology. This disjunction is often effected by using gender symbolism to concretise the hierarchical contrast. Sexuality is set in opposition to fertility as women are opposed to men.

Again the Lugbara case provides us with an illustration. We have already noted that here the untamed sexuality of women is identified with the dangerous, socially-unproductive wild. This contrasts with the fertility associated with the compound, the ancestral shrine, and the authority of elders – a sacred ancestral fertility controlled by men in which women would appear to be but passive partners. What is more, it is not only female sexuality which belongs in the bushland but also parturition, for during her labour a woman is surrounded by taboos which symbolically remove her hut from the settlement and relocate it in the wild. It is not until the biological process has been disposed of that the new-born child can be introduced into the social world as a gift

19

made by the elders by virtue of their control over the source of *legitimate* fertility. Sexuality, biological birth and death are made to represent an intrusion of the wild, the natural sphere of women – an intrusion acted out in the unrestrained and orgiastic sexual pairing which occurs *outside* the homestead during the death dances and which *cannot* result in conception. Consistent with all this, the Lugbara myth of the origin of death (and also incidentally of the origin of social division) places the blame squarely on a woman, who cut the rope (or tree) by which men could return to converse with Divinity.

In such a context it would be wholly misleading to interpret the symbolism of sexuality in terms of a regeneration of fertility. But this, we suggest, is precisely the flaw in Huntington's striking and suggestive discussion of the funerary rituals of the Bara of southern Madagascar (Huntington, 1973; Huntington and Metcalf, 1979:98–118). Life for the Bara, Huntington argues, is a precarious balance between the sterile forces of 'order' associated with bone derived from the father, and the chaotic forces of 'vitality' associated with flesh derived from the mother. In death the balance is upset: the corpse is reduced to bone, order and sterility; and the purpose of the mortuary rituals is to restore the equilibrium 'through a symbolic increase in vitality' induced by unrestrained sexuality. So on this analysis the roles of women, flesh and orgiastic sexuality in the mortuary rituals are as agents of a regeneration brought about by the restoration of the female components of the person.

In the light of this interpretation it is perhaps surprising to find that the first and temporary burial of the corpse is clearly intended to effect a complete separation of the bones from the flesh, and that once exhumed the bones must be cleansed of any residue. If, in other words, the object is to restore the female element, it seems somewhat paradoxical to insist on the complete elimination of the flesh (the quintessentially female component of the person) – the more so since in other Malagasy societies (like the Merina) we find that people go to some lengths to retain *both* the bones and the flesh (in the form of the dust of the corpse).

It is, incidentally, tempting to see this variation as associated with the fact that the Bara stress exogamy while the Merina stress endogamy. More generally, it would seem that those systems which make a distinction between kin and affines are the ones which are likely to pick up on the common contrast between male bones and female flesh, and to be concerned to separate them at death (e.g. the Bara and the Chinese example discussed here); while those systems which allow no such distinction and which stress endogamy as an ideal are much more likely to be concerned with the corpse as a whole (e.g. the Merina and the Laymi of pre-Catholic times).

Another interpretation of the Bara data, more consistent with this aspect of their mortuary practice and more in line with the case we are arguing, is however possible. Immediately after death two huts are cleared: one for the men and one for the women (from which males are rigorously excluded). The corpse is secluded in the latter for a period of three days and two nights. During the daytime the people mourn, while the nights are given over to promiscuous sexual pairing initiated by the erotic dancing and provocative singing of the girls – behaviour which would be completely unacceptable to the Bara at other times. This period is terminated by what Huntington describes as a 'burial by capture'. The men go to the women's hut and forcibly remove the corpse over the anguished protests of the female mourners. Relays of young men run with the coffin towards the mountain of the ancestors, pursued by a group of young girls – hair dishevelled and clothes in disarray – who try to hinder their progress.

Often the girls intervene physically to stop the journey to the tomb and there ensues a tug-of-war over the coffin as the girls try to pull it back to the village. When this fails, the girls may run ahead and line up across the boys' path. The boys charge, using the coffin as a battering ram to penetrate this female barrier and continue toward the tomb. (Huntington and Metcalf, 1979:115–6)

Having reached the tomb, the deceased is reborn (head first like a foetus) into the world of the ancestors.

All this suggests a ritual drama in which women are given the role of an unacceptable obscene sexuality, in which they deliberately endeavour to implicate men, which takes place at night and which must be broken through during the day – as the obstructive cordon of girls must be broken through – in order to attain a proper rebirth into the world of the ancestors. In other words, it is the necessary defeat of women, sexuality and biology which is enacted, rather than their indispensable part in the re-creation of life. In this case then – as with the Lugbara – sexuality is, we suggest, opposed to fertility. It is associated with flesh, decomposition and women, while true ancestral fertility is a mystical process symbolised by the tomb and the (male) bones. Consistent with this ultimate repudiation of sexuality is the fact that a Bara woman is buried in her father's tomb and never in her husband's (Huntington and Metcalf, 1979:107). As with the Dobuan case, which we will consider later on, the final triumph over death is also a triumph over the necessity for affines and over the world of sexual reproduction which they represent.

Maurice Bloch and Jonathan Parry

Women and putrescence

On our analysis, then, the symbolism of the mortuary rites of the Bara and Lugbara identifies women with sexuality, and sexuality with death. Victory over death – its conversion into rebirth – is symbolically achieved by a victory over female sexuality and the world of women, who are made to bear the ultimate responsibility for the negative aspects of death. In line with this, the sexuality of women is often closely associated with the putrescence of the corpse as, for example, Pina-Cabral's (1980) fascinating discussion of the cults of the dead in contemporary North-western Portugal shows.

Here the flesh (as metonym for the body) is what binds the soul to the mundane world, and its corruption is a necessary step towards spiritual purification. Three or four years after the burial the grave is opened and the bones are cleaned in order to rid them of the flesh, thus marking the final separation of the deceased from the living. But sometimes (surprisingly often) the disinterred corpse has not decomposed. There are two possible interpretations of this. The first, favoured by the priests, is that the deceased must have died with a large burden of unexpiated sin. This calls for a ritual 'lifting of excommunication' which consists of whipping the corpse while reciting prayers so as to unify him (or her) with the body of the church – (the incorrupt flesh being the material manifestation of his exclusion from it) – and to allow the soul to go to heaven. The laity, however, generally interpret an incorrupt corpse as an indication of sainthood, and if the body is reburied after the ritual whipping and still does not decompose, then the popular view is held to have been vindicated and the priests will be forced to take it seriously.

The significance of this material for our argument is that the female corpses which are found to be incorrupt – or at least those amongst them which eventually come to be venerated – are the corpses of women who are held to have been paragons of sexual purity. (The incorruption of male corpses, by contrast, is attributed to exemplary social and economic behaviour.) The parallel here is with the Blessed Virgin whose Assumption was in corporeal form, and whose ascent to heaven was not conditional on the decomposition of her immaculately conceived and virginally intact body. It could hardly be clearer that it is women's sexuality which causes the corruption of their flesh. Putrescence is a consequence of concupiscence, and an eternal preservation of the body is the reward of those who renounce its pleasures.

This association between (female) sexuality and decomposition is implicit in several of the case studies provided in this book. One of the

22

most remarkable features of Watson's Chinese material is the extent to which the corpse itself is an object of terror and its putrescence is the source of severe pollution. It is even said that marauding brigands have been kept at bay by the false report of a death in the village. The first burial allows the flesh to rot away, and when the body is later disinterred the bones are meticulously cleaned of the last vestiges of flesh before being reburied. Once this has happened the bones emanate a power which, if properly tapped, promotes the fertility of the descendants.[1] It is, as one might by now expect, the men who handle this aspect of matters, while the married women (as opposed to unmarried girls) are crucial in the ritual sequence dealing with the putrescent flesh – from which the men absent themselves if they possibly can. True they have some excuse, for a man's male essence (*yang*) is depleted every time he handles a corpse, and by the seventh occasion he is permanently polluted, while a women is not affected in the same way. The hair is absorbent, like blotting-paper, and the women rub their hair on the coffin 'out of respect' – thus symbolically soaking up the pollution of the decaying flesh. In other terms, what seems to be happening is that at death the women reabsorb the flesh that is their contribution to the child at birth, and Watson demonstrates that this in turn renews their powers as biological reproducers.

Both the theme of a particular affinity between women and rotting corpses, and an ambivalence about biological reproduction similar to the one we have encountered elsewhere, are worked through with emphasis in Gimi culture as Strathern's paper shows. 'Out of compassion' the women short-circuit the normal process of putrescence by consuming the flesh of a deceased male, thus freeing his spirit to return to the pre-eminently male domain of the rain forest which is ideologically represented as the source of productivity in the Gimi universe, and which is the abode of the ancestral spirits who 'collectively constitute a forest reservoir from which emerges the animating life-force of new generations' (Gillison, 1980:154). The recycled spirit is redeposited in women by men so that they may nurture it, but special ritual measures must be taken to force them to relinquish it at the proper time, for 'the female tends permanently to retain and in that way destroy (i.e. reabsorb) what she nourishes' (Gillison, 1980:148).

In a number of ways we are dealing with a complex set of representations which endeavour to overcome the spectre of a tyrannous biology. Not only is the good death a controlled release of life and copulation an insufficient cause of procreation, but even birth itself is (as in the Gimi case) induced by male authority, or (as in our

Lugbara example) represented as an act of patriarchal benevolence to which the mother's travail in the 'wild' of the confinement hut is seemingly little more than a regrettable prelude. In this attempt to master the world of biology, gender symbolism often provides – we have suggested – the crucial mechanism. Fertility is separated from and made superior to the biological processes of sex and birth by analogy with the taken-for-granted difference between the sexes.

Bloch outlines a very general model in terms of which these various elements are combined, though his discussion starts out from the specifics of the Merina case. Merina women are identified with the domestic sphere of the household, the individual interests of which are seen as a threat to the unity of the undivided deme. In the rituals women are thus given the dramatic task of representing the divisions which are to be overcome. Consistent with our earlier discussion of the deceased as representative of individuality and duration, it therefore makes perfect sense in terms of Merina cultural logic that women should be associated with the polluting world of the time-bound individual with which the first funeral is concerned, and which must be transcended by the second burial. This transcendence is demonstrated by the elaborate assault on the world of women which occurs during this ceremony, when the de-personalised ancestor is incorporated into the collective tomb which is the source of pure fertility. A similarly antagonistic dichotomy applies to birth: physical birth – which is represented as an exclusively female activity – is polluting, and is subsequently transcended by the circumcision ceremony at which the child is torn away from the divisive and impure world of women to be reborn into the pure and undivided world of the descent group. Merina women may thus be said to act as representatives of that aspect of people which must be removed (biology and individuality) and are therefore associated with the decomposition of the corpse and the pollution which this causes. They take upon themselves the negative aspects of death and act as the defeated protagonists in a mock battle from which rebirth and fertility emerge victorious.

In this case it is the undifferentiated category of women which is associated with the pollution of the corpse. Among the Cantonese, however, this role is given only to married women; while elsewhere a distinction is drawn between women as daughters and sisters, and women as wives and mothers. In Ngubane's (1976) discussion of the Zulu, for example, we find that the chief mourner is always a married woman, who is aided by other married women of the lineage. The ethnography again reveals the association between, and devaluation of, biological birth and biological death, for it is almost as if she is made to give birth to the corpse.

When a widow delivers a corpse to the lineage men at the doorway, her action represents delivering a baby to the lineage at birth. The corpse is tied up in such a manner that it more or less represents a foetus in the womb – with its knees and arms bent up. The hut in which the corpse and the mourners are, symbolizes the confinement hut as well as the womb itself ... Having delivered the corpse to the men, in a dramatization of birth, soon afterwards the conception is dramatized, when the chief mourner enters the round hole (representing the womb), receives the corpse from the lineage men and places it in the niche – to be born into the other world. (Ngubane, 1976)

In terms of the present discussion, the really significant point is that among the Zulu it is as wives and mothers that women are associated with negative polluting mystical forces, while as daughters and sisters they deal as diviners with positive mystical forces. It is tempting to see the significant variables here as exogamy, versus the endogamy of the Merina who do not in the matter of mourning significantly discriminate between different categories of women.

While an intimate association between women and the pollution of death appears to be extremely widespread it is not universal. It is absent from the South American Laymi case where the ideology continually stresses, not the subordination of one sex to the other, but rather their parallelism and complementarity. Nor would it seem to be a particularly prominent feature of the Hindu mortuary rituals – which is perhaps partly to be explained by the fact that here there are Untouchables, low-grade Funeral Priests and other specialists to shoulder the burden that is elsewhere assumed by women (Parry, 1980). Even where pollution is as far as possible off-loaded on the women, they are not of course the only ones to be infected by it. In our Cantonese case, for example, it is also absorbed and removed by the funeral specialists (who are paid for their pains), and by the direct heirs of the deceased (whose recompense is explicitly conceptualised as a share in the inheritance proportionate to the amount of pollution they soak up).

But whether or not putrescence is associated with women, an apparently superfluous emphasis on its horrors is common to a wide range of different kinds of society. This highlighting of decomposition is particularly striking in the case of the Cantonese with their endless insistence on averting their gaze from the corpse at critical junctures of the ritual. During the second burial the Merina display an uncompromising determination to force the participants into the closest possible proximity to the terrifying decomposed corpses. Again, the theme of decomposition seems to have held a particular fascination for the western European mind during the late Mediaeval period – witness those funerary monuments which not only represent the putrescent corpse but for good measure also remind us of the worms wriggling in and out of it. But no more dramatic instance of this luxuriance in putrescence is perhaps to be found than that of the Aghori ascetics who live on the cremation grounds and consume their food out of human skulls.

It is, of course, obvious that such symbolism provides a potent warning against the vanities of the flesh and the transience of the sensual world – a denigration of the world of the senses which is particularly clear in the Aghori case, but which also seems to underlie the fifteenth and sixteenth century European fascination with decomposition which Huizinga (1965:136) suggestively describes as 'a spasmodic reaction against excessive sensuality'.

It is, however, to a different aspect of this hyperbolical elaboration that we would draw particular attention here. In all these systems death is harnessed to the cycle of regeneration and converted into birth. One of the key ways, we suggest, by which this restitution of life is dramatised is by the elaborate construction, and subsequent negation, of its antithesis – decomposition and decay. An emphasis on biological processes is used to darken the background against which the ultimate triumph over biology (and hence over death) can shine forth all the more brightly. This is perhaps clearest in the two Malagasy cases we have cited, where that which is to be overcome is carefully set up in order to be the more emphatically knocked down. But it is also significant that above the late Mediaeval representation of the maggot-infested corpse we may sometimes discover the pure, radiant and incorrupt soul leaving behind its corruptible shell and arising into heaven. Symbolically it is the corruption of the corpse which *creates* the purity of the soul – a point which Catholic belief itself comes close to recognising in the notion that it is the flesh which binds the soul to the profane world, putrescence thus becoming a necessary prelude to spiritual purification (see above p.22). Again, in the Cantonese case, it is the decomposition of the flesh which will eventually permit the recovery of fertility from the bones. From the participants' point of view, then, putrescence is in all these instances seen as a prerequisite for the distillation of life out of death. From the outside analyst's point of view it would, however, be preferable to say that the symbolism of regeneration actually derives its force from its juxtaposition to the antithetical symbolism of decomposition. The vigil of the Aghori on the cremation ground reveals this process clearly, for his morbid revelry in putrescence only serves to underline his claim to have transcended the world of biology and pollution, and to have conquered death. By wallowing in decay and death the Aghori histrionically proclaims his victory over them. In the light of all this it becomes significant that where – as in the four hunter–gatherer societies discussed by Woodburn – the symbolism of regeneration is weakly elaborated, there is little or no symbolic preoccupation with the process of decomposition, for nothing here is created in antithesis to it.

We have suggested, then, that the *negative* aspects of death are commonly seen as inseparable from other biological phenomena (like copulation and parturition); that in common with other biological processes, decomposition and decay are often (though not always) pre-eminently associated with women; and that this world of biology is elaborately constructed as something to be got rid of so as to make way for the regeneration of the ideal order. It is to this reconstituted ideal order that we turn our attention in the two sections which follow. The first of these focuses primarily on the commentary which this ideological representation of the community makes on marriage and exchange. In this connection, the Dobuan data from Melanesia with which we start, provides us with a crucial case. In the second section we shall pick up on a prominent theme to emerge from our re-analysis – the role of the tomb as a crystallised embodiment of the ideal community.

Eternity and the end of affinity

Perhaps the most dramatic feature of Fortune's (1963) ethnography concerns the Dobuan view of affines – 'Those-resulting-from-marriage' – as a constant danger to the exogamous matrilineage (*susu*). All deaths are caused by a human agency, and the first suspicion of 'treacherous secret murder' by sorcery falls on the village kin of the surviving spouse, for

One marries into a village of enemies, witches and sorcerers, some of whom are known to have killed or to be the children of those known to have killed members of one's own village . . . In the dark spaces between villages (at night) the agents of death roam – and death dealing spirits of women and men of all other villages, witches and sorcerers all. (Fortune, 1963:23)

It is hardly surprising, then, that marriages are extremely tense affairs and that the conjugal bond is fragile. A man is only really safe with his village 'sisters', with whom marriage is strongly discountenanced because such a union would not set up economic exchanges between two villages (Fortune, 1963:69). 'Incestuous' relations between classificatory 'brothers' and 'sisters' are, however, common; and the constant suspicion that one's spouse is conducting an affair with a sibling may prompt a jealous husband to time his wife's absences when she goes to the bush to defaecate, or to recruit children as spies.

A kind of suppressed yearning for the safety of incestuous reproduction is clearly apparent in Dobuan notions about plant biology, and in particular about the yams on which their subsistence is based. The particular strain of seed yams which any gardener cultivates is exclusively inherited within the *susu*; and although husbands and wives pool their production, they cultivate separate gardens in which they each tend yams of their own matrilineal strain. This is no mere matter of an idiosyncratic culinary preference; no other variety would grow for them. Just as seed yams remain within the lineage, so the garden magic which promotes their growth can, in theory, only be transmitted within the descent group.

All this is more than an question of a particular strain of yams being *associated* with a particular lineage; it is rather that the yams are *part* of the lineage. For the Dobuans all creation is the result of the metamorphosis of one thing into another. Yams are metamorphosed people, and they still retain many of their human characteristics. They have ears and hear, are susceptible to magical charms, walk about at night and give birth to children – though significantly there is no mention of them propagating sexually. They are *tomot* – 'human beings' (as opposed to Europeans who are of a different species). But further than this, they are lineage kin descended from the founding ancestress of the *susu*. Their flesh – the Dobuan idiom – is planted in the gardens as the corpses of the ancestors are planted in the village mound which is the focal point of the settlement. What reproduces the lineage in a material sense, then, is – in Dobuan ideology – the flesh of its own kind. The consumption of yams, or at least of the yams grown from one's own lineage's seed strain, thus amounts to an act of symbolic endo-cannibalism.

Eating on Dobu is an intensely private affair. Meals are generally only shared by the members of a single conjugal unit (Fortune, 1963:74) though the key element in the formal recognition of marriage is the feeding of the bride and groom by their respective mothers-in-law (p.26). Commensality is closely associated with affinity and more loosely eating with sexuality. Consuming one's own yams becomes a metaphor for consuming one's own sisters. What we seem to have here, then, is the symbolic equation between cannibalism and incest that is such a pronounced feature of Strathern's ethnography.

This metaphorical association between yams and women, and

between sexual and alimentary consumption, is further revealed by the elaborate magical procedures which are directed as the seduction of other people's yams. 'Just as it is considered good form to try to seduce other men's wives whenever possible, so in gardening ... every man should try to entice the yams, greatly desired personal beings in metamorphosised form, from other persons' gardens' (Fortune, 1963:134). With regard to both the objective is the same: to appropriate what belongs to others while hanging on to your own. But what needs to be kept firmly in mind is that such predation has a limited pay-off not only in that it invites mystical retribution, but more importantly in that stolen yams are barren. It is only your own yams which will reproduce, just as it is only your own sisters that can reproduce the lineage. The symbolic assimilation of women to endogenous yams thus denies to affines any real role in the propagation of the descent group. Dobu is not after all so remote from the Trobriand Islands with their famous denial of physiological paternity.

Not surprisingly, this desire of the lineage to turn in on itself and abrogate all relations with outsiders emerges as a central feature of the symbolism of Dobuan mortuary practices. In life the pattern of alternating residence means that individuals must spend half of their time in the dangerous and hostile world of their spouse's village. Even at home one can hardly be safe, for the settlement will include the spouses of one's own brothers and sisters, who are serving time in *their* affinal village and who are probably witches and sorcerers.

All this however is only a problem of life, for at death one attains a permanent haven in the village mound where one is at last free from untrustworthy outsiders. This liberation of the deceased (as well as the liberation of the survivors from the affinal relationship which he or she contracted and which may well have been the cause of the death) is dramatised in various aspects of the funerary sequence. The house – which is the key symbol of the conjugal unit and from which all others are excluded – remains deserted until the end of mourning, when it is razed to the ground. The corpse itself is claimed by the *susu*, while 'Those-resulting-from-marriage' kneel outside and can neither look on it, nor participate in its subsequent display, decoration and interment.[2] After this the surviving spouse remains a kind of prisoner in the deceased's village until the end of an arduous year of mourning. Initially the spouse is incarcerated, with blackened body and a black rope around the neck, in a small walled enclosure of plaited coconut fronds which is built underneath the now abandoned house, where he or she remains 'sitting on a mat all day, walled off, speaking to no one and seeing no one' (Fortune, 1963:11). After a couple of months the survivor emerges to do toilsome work for the deceased's lineage kin, but must hide when the skull of the deceased is brought out. At the end of this arduous regime the widow, or widower, is led out of the village and may *never* return.

All this has to be placed in the context of a situation in which the rules of residence ensure that the empirical manifestation of the descent group is highly problematical in that its living representatives have no territorial integrity. Yet the *susu is* geographically anchored – by the large communal burial mound which stands at the centre of its notional settlement, and around the periphery of which are grouped the individual houses of the various conjugal families who are the part-time members of the local community. The physical marginality of these houses, and their impermanence provide a fitting symbol of affinity itself. The burial mound, by contrast, is a place of permanence and stability. Here the ideal unity of the *susu* is finally realised after the aggravating flux of life. It is not too much to say, then, that burial constructs a Dobuan vision of Utopia in which the boundary between one descent group and another is hermetically sealed. What is achieved when 'Those-resulting-from-marriage' are sent packing after death is the creation of the ideal community represented by the mound where the generations succeed each other without the unpleasant necessity of exchange – in much the same way as the lineage yams reproduce themselves asexually.

A similar ambivalence about exchange is, as we read the evidence, implicit in much of Strathern's ethnography. According to the Melpa theory of genetics, bone comes from the father, while from one point of view flesh is the contribution of the mother. In another way however, this is denied, for the flesh of the living is also seen as a product of the fertility brought about by the putrescence of the dead, whose bodies regenerate the soil and feed the plants on which the living subsist and which creates their substance. In a further respect, too, Melpa symbolism seems to suggest an attempt to deny – or at least replace – women, if not as the source of birth then as the source of the nurturing towards adulthood. Shortly after birth, the child's navel-string and its mother's placenta are buried together, and a cordyline or a banana tree is planted over the spot. As the plant grows, so does the child. 'The navel-string', says Strathern, 'which once connected the child to the mother in her womb, now connects it to the earth, and the link is represented by the cordyline . . . '. What this seems to suggest is that as soon as they possibly can, the Melpa replace women by the clan territory. They would seem to be working out the same phantasy as is revealed by their proclaimed abhorrence of cannibalistic consumption – the phantasy of a world without exchange. But whereas – on Strathern's analysis – cannibalism shows the disadvantages of such a world, this ideological displacement of women would seem to display a surreptitious yearning after it. Our own interpretation of Melpa cannibalism, however, would be rather different; and would be consistent with – rather than contradict – what we have said about the replacement of women. That is, we would argue that Strathern's interpretation should be turned on its head: since the typical cannibal is an in-marrying wife, the problem which cannibalism highlights is not so much the dangers of non-exchange, but rather the dangers attendant on the necessity of exchange with others exemplified by a reliance on outsider women. Seen like this, the difference between the Melpa and the Etero is less extreme than Strathern suggests. It is not so much that the beliefs surrounding the imaginary cannibalism of the Melpa are (as Strathern's analysis would suggest) an emphatic repudiation of what the Etero practice, but rather that Etero practice corresponds to the Melpa phantasy of an enviable order without exchange – an order which they create in their rituals but which their society, based on the foundation of exchange, makes impossible.

While Melanesian peoples in general are commonly associated with a maximum ideological elaboration of exchange, the two Melanesian societies we have looked at here *simultaneously* entertain the countervailing vision of an ideal order without exchange. This observation does little more, however, than echo what Lévi-Strauss expressed in far more general terms and in far more vivid language in his concluding paragraph to *The elementary structures of kinship and marriage*:

To this very day, mankind has always dreamed of seizing and fixing that fleeting moment when it was permissible to believe that the law of exchange could be evaded, that one could gain without losing, enjoy without sharing. At either end of the earth and at both extremes of time, the Sumerian myth of the golden age and the Andaman myth of the future life correspond, the former placing the end of primitive happiness at a time when the confusion of languages made words into common property, the latter describing the bliss of the hereafter as a heaven where women will no longer be exchanged, i.e., removing to an equally unattainable past or future the joys, eternally denied to social man, of a world in which one might *keep to oneself*. (Lévi-Strauss, 1969:496–7).

To these observations we would however add that in the converse case – where the exchange of women between groups is ideologically discountenanced – certain aspects of ritual life may express an equally ambivalent attitude towards the consciously articulated values. This is illustrated by the striking contrast between the (imagined) cannibalism of the Melpa and the necrophagy of the Aghori ascetics. That the former is associated with greed and consumption while the latter stands for an ascetic denial of normal consumption should be obvious enough. But what is more germane to the point at issue is Parry's observation (chapter 3) that 'with the destruction of boundaries implied by the consumption of flesh, excrement and so on, goes an affirmation of the irrelevance of caste boundaries'. In this respect also the symbolic load carried by Aghori necrophagy would seem to be precisely the reverse of the message encoded in the myth of Melpa cannibalism. In both instances cannibalism represents an antithesis to the prevailing order. But while for the Melpa it stands, we have argued, for the dangers of exchange in a world premised on the principle of exchange, in the Aghori case it stands for the suppressed potential of the exchange of substance to dissolve the social barriers between groups in a world premised on their exclusiveness and closure (the orthodox Indian ideal being much more like that of the Etero, for whom bodily substance is to be conserved rather than exchanged).

At another level, however, this contrast with the Melanesian material disappears. In the Dobuan case, we have argued, the eternal order is created by the repudiation of exchange. But there is a sense in which this is also true of the Aghori. Exchange not only presumes an alter, but also creates or maintains differentiation and – where it takes an asymmetrical form – the hierarchy of castes. But all this is precisely what the Aghori denies. For him everything in the universe has the same essence, and the distinction between ego and alter, or between Brahman and Untouchable, belongs merely to the world of illusory appearances. By realising this state of non-differentiation through his ascetic discipline, he attains an eternity in which there is neither death nor birth. As with the Dobuans, then, permanence is only achieved by overcoming the differentiation on which exchange is based. There are no others in eternity. In the Dobuan case they are eliminated by the suppression of affinity, while in the Aghori case they are eliminated with the boundary-maintaining pollution practices that separate alter from ego, and both from perpetuity.

Tombs and the social order

If the avoidance of exchange constructs the image of permanence, we have seen how, in the Dobuan case, this construction takes a material form in the burial mound.

A further example of the graveyard as a symbolic representation of the social order is given in Firth's (1936) famous ethnography of Tikopia. The focus of traditional Tikopian social organisation is the *paito*, a term which Firth has variously translated as 'house' or 'lineage', but which might also have been glossed as 'tomb'. The *paito* is given its identity by the house-site on which it stands and from which its members take their name. This name identifies its bearers as the heirs to a long line of previous residents on the site, and therefore merges descent with locality. But that is not all. One half of the traditional Tikopian house is not actually lived in because underneath the mats which cover the floor are buried the former occupants of the house; the previous bearers of the name. Tikopians live, therefore, on the cramped borders of their tombs and take their identity from what is essentially a necropolis. As in Dobu, tombs in Tikopia are the enduring units of society and provide the material symbol of their continuity.

W.A. Douglass' ethnography of a Spanish Basque village, *Death in Murelaga* (1969), describes a situation reminiscent of the Tikopian case. Here the primary unit of social organisation is the rural farmstead, or *basseria*, which is managed by one domestic group (or household) consisting of a couple, their children, and perhaps also an aged parent (or parents) and any unmarried siblings. Only one of the couple's children will be appointed as the heir to the farmstead, while the other children will be given a share of the moveable property and expected to set up on their own. A *basseria* cannot be dismembered by sale or inheritance and, like the Tikopia *paito*, theoretically exists in perpetuity: 'in rural Basque society social continuity is provided not by descent groups but rather by the immutability of households' (Douglass, 1969:88). People derive their names from the farmsteads on which they reside; their social identity is completely bound up with a specific household and they interact with others as members of it (p.115).

Each *basseria* is associated with a *sepulturie* on the floor of the local church, which is not only a family stall in which the women sit on Sundays, but also a symbolic burial plot and the focus of mourning rituals and rites to the dead. This *sepulturie* is the responsibility of the heir of the farm. Up until the late eighteenth century it was the real burial site, and is still seen by people as a family tomb. Today, however, corpses are buried in the graveyard outside the church in plots allocated by household. But the real grave is of little importance.

Whenever there is a death, the gravediggers exhume a previously buried corpse, deposit the bones in the ossuary, and then bury the newly deceased. Little attention is paid to where the individual is buried. In a few months the weeds claim the grave, and it is often impossible to distinguish the outlines of the grave plot. (Douglass, 1969:72)

Such neglect contrasts with the attention devoted to the *sepulterie*. On Sundays the women surround it with candles and during mourning it is the focus of Masses said for the collective dead. If the *basseria* is sold, the new owners assume full control of the *sepulturie* and the vendors relinquish all rights. Masses said for the collective dead are devoted to *all* former owners of the farmstead traced through any line of descent or none, but excluding kin who have moved out. In this way the *sepulturie* represents the uninterrupted integrity of 'the basic unit of rural society and economy' (Douglass, 1969:6).

The role of the tomb as a symbol of the continuity of the property-holding kinship group is also nicely illustrated by the scene in Galsworthy's novel *To Let*, where Soames sits by the family vault in Highgate cemetery morosely pondering the end of the old order and the dispersal of the Forsytes, augured by the cremation of Susan Hayman and the uncertain future of the family mausoleum. This volume offers several other examples of groups creating themselves and sealing their association with a particular locality by the construction of sepulchres. Harris' discussion of the Laymi illustrates well how the location and inclusiveness of the cemetery reflects changes in the character and autonomy of the local community. Consistent with their objective of undermining the relative independence of the pre-colonial local groups, the Spanish authorities centralised the cemeteries. Now the trend is again towards the political detachment of the local community from the wider society, and is in turn reflected in a renewed dispersal of the graveyards.

Perhaps clearest of all is the Merina case. The fundamental unit of Merina social organisation is the deme, an ideally endogamous kindred associated with a specific territory by a number of tombs. The tombs not only contain the remains of members of the deme but may actually be said to create the deme, which – like the Dobuan *susu* – has no territorial integrity this side of eternity since most of its members may actually reside elsewhere. After death, however, the expatriate Merina returns 'home'. This regrouping of the dead, which is a central symbol of the culture and which underlies the joy of the second funeral, is achieved by the entry of the new corpses into the collective mausoleum. In this way the tomb and the reunited dead within it represent the undivided and enduring descent group, and as a result is the source of blessings and the fertility of the future.

The force of this symbol of the tomb as the representation of the eternal undivided group can only be sustained by down-playing the individuality of the corpses which enter it – which the Merina do by breaking up their individual dead in order to 'group' them. The same process is also found in a less material form among the Laymi. At the festival of All Saints 'the spirit is first welcomed and mourned individually and then there is a move towards collectivity in the graveyard'. The collective tomb or cemetery in which the group finds continuing life brooks no individuals, or is at least antithetical to the long-term maintenance of individual memory.

On the face of it the generality of this anti-individualism in funerary rituals would appear to be completely undermined by those cases in which the tomb of a single individual – for example, a king – becomes the focus of the continuity and fertility of the community. Such a situation has been discussed by Bloch (1981) for western Madagascar, though probably the most obvious example is that of the Egyptian pyramids (Frankfort, 1948). In passing we may observe that in such cases the growth in the size and significance of royal tombs seems to be accompanied by a diminution, or even a total eradication, of the tombs of the subjects as permanent objects. The central problem, however, is that the renewal of life implies the denial of individual death; yet the identification of the royal tomb as the source of regeneration comes close to emphasising an individual lifespan. One solution to this dilemma is to stress – as do the Merina – the royal *line* rather than the individual monarch. In the ritual of the royal bath the living Merina king goes to the tomb and washes himself with water associated with the *collectivity* of his forebears. He thereby proclaims his complete mystical identity with his predecessors and successors. Another and more radical possibility is to deny altogether the transient nature of the ruler's life by transforming his body into a permanent death-transcending mummy. In the one case it is the individuality of the king that is denied, in the other it is also his mortality.

In this section we have focused on the way in which tombs are used to construct an idealised material map of the permanent social order. It is worth pointing out, however, that the general process we are dealing with does not necessarily require the corpse in its entirety, or even any of the physical remains of the deceased. The same result can also be achieved by utilising only a part of the corpse (as appears to have been the case with the skull houses of the Melpa), or some immaterial aspect of the deceased. This possibility is realised by the Lugbara (as well as by many other African peoples). Here what is retained of the deceased is his 'soul', which is established in a shrine as a 'ghost' after the threatening individual aspect of the deceased's person has been cast away into the 'wild' thereby allowing his moral lineage aspect to be created anew in the 'home'. If we bear in mind that there is a sense in which ancestor worship creates the lineage in such societies, it is clear that we are once again dealing with the fabrication of an ideal social order out of the transformed remains of the dead.

These various systems – the Dobuan, Tikopian, Laymi, Merina and Lugbara – are all cases where the community in its enduring aspect is constructed by reference to the dead. Whether this is actually accomplished by means of skulls, corpses, tombs or shrines is perhaps of little significance in terms of the overall logic of the ideology – which only goes to show how misleading it may be to extrapolate collective representations about death directly from the evidence of material culture. In all these instances what is created by the mortuary symbolism is a particular group or division of society – a lineage, for example, or a local community. But this is not – as Parry's discussion of the Indian data indicates – invariably the case.

At first sight Hindu funerary practices could not be more different than the cases we have just considered. In Hinduism nothing of the individual is preserved which could provide a focal symbol of group continuity. The physical remains of the deceased are obliterated as completely as possible: first the corpse is cremated and then the ashes are immersed in the Ganges and are seen as finally flowing into the ocean. The ultimate objective seems to be as complete a dissolution of the body as possible.

This last statement needs however to be qualified. The Hindu concept of the 'body' (*sharira*) does not entirely correspond with our own, and the real aim of the mortuary rites is more specifically the radical destruction of the 'gross' physical body (*sthula sharira*). The limb by limb creation of a new body for the deceased is the central purpose of the ritual sequence of the first ten days after cremation. But this new container for the soul is a 'subtle' or 'ghostly' body (*suksham* or *preta sharira*)) of a more refined and less elemental form. What is more, the *preta sharira* appears to be a transitory form which will also soon be dissolved, or transformed, with the assimilation of the deceased into the category of the ancestors. A ball of rice representing the newly created body of the deceased is laid alongside three other rice balls representing his father, father's father and father's father's father. It is then cut up into three pieces, the first of which is merged with the father's rice ball, the second with the grandfather's and so on. In Benares the three ancestral balls (which now contain the three fragments of the deceased) are subsequently rolled into one and immersed in the Ganges. In other words, the process of generation is reversed so that the generating absorb the generated (until – as the ultimate immersion of the consolidated rice ball perhaps suggests – total annihilation). It is as if the genealogy of the dead had been reversed. Whether, when all this is done, the deceased can be said to exist in bodily form is not altogether clear from informants' statements. The theologically unsophisticated tend to talk as though he now exists in a purely incorporeal state in the 'form of air' (*vayu rup*), while those who are better versed in the texts present it as a matter of acquiring an even more ethereal bodily envelope. But whichever view one takes, the underlying progression is the same: a gross material body is replaced by more and more refined forms.

All this bears testimony to the influence of the ascetic ideal and to a preoccupation with abandoning the sensual, material order. The Brahmanic theory of the four stages of life supposes that at the end of his life a man will eventually renounce the world and become a wandering and homeless ascetic. In fact, of course, this ideal is hardly ever realised in practice. But it is here, we suggest, that cremation fits in as a kind of surrogate for the ascetic's abrogation of the body. It is a kind of catching up on the renunciation of carnal existence which should ideally be the conclusion to every (male) life. Cremation must therefore be represented as a *voluntary* act of self-sacrifice consciously undertaken by a living individual. The conventional observation that renunciation is a kind of death may thus be reversed: death takes the form of a kind of last-ditch renunciation. Here we have one explanation of why the ascetic himself is not cremated. He has already accomplished what cremation belatedly achieves for the householder. To burn his corpse would not merely be redundant; it would also be to insinuate that his renunciation had been inadequate. Cremation and renunciation are both directed towards the same end: a repudiation of the 'gross' body. This repudiation is somewhat melodramatically proclaimed by the Aghori ascetics whose practices demonstrate that they can with impunity reverse what remains essential for those who are still bound to the mundane world and are still carnal beings. Having reached beyond carnality, they bombastically declare themselves impervious to the most polluting substances and actions.

The Hindu case, with its insistence on a total destruction of the physical body, is therefore quite different from the Malagasy, Dobuan, Laymi and Lugbara cases where an attempt is made to retain a pure and regenerating aspect of the deceased in order to construct and reproduce an ordered group. Beyond this difference there is however a more fundamental similarity. The overwhelming evidence is that the theme of life out of death is as central to Hindu thought as it is to any of the other systems we have considered. But while elsewhere the mortuary rituals guarantee the continuation of specific groups, in Benares they re-enact the creation of the whole universe and regenerate the cosmic order. The real difference between this case and the others is the difference between a system in which the mortuary rituals dissolve the fundamental units of society into an *undifferentiated* universe, and those systems where they shore up these units and give them a permanent and transcendental value. In the eyes of the Hindu ascetic (traces of whose ideology we have discovered in the mortuary practices of the householder) this world of appearances – where caste is divided from caste and man from god – is merely, after all, the product of illusion (*maya*).

We are back, then, with the contrast with which we ended the last section. On the one hand we have those systems where the eternal order is achieved by the abolition of exchange relations between groups, which produces a static fossilisation of these groups in their sepulchres. On the other hand we have the Hindu system where – in order to attain a timeless eternity – exchange is abolished by the destruction of the internal divisions of society, whose existence implies the necessity of exchange.

The limits of the ideological representation

In the previous sections we have discussed how 'fertility' is created out of death. In order that this eternal, stable, life-giving element can be constructed, it is antithetically contrasted with another order built up by reference to such notions as 'biology', 'individuality', 'flesh', the 'gross body', and 'exchange'. What all these things have in common is that they refer to life and people as they are known in the everyday world, though seen for the purpose of the ideology in a particularly hostile light.

The elimination of this element creates the transcendent but this process is, as we have already noted, inevitably problematic. The problem lies in the very use of the antithesis. It recognises what it devalues. We saw, for example, that funerary rituals which deny death in order to construct an eternal source of fertility where life and death are merged, have first to revel in decomposition, biology and the dangers of exchange.

There is clearly, however, an even more fundamental reason why ideology cannot completely eliminate the natural world of biological process or the social world of exchange. To refuse the first would be to jeopardise the physical continuity of the group, while to refuse the second would be to deny society itself. That there is a real problem here is shown by the Aghoris who come close to repudiating all social relationships, and even more clearly by the Dinka Spearmaster who does indeed defeat the contingency of biological events, but only at the cost of abolishing himself. As illustrated by both these instances, the ultimate irony of death is that its final conquest is only achieved by embracing it oneself.

Such a solution is clearly not available to any on-going social system, and this fact most poignantly reveals the limits of ideology. What is more, the ideology has to be put to work in that very world which it denies, and it must therefore be compromised. This compromise is manifested symbolically and this explains certain aspects of the funerary rituals we have not so far examined, and which take the form of the reintroduction, in certain ritual contexts, of what had enthusiastically been denied in others.

Lugbara funerary practices, for example, expel that part of the person – the 'spirit' – which is symbolically and linguistically associated with the 'wild', and project an image of uncontrolled sexuality as sterile. But it is then as if the amorphous and destructive power of the wild must be, with the greatest caution, reintroduced so that it can augment the fertility of the ancestors. This power is brought into the 'home' by women; and more particularly by their sexuality, which by itself is dangerous and unproductive, but which – like fire – is at the centre of social life once it has been tamed. Control of the wild always remains problematic, though divination is one means to this end. A more successful attempt to channel its power seems to be that of the rain-maker who is able to contain within himself the force of divinity and to control it for the benefit of man.

The same dialectic is found in a different form in the Cantonese example. There the key symbols of legitimate authority and the enduring lineage order are the ancestral halls and the ancestral tablets, which must at all costs be protected from the contamination of the corpse. This terrifying object is to be disposed of as quickly as may be. Yet the elements of which it is composed must not be irretrievably lost. The flesh is, as we have seen, recouped by women – through their hair and by way of the absorbent green cloths which they wear at funerals and which reappear in the harnesses they use to carry their infants. However the greatest power resides in the bones, and this can only be recovered under the strictest precautions. In order to confer fertility and good fortune on some or all of the deceased's descendants (who are merely a segment of the wider descent group) his bones must be located according to the finest geomantic calculations, which if inaccurate may – like an uncontrolled intrusion of the Lugbara 'wild' – also bring disaster. The Chinese symbolism of the bones and flesh would seem therefore to be significantly different from the apparently similar bone/flesh dichotomy we have encountered among the Bara and the Melpa. In these latter cases the bones stand as symbols for the permanent units of society. But in China this symbolic function pre-eminently belongs to the ancestral hall and the tablets it contains; while both bones and flesh represent a dangerous vitality which can only be recovered under strict control. As Freedman (1966:143; 1967) made clear, the bones stand for the amoral advantage of some as against the moral authority wielded over the collectivity by the ancestral spirits in the lineage hall.

By contrast with these cases, the main concern of the Laymi would seem to be to expel the dead altogether, without retaining any aspect of their personality. The community, cannot, however, exist without the fertility which they control. However regrettable the necessity, the dead must therefore be brought back at the festival of All Saints so that they can preside over the growth of the crops in the months which follow. But these ancestors are half devils, who belong to the evil sphere and whose power is potentially malevolent. The period during which they remain in the world is a period of sadness, toil and restraint; and the festival which welcomes them emphasises social differentiation and is a time for fighting and battles, for the blood spilt is necessary for the earth to bring forth its harvest. The dead confer fertility, but the price which has to be paid is high and they are inseparably associated with the world of particularistic interests. At Carnival, however, this world is abolished, fights are prohibited, individuals are made anonymous, individual rights are transcended (as, for example, in the legitimised stealing of the standing crops), and the ancestors (whose work is now done) can at last be called devils to their face and unceremoniously driven out of the village to make way for a season of sociability and communal solidarity.

As with the Lugbara and the Chinese, we are once again confronted with a recognition of the necessity of coming to terms with what ideology would prefer to eliminate altogether, and with the dangers of doing so. This danger is again revealed by the special vulnerability of pregnant women to funerals which we find among the Laymi, the Merina and the Chinese. It is as if their condition makes them peculiarly susceptible to the untamed power which is unleashed, as a consequence of which they would – as the Merina believe – bear anti-social monsters.

Death and the legitimation of authority

The unavoidable compromise which the ideology has to make with the practical world of nature and exchange is however mitigated by its careful reintroduction under the strict control of authority. This brings us back to the political significance of the representations we have been considering. At several points we have stressed the relationship between mortuary beliefs and practices and the legitimation of the social order and its authority structure. This relationship is perhaps clearest in those instances where that order is built up by transforming the dead into a transcendent and eternal force – as, for example, in the Lugbara, Cantonese and Merina cases. In these instances the social group is anchored, not just by political power, but by some of the deepest emotions, beliefs and fears of people everywhere. Society is made both emotionally and intellectually unassailable by means of that alchemy which transforms death into fertility. This fertility is represented as a gift made by those in authority which they bestow by their blessings.

If the political implications of funerary practices which emphasise the permanence of distinct social groups are clear enough, it is by no means obvious that any such significance can be attached to the apparently radically different Hindu case, where the mortuary rites do not eternalise distinct social groups but actually seem to do the exact opposite. However, even in this case, the pattern is recognisable. The transcendent authority of the Brahmans, who sacralise the social order, is reinforced by the theory of death as a cosmogonic sacrifice, for this theory locates the ultimate source of regenerative power in the ritual sphere, and places its control in the hands of those who operate the sacrifice. As for the ascetic who is striving after liberation from the cycle of rebirth, his whole endeavour is founded on an attempt to escape the inexorability of *karma*. He thereby acknowledges its reality for the man-in-the-world, and hence the principal ideological justification for the inequalities of the world.

The contrasting position of the Brahman and the ascetic illustrates well the complexity of the relation between the ideological construction and authority. The difficulty is that a position of real authority cannot be entirely rooted in a pristine ideological order, since as we saw in the previous section, this removes the actor from the world where his authority is to be exercised. He must at once be part of the

Maurice Bloch and Jonathan Parry

ideal world where death is replaced by eternal fertility and part of this world where death and time remain. As a result he has to keep a foot in both camps. Viewed in another light, the intellectual problem of the limits of ideology, discussed above, is also a political problem of authority. The challenge is one of achieving a workable balance between the ideological construction and the reality of death, duration, exchange and power.

It is not surprising, then, that this legitimating function is necessarily entirely hidden from the actors themselves. At certain points in history the political significance of such practices may become transparent – as, for example, during the Maoist period in China, when on the other side of the border a systematic propaganda campaign was launched against the kind of mortuary system which Watson describes for the Cantonese of Hong Kong. Similarly, in the Andean example it is evident that the Spanish conquerors well appreciated the significance of the Laymi graveyard in the ideological reproduction of the autonomous local community and therefore attempted to destroy it.

There are cultures, however, in which the handling of death is not put to work as a device for the creation of ideology and political domination. The four hunter–gatherer societies discussed by Woodburn are cases in point. In none of these instances is there any systematic attempt to transform death into a rebirth or a regeneration of either the group or the cosmos. 'When you're dead that's an end of you', say the Baka. Indeed, as Woodburn points out, the force of the analogy between death and rebirth is missing when you not only enter and leave the world naked, but remain naked while in it; where there is no transcendental authority to be created the dead can be left alone.

NOTES

We would like to thank the following for comments on an earlier draft: C.J. Fuller, R.L. Stirrat and R. Thomas.

1 A fascinating detail is that the power of the bones is transmitted through the medium of the flesh of a roasted pig. Though it is going beyond the evidence available to us, it is tempting to see in this an element of the symbolic necrophagy which is suggested by the comparison with the symbolism of Melpa pig prestations discussed by Strathern.

2 The widow's (or widower's) family must pay an arm-shell to the *susu* representatives who dig the grave. The arm-shell is an essential brideprice payment, and a case is cited in which a nubile daughter was given in lieu (Fortune, 1963:194). From this we may infer that the payment is a kind of replacement for the deceased. It is almost as if the affines were acknowledging their complicity in the death.

REFERENCES

Bachofen, J.J. 1967. *Myth, religion and mother right*. (trans. E. Mannheim) London: Routledge and Kegan Paul.

Barth, F. 1975. *Ritual and knowledge among the Baktaman of New Guinea*. Yale: Yale University Press.

Bloch, M. 1981. 'Tombs and states', in *Mortality and immortality: the anthropology and archaeology of death*. ed. S.C. Humphreys and H. King. London: Academic Press.

Douglass, W.A. 1969. *Death in Murelaga: funerary rituals in a Spanish Basque village*. Seattle: University of Washington Press.

Durkheim, E. 1952. *Suicide*. London: Routledge and Kegan Paul.

Eliade, M. 1965. *The myth of the eternal return*. Princeton: University Press (Bollingen Series XLVI).

Evans-Pritchard, E.E. 1948. *The divine kingship of the Shilluk of the Nilotic Sudan*. The Frazer Memorial Lecture of 1948. Cambridge: Cambridge Unniversity Press.

Firth, R. 1936. *We, the Tikopia: a sociological study of kinship in primitive Polynesia*. London: George Allen & Unwin Ltd.

Fortune, R. 1963. *Sorcerers of Dobu: the social anthropology of the Dobu Islanders of the Western Pacific*. London: Routledge and Kegan Paul.

Frankfort, H. 1948. *Kingship and the gods*. Chicago: University of Chicago Press.

Frazer, J.G. 1890. *The golden bough*. London: MacMillan.

Freedman, M. 1966. *Chinese lineage and society*. London: The Athlone Press.
　1967. 'Ancestor worship: two facets of the Chinese case', in *Social organization: essays presented to Raymond Firth*. London: Frank Cass & Co. Ltd.

Gillison, G. 1980. 'Images of nature in Gimi thought', in *Nature, culture and gender*. eds C. MacCormack & M. Strathern. Cambridge: Cambridge University Press.

Goody, J. 1962. *Death, property and the ancestors*. London: Tavistock.

Harrison, J. 1912. *Themis*. Cambridge: Cambridge University Press.

Hertz, R. 1960. 'A contribution to the study of the collective representation of death', in *Death and the right hand*. (trans. R. & C. Needham) London: Cohen & West.

Huizinga, J. 1965. *The waning of the Middle Ages*. Harmondsworth: Penguin Books.

Huntington, R. 1973. 'Death and the social order: Bara funeral customs (Madagascar)'. *African Studies*, **32**(2):65–84.

Huntington, R. & Metcalf, P. 1979. *Celebrations of death: the anthropology of mortuary ritual*. Cambridge: Cambridge University Press.

Leach, E.R. 1961. 'Two essays concerning the symbolic representation of time', in *Rethinking anthropology*. London: Athlone Press.
　1966a. 'Anthropological aspects of language: animal categories and verbal abuse', in *New directions in the study of language*. ed. E.H. Lenneberg. Cambridge, Massachusetts: The M.I.T. Press.
　1966b. 'Virgin birth', in *Proceedings of the Royal Anthropological Institute of Great Britain and Ireland*.

Lévi-Strauss, C. 1969. *The elementary structures of kinship and marriage*. (trans. J.H. Bell, J.R. von Sturmer & R. Needham) London: Eyre and Spottiswoode.

Maurice Bloch and Jonathan Parry

Lienhardt, G. 1961. *Divinity and experience: the religion of the Dinka*. Oxford: Oxford University Press.
Malinowski, B. 1948. 'Baloma; the spirits of dead', in *Magic, science and religion*. London: Faber and West.
Morin, E. 1970. *L'Homme et la mort*. Paris: Edition du Seuil.
Ngubane, H. 1976. 'Some notions of "purity" and "impurity" among the Zulu', *Africa*, **46**:274–83.
Parry, J.P. 1980. 'Ghosts, greed and sin: the occupational identity of the Benares funeral priests', *Man* (n.s.) **15**(1):88–111.
    1981. 'Death and cosmogony in Kashi', *Contributions to Indian Sociology*, **15**:337–65.
Paulme, D. 1940. *Organisation sociale des Dogons*. (institut de droit compare: Etudes de sociologie et d'ethnologie juridique, **32**).
Pina-Cabral, J. de 1980. 'Cults of death in Northwestern Portugal', *Jouurnal of the Anthropological Society of Oxford*, **9**(1):1–14.
Raglan, Lord 1945. *Death and rebirth*. London: Watts & Co.
Thomas, L-V. 1975. *Anthropologie de la mort*. Paris: Payot.
Van Gennep, A. 1909. *Les rites de passage*. Paris: Emile Nourry.
Wilson, G. 1939. 'Nyakyusa conventions of burial', *Bantu Studies* **13**:1–31.

2 The dead and the devils among the Bolivian Laymi

OLIVIA HARRIS

Introduction

... the dead go directly to Puquinapampa and Corapona. There they meet together and it is said that there they enjoy much feasting and conversation between the dead men and the dead women; and that whenn they leave there they go to another place where they endure much work, hunger, thirst and cold, and when it is hot the heat is too great; and thus they bury them with their food and drink. And they always take care to send them provisions to eat and drink; and after six months they make another similar feast for the dead, and after a year another; but they do not take out the said deceased in a procession as they do in Chinchaysuyu, they leave him inside his cave and underground chamber and they call the town of the dead *amayan marcapa* (town of the ghosts). (*Waman Puma, 1613 (1936:294)*)

Waman Puma here relates the burial customs of Qullasuyu, which included what is today highland Bolivia, and formed the South-eastern quarter of the fourfold Inka state. His description, though separated by 350 years from the present day, offers illumination for the account that follows of mortuary rites in the Laymi ethnic group of northern Potosí, Bolivia. The Andean writer expresses a poignant contrast between the time of feasting and 'conversation' and the subsequent hard labour and suffering experienced by the dead. While he does not connect this polarity directly with calendrical rites, he does note that ceremonies for the dead are performed twice a year; the divided experience of the deceased is echoed in a temporal arrrange-ment that divides the year into two halves. Today too the Laymi divide their year into two contrasted halves, each marked by a feast of the dead; one half is a time for sorrow and hard work, while the other is dedicated to feasting, pleasure and rest from their labours.

In other respects what we know of the mortuary practices of pristine Andean cultures stands in stark opposition to the present; the break was effected historically through the 'extirpation of idolatrous prac-tices', the veritable military campaign waged against autochthonous Andean religion by the Christian priests and their heirs in the first century of European imperial rule.[1] Many of the sixteenth-century

45

Olivia Harris

Spanish 'chroniclers' give some account of the Inka practice of embalming, and describe the ceremonies for the royal mummies who retained their own lands and servants, were fed and clothed daily, and were publicly honoured with periodic ceremonies. Other sources give comparable information for the local level; each ethnic group apparently venerated its own ancestors, or at least those of the lords, often embalmed or in the form of an 'idol', and held sacred the tombs or caves where the relics and images were preserved.[2] These ranked high in the indigenous pantheon, and bestowed strength, good fortune and prosperity on those who worshipped them. Particularly significant for the context of this book is the information that mummies of the ancestors were identified closely with the land they once had worked, and with its continued fertility.[3]

A priest of the Archbishopric of Lima in the early years of the seventeenth century wrote a manual on how to discover and eliminate idolatry; he was particularly concerned with the discovery that the Andean population was disinterring the dead and taking them back to their traditional resting places in the fields:

They pour chicha discreetly into the tomb so that the dead may drink, and they make a show of doing him honour, placing cooked meals and roasts upon the grave for him to eat. For this reason, it has been forbidden them to place anything of this sort upon a grave on All Saints Day.

Their greatest abuse is to disinter the dead and remove their bodies to their machays, or burial places of their ancestors in the fields. In some localities they call these *zamay*, which means tomb of rest. At the time of death they cry out: 'Zamarcam', that is, 'Requievit'. On being asked why they do this, they say that this is cuyaspa, for the love they bear them. They say the dead lying in the church are in great torment and bound to the earth, whereas in the fields, because they are in the open air and not buried, they have more rest. (Arriaga, 1621 (1968):56)

Arriaga's response to these pagan practices was a catalogue of subtle manoeuvres to outwit the Indians: in the last instance mummies were to be assembled in the village plaza and publicly burnt. The ashes should then be thrown in the river and thus obliterated from memory and experience.

While practices for disposing of the dead differed throughout the Andes,[4] it seems clear that they were worshipped in a material form, and that the images and relics of the dead lords enshrined memory, wisdom, power and fertility. Small wonder then that so much missionary energy was directed towards this fundamental source of social existence. While I am here concerned with the present-day, attitudes towards death must be viewed through the optic of the past – both what is remembered and what is forgotten. Laymi beliefs about

46

the dead today illuminate historical knowledge, and are rendered more intelligible through appreciating the extent of the catastrophe suffered by Andean cultures in the sixteenth century and by trying to chart the complexity of the Catholicism which they espouse today.

The Laymi ethnic group, land and the State

Laymi are Aymara speakers, though most also speak a second Andean language – Quechua. Their territory is divided into two radically contrasted ecological zones, the highland *suni* (11000–15000 ft) and temperate intermontane valleys known as *likina* (7000–10000 ft). The ethnic group as a whole numbers some 8000, of which about two-thirds lives in the treeless highlands, and the rest in the valleys. The staples of the *suni* are indigenous tubers, including a wealth of potato varieties, and Old World cereals; most households own flocks of sheep and llamas. In the *likina* (at a distance of several days' journey), a radically different ecology produces maize and squashes as staples, and goats and some sheep are raised. There is a sharp contrast and a consciously-articulated sense of difference between these two 'tiers' of Laymi territory; nonetheless through the various historical experiences of political and administrative separation the Laymi have remained until the present a single integrated ethnic group, proclaiming through the internal circulation of produce, their overwhelming endogamy, their intricate and highly-distinctive aesthetic in textile production, an identity that transcends separation and opposition.[5]

Any traditional agrarian society must be oriented towards the past. Land, the source of life, has been cleared, cultivated, improved and handed on from one generation to the next. For the Laymi, relations with previous generations are represented through rights to land and inheritance of houses. Inheritance of fixed property is traced through agnatic links. Men inherit from their fathers and remember the forebears through whose hands their land has passed. Usually the furthest back they recall is the 'original' landholder whose titles were recorded in the last general cadastre of land rights carried out in 1884.[6] Agnatic lines of named forebears go back three or at most four generations where fixed property is involved. There is thus an agnatic bias in the returning of the dead; nonetheless the pattern of memory always includes four lines for any individual: father's, father's mother's, mother's father's, and mother's mother's. These cognatic ancestors are remembered through the pouring of libations on many ritual occasions. In some rituals the emphasis is on the personal forebears of the individuals who have organised the ritual, for example in house-building ceremonies; on other occasions however all the dead of the locality (*wisinu alma*) are remembered as a group, for example feasts which confirm rights of access to community land.

The important place given in ritual libations to the dead of the locality reflects the significance of the local land-group. As we shall see, all residents of a hamlet are implicated in the death of one of the vicinity, and celebrating the dead is the responsibility both of the kin and of the hamlet as a whole. But the contrast between the kin-group and the locality is not a sharp one in a context where most people marry close to home and where cognatic links are much emphasised. The ethnic group is overwhelmingly endogamous, and people circulate as spouses and as a source of labour throughout Laymi territory. While there are clear agnatic groups who own titles to, and work particular parcels, their identity as unique groups in opposition to other similar groups is diffused by the importance of the local land-group which usually embraces families from a variety of agnatic groups, as well as families with no direct access to land, who work land loaned by members of the vicinity. As such, demographic accumulation of particular groups in opposition to others is little emphasised.

In Laymi culture land is paramount; humans must serve the land both directly by cultivating it and through worship of the telluric spirits. The dead too, as we shall see, direct their energies towards agriculture and animal husbandry. Large families are frowned on by Laymi because they upset the balance between humans and land. When ritual libations are poured to celebrate natural increase, human fertility is never singled out as a primary value. Rather it is metaphorically transposed into the key of vegetation: the most common symbol of fertility is that of flowers.

One ethnographer of the Titicaca region some 200 km to the north writing 35 years ago, spoke of the 'strong ancestralism' and gerontocratic organisation of Aymara culture (La Barre, 1948:135).[7] But in Laymi society today there is little concentration of authority whether gerontocratic or not. Within the agnatic group authority is highly diffuse; inheritance is by ultimogeniture, and while land is mainly passed down agnatically, women too own property. Sexual parallelism and complementarity is fundamental to the way that authority is represented, such that it is multiple and shifting, rather than focused on a particular figure.[8] Within the land-holding communities, all traditional political offices, both the local headman and the dual authorities for the ethnic group as a whole (*segundas mayores*), rotate annually amongst adult male landholders. Offices in the national peasant union, established in the aftermath of the 1953

Agrarian Reform, do not rotate but are for the Laymi permanently elected positions; but the centres of power lie outside the ethnic group, controlled through the administrative system of the Bolivian state, careful surveillance by the army and manipulation of the union.

The Laymi of today have forgotten the times when they embalmed their dead to negate the corrosive effects of time on the decomposition of human flesh and memory. Control over the dead was a cornerstone of Christian policy for shedding the light of true religion in the lives of the heathens. The village church became the only acceptable place of burial; part of a wider colonial policy to concentrate the indigenous population into large villages (*reducciones*) in order to facilitate the administration of the new subject peoples of the Empire. The ancestors no longer exist in material form to which cult can be made. Nonetheless some trace lives on, particularly in the pre-Columbian burial chambers known as *chullpas*, found widely throughout the altiplano, and dating from the period preceding Inka hegemony (Hyslop, 1976). As Cieza de León commented in the early years of Spanish rule:

The things which, to my mind, are most worthy of notice in the Collao, are the tombs of the dead . . . I was truly astonished to see how little they cared for having large and handsome houses for the living, while they bestowed so much care on the tombs where the dead were interred. (Cieza de León, 1553 (1947))

Near the Laymi village of Qalaqala there is a huge ruined *chullpa* whose adobe walls tower above the single-storey houses nearby. In other areas, bones are used for divination and agricultural magic (La Barre, 1948:137). Laymi *chullpas* appear to have been sacked of all their relics, but they are still places of ambiguous power. The dead today are viewed with a repugnance which is never fully transcended. The absence of monuments or shrines to the dead is perhaps an indication of their ambiguity. Just as the Laymi are subject to the workings of a state over which they have little control, they are unable to harness fully the potential power of the dead for the reproduction of their own society.

The process of death

The dying are watched over by their kin and neighbours, who chew coca leaf and smoke cigarettes constantly as a prophylactic against the devils afflicting the sick person. When the person's soul has finally left the body, a three-stranded string is spun counter-clockwise (the spindle is normally twisted clockwise) with which to tie the neck, hands and feet of the deceased and thus to prevent the ghost from escaping. In the Titicaca region the corpse is actually strangled, ostensibly to prevent the stench from escaping (Carter, 1968; Buechler, 1980). The Laymi, too, from the moment of death refer continually to the stinking state of the corpse, using always the same term of disgust (*wali th''usqa*) to a degree which suggests that it is a categorical rather than a descriptive statement. The kin then cover the corpse and lay it on blankets; on top of it a hastily-made cross is placed, and some good-quality cloth, a hat and a bag for coca leaf. A candle, made from animal fat, is lit by the head and some piece of clothing closely associated with the death is thrown up on the roof.

At the same time, the family go to notify close bilateral kin and ritual kin in the neighbourhood and these come to assist the bereaved. As soon as the corpse has been hastily prepared a grand mobilisation of hamlet resources must be organised. First of all, quantities of coca leaf must be acquired in order to protect all who come to mourn and keep vigil from the malignant ghost. In Laymi territory there are virtually no shops, thus amassing sufficient coca leaf usually involves visits to several households. In the *suni* it is by now common custom to drink cane alcohol through the vigil and the wake; this again must be acquired rapidly from whoever has some stored. Next the bereaved must go round the hamlet soliciting help with an offering of coca leaf. Men must be persuaded to go in search of firewood, women to bring water; quantities of food must be assembled, an animal to slaughter is chosen or if necessary bought, a man and woman must be persuaded to organise the preparation and distribution of food, drink and coca leaf, another man requested to dig the grave, and older men or women to wash the corpse.

Once these basic provisions have been made, the close consanguines return to stay beside the body of the deceased until it is prepared for burial. They must keep a vigil for at least one night, chewing coca leaf, and if possible drinking cane alcohol, with constant offerings and libations to all deities, spirits, and souls of dead people. The following day a funeral feast is prepared for the whole hamlet and anybody else in the vicinity. To stay away deliberately from the feast endangers the whole community; on the other hand, little attempt is made to notify kin in other communities, and it will be a matter of luck whether they hear the news in time to attend.

After the feast, of which the deceased takes an honoured – if token – share, the body is washed and clothed in a white habit and hood that have been hastily sewn together from cotton flour-sacks. On its feet are placed rough sandals made from llama hide, worn by all Laymi until the recent introduction of the more durable and now ubiquitous rubber-tyre footwear. Men, and sometimes women past childbearing age, not close consanguines, perform these tasks while women prepare a bundle for the ghost to take on its long journey to the land of the dead; it contains food, coca leaf and a few household and personal articles, and also money so that the ghost can buy food and a house when it arrives at its destination. During these final preparations young men play games in order to build a house for the soul's future life. One, played with sheep knuckle bones, resembles dice, while the other is a form of bowls played with large stones. While I found it impossible to grasp the principles of scoring, the games were non-competitive and appeared to consist of reaching a round number and starting again. They provided a means of harnessing the energy of the young men to work for the future wellbeing of the deceased. The occurrence of games of chance at funeral ceremonies has been noted by various writers; their significance may lie in the repetitive elaboration of arbitrariness (for example in how the knuckle bone falls). In this way culture is able to play with and reorder the unanswerable arbitrariness of death.[9]

In the highlands, graveyards lie outside the nucleated hamlets, enclosed by high adobe walls and the single entrance blocked up with large stones. Where there is a burial ground there is often also within the settlement a small church or chapel, and the funeral party stops in the place of Christian worship to chew coca leaf, pour alcoholic libations and ask the protection of gods and saints for the soul now setting out on its long journey. In the graveyard a man not closely related to the deceased, again fortified by coca leaf and alcohol, has dug a grave three or four feet deep. Since graveyards are small and the digger is bound to unearth old bones, but those whose memory lives on must rest undisturbed; only those whose mortal remains bear no name can be viewed dispassionately and shoved aside to make way for newcomers.

The corpse is carried on a blanket strung between two poles by teams of men, who run from the funeral house to the graveyard, stopping only at ritually-appointed places, one yoke replacing another as they run. On this final earthly journey the ghost desires urgently to escape; by running with the corpse humans hope to outwit its intentions. In the highlands the nearest graveyard may lie some three or four hours' walk from more distant hamlets; in the temperate lowland, distance is compounded with steep ascent, since graveyards in this lower zone are located on mountain tops, unfenced-in but above the level of cultivation or habitation.[10] To transport the corpse running up the mountainside, after two days of mourning and a night of sleepless vigil, would in itself be a defiance of mortality. The allusion seems however to be more precise; the teams of men are called by the Laymi by the same term (*yunta*) as is used of the yoke of bulls who open the earth for sowing. The semantic link is found most clearly in a ritual that takes place at the sowing season to celebrate the Pachamama (the Andean earth mother, in whom are incarnated both space and time), when pairs of young men are yoked to the plough and driven across the fields opening the first furrow; they are bulls, and like bulls they are strong and uncontrollable. The wilder they are, the harder they run, the more efficacious is the ritual, the more glorious their show of strength. Not only their strength, but also their paired duality under the plough makes of bulls a primary expression of the integral bond between humans and earth. The way that the corpse is taken to be placed in the newly-opened earth is thus explicitly reminiscent of a ritual which embodies the critical act of cultivation. This interpretation gains support from a comparable procedure in the Qullawaya region to the north. In the precipitous landscape of Kaata, Old World bulls and ploughs have not replaced the native Andean foot plough; there the manner in which the grave itself is dug, using the foot plough, bears striking resemblance to the way that fields are tilled and potatoes planted: in the words of the ethnographer 'the grave-digging was a relay race; they plowed and shoveled in pairs to the point of exhaustion and then were replaced by another pair' (Bastien, 1978:125).

All those who accompany the corpse enter the graveyard for a final moment to wail and offer libations and coca leaf, and then household members, women of childbearing age and any children present must leave as three foot of earth is heaped over the corpse, topped by thorns and a cross. In this final moment of dispatch the ghost tries desperately to seize another person for company; women, children and close kin are the most vulnerable. After the burial more food is distributed to all who took part and they then return home. Immediate kin and household members remain in heavy mourning for eight days, wearing black, and abstaining from salt and chilli pepper in their food. The end of this first period of mourning is marked by washing the clothes and other possessions of the dead; libations are poured and the washers build in the stream-bed little houses and gardens for the deceased to inhabit and cultivate in the land of the dead. The mourners may cease to wear black; the dead person's property is allocated now, though it is not yet distributed.

The participants in Laymi mortuary rites are first and foremost immediate kin and household members. After making the initial preparations they remain beside the corpse until the moment of burial.

The active tasks on the other hand are the responsibility of those whose relationship with the deceased is less direct: affines and ritual kin play an important part, since they are less vulnerable to attack. The role of in-marrying women, or men, is often ambivalent. Young in-marrying spouses appeared to stay apart from the central mourning group, while older people married away from their genealogical kin, more fully incorporated, are likely to join completely in mourning for their affines. The man who distributes coca leaf and sometimes alcohol to mourners is also responsible for urging them to weep and display their sense of loss; he himself is less likely to mourn. Close female kin usually lead in wailing and keening, but men too show great emotion and behave like the women. This is especially evident when alcohol is flowing; however the parallel behaviour of women and men in mourning is not simply the result of intoxication, but conforms to the overwhelming parallelism and complementarity between the sexes typical of Andean culture as a whole (Harris, 1978a). In conformity with Laymi ritual practice overall, the participation of both sexes is obligatory, but at any one time, there will be far more men than women in attendance. Few women join the vigil, and during the day too most women remain outside the house of mourning, helping in preparation of the funeral feast, while the men sit beside the corpse itself. When the deceased was a woman, there is likely to be greater involvement of women as mourners, but in this case too it is men and post-menopausal women who mediate the dangerous world of ghosts because of women's great vulnerability to them.[11] This vulnerability is stressed in various contexts. The implications are clear. In Andean culture women do not mediate between the dead and the living, representing simultaneously all bodily functions whether of birth or decay (unlike for example the account of Watson, this volume). Rather the dead are represented here as antithetical to the living, and women of childbearing age are correspondingly the category of people who must be most rigorously separated from the ambiguous activities of the dead (Harris, 1980).

From the many rituals associated with the period after death, it is clear that the dead are a danger to the living; the spirit must be restrained in its own body (by tying the neck, arms and feet after death, the use of thorns to prevent it escaping, and running to the graveyard), and the living must protect themselves from it (through constant chewing of coca leaf, wailing, leaving the grave prior to burial, putting up thorns and knives to keep it from the house, taking care not to sleep or walk alone at night, and avoiding the graveyard at all times, especially at night which is the time of ghosts). The dead are 'envious';

if they are not given their due whether of food, animal sacrifice, coca leaf, or display of sorrow from their kin they will haunt the abode of the living. Thus the major concern is to get rid of the ghost, and much of the ritual is performed with this aim. The corpse itself is polluting: we have already mentioned the frequent references to its fetid state, and all those who go in to pay their final respects, particularly those who actually prepare the corpse, must wash themselves in water in which cleansing herbs (*ismillu*) have been boiled. After the corpse has been taken away for burial the whole house is swept with a broom made of the same herbs, and then more of the water is sprinkled throughout. The sweepings, like all ritually-dangerous substances, must be taken to the river or stream for the devils to eat.

But the ghost is from the start a more substantial threat than the body; in death as in life, bodily functions scarcely pollute. Today Laymi representation of death exemplifies the common duality that opposes what disintegrates to what survives. In previous epochs the preserved mummies were objects of worship and power; today only the spirits of the dead survive, while respect for mortal remains is contingent on human memory. However, while Christian teaching must have reinforced a dualistic understanding of death in the separation of body and soul, it did not take full control of the spirits of the dead. As we shall see, Laymi beliefs about the afterlife imply either that they were given to understand that heaven was not for the likes of them, or more probably that the dead had other responsibilities which outweighed possible elysian pleasures.

Feasting the dead and the devils

While immediate mourning may be brought to a close after eight days, the deceased is still close to the world he or she has left behind. The central moment of separation comes in the annual celebration of the feast of All Saints on November 1st, followed by All Souls on the 2nd. The month of November was dedicated to the dead also in the Inka calendar (Valcarcel, 1948:474), and there is evident continuity in the extraordinary complex of rituals practised today.

The souls of the dead arrive the night before All Saints, and those households where someone has died in the course of the previous year must hold a feast for the soul. Previously they have brewed chicha and baked quantities of bread, much of it shaped as 'babies' (*wawa* in Aymara and Quechua) in the form of humans, animals, celestial and mythological beings.[12] Wild flowers, heralding the spring and the onset of rain, are placed on the roof to welcome the dead (*wayllura*); a llama is slaughtered in its honour; a table is prepared, typical of all offerings to telluric spirits and similar to the one at the wake itself, except that now a greater variety of luxury foods is offered to the spirit. Close kin keep vigil through the night pouring libations for it and all spirits of the dead, remembered and forgotten, and for all celestial beings, spirits and guardians of the community. The vigil is brought to a close with a ritual breakfast of maize porridge (*qalapari*). On the day of All Saints itself, the bereaved family offers festive food to the entire community. Where there is more than one soul to be feasted it is so organised that everybody can go in succession from one feast to the next. It is important that all should attend and celebrate together. After the feast, the clothes and personal property of the deceased are again ritually washed. In addition to the washing itself, all participants and the objects themselves must cross over the stream. The water signals an effective separation from the deceased; souls cannot cross water unaided.[13] The property can then be distributed, and any old or worn items will be burnt.

The day of All Saints itself is a transition from the celebration of an individual ghost to a more collective ritual. Members of all the communities who use a particular graveyard converge on it. Graves of those who have died in the previous two years are covered by stepped altars 7–8 feet high, known as *escaleras* (Sp. = ladder) on which the souls will supposedly ascend into heaven. Their passage is assisted by prayers of all who go to the graveyard; those who can make long recitations in Latin are much in demand, but even a short prayer in Spanish is welcomed by those who preside over the 'ladders' of their dead kin. To this structure have been tied as many offerings as can be crammed on: bread icons of the sun and moon at the top, together with a Bolivian five peso note, and below them all forms of delicacy – bread babies, fruit, specially-prepared maize, chilli peppers, dried meat, coca leaf, cigarettes. All who pray are 'paid' with food, chicha, alcohol, coca leaf, and after a few hours emotions have risen to a crescendo. When I attended this feast in the highlands, a few weeks after I arrived, the chaos was indescribable; it poured with rain and the walled-in graveyard was simply not large enough to contain all who had come to mourn and pray. All around people were wailing drunkenly and reciting prayers which grew shorter and shorter as the afternoon wore on, embracing each other and calling on the dead. The bread and food they earned was quickly hidden away in the folds of their clothes, since it could not be consumed until the feast of the dead was completed. When night fell more food was handed round, and drinking, singing and dancing continued in and around the graveyard until the following day. When the ladders had been dismantled and the graveyard unceremoniously abandoned, feasting and drinking continued for another day or two in the households of the deceased, and then the ghost was ritually despatched. On such occasions the family once again provides food for its journey and with this parting gift they shoo it away from their home. However even this somewhat dismissive act is recast as an offering from the earth to the participants. As they return they collect up bits and pieces – on the occasion I witnessed we gathered maize stalks, sheep dung and stones – which are distributed, as the property of the deceased, to enrich those who have paid their dues. I myself received a 'cow' and a 'grinding stone'.

The timing of an individual death is arbitrary. In the feast of All Saints, death is tamed, becomes cyclical, is transformed into a ritual in which all join together; after this celebration the bereaved may take off their mourning clothes. However, while all attend, the festival also emphasises social divisions. Mourning of the dead is organised by their kin, who are united as a group by their need to propitiate the dead. Those who have prepared the ritual tables and 'ladders' use the opportunity to ask for prayers for all their other dead kin, thus reiterating the particularity of their own genealogical position.

Again, the very disposition of the graveyard emphasises social distinction within the ethnic group; graves are arranged according to group affiliation, both by moiety and sub-divisions within each moiety. Each part of the graveyard is associated with a local section of these sub-groups. The division is not merely a spatial one; at the level of moieties it finds expression in the ritual battle (*tinku*) which is fought at All Saints as at most feasts throughout the year. The composition of the units ranged against each other in a *tinku* differs according to the feast and who is present, but Laymi fighting at All Saints is particularly associated with the opposition of moieties within the ethnic group. These moieties are not primarily marriage classes, rather affiliation derives from landholding; Platt argues for the neighbouring Macha that the ritual battles are in part assertions of rights to land, and that the blood spilt is necessary for the earth to bring forth the harvest (Platt, n.d.).

All Saints in the Andes is a spring festival, marking the time for sowing and planting, and the start of the rains. The initiation of the agricultural cycle is, then, marked by the 'socialisation' of the graveyard which at all other times is a place avoided with fear and repugnance. In the attention paid to the souls of the dead, there is a movement from obligatory mourning, to release from the ghosts and festive celebration. In the calendrical cycle however, All Saints is a moment of transition away from festivity since the season of rains, the period of growth and maturation, is marked by taboos and restraint, and is a time of sadness. During this period contact with water and washing is restricted; small round mirrors, the festive decoration of the young and unmarried, must not be worn. Above all, All Saints initiates the time of *wayñus*, melodies played on wooden flutes whose explicitly mournful tones pervade the whole season and attract rain.

The end of the rains is celebrated at Carnival (February/March) which is the most important feast of the Laymi year, singled out from all others, and marking both the First Fruits and the New Year. Its name in Aymara is *Anata*, the time of play; it is also known as the feast of the devils. Celebrations continue for up to ten days and embrace a wealth of different rituals. As the festival of First Fruits it is a time for rites of increase; armfuls of wild flowers are collected and placed on the houses, the ritual altars, in the animal corrals and in the ritual bundles carried by individual sponsors of the feast. Plants from the maturing crops are stolen from the fields and carried triumphantly as offerings for those who provide chicha and food for the festival. Special rites are held for the flocks to encourage their continued increase.

Carnival is a most dramatic proclamation of community. It is the only feast of the year in which fighting is forbidden, and ritual battles are never fought.[14] A highlight of the feast is the visits paid by people of all ages to villages and hamlets within, and sometimes beyond the confines of the ethnic group. It is the feast in which women enter most fully into the celebrations; on other occasions married women are often prevented from joining in the dancing and singing, but at Carnival they too stay up all night, and go visiting. Young people will make sure to visit other communities where girls from their own hamlet have married, thus reuniting briefly those whose lives have been separated by virilocal residence. Wherever they visit they offer plants from the fields, and sing and dance; in return they are given food, drink and coca leaf.

These visits are marked vividly by the display of cloth and clothing. Girls and young men take their entire wardrobes and more, hanging what they cannot actually wear from cloths or ropes strung across their backs. This is personal display, but it also has the effect of reducing individuals to virtual anonymity beneath the weight of cloth. The anonymity is complete for those who wear what is known as *sintapulla*, cow-hide helmets worn by warriors and entirely covered over with brightly-coloured ribbons (*sinta*) which hang almost to the ground. It is virtually impossible to identify the wearer, and even sexual distinctions are blurred. There is a deliberate creation of mystery, an attempt to avoid being recognised as long as possible.[15]

Another form in which individuality is suppressed is the shared vulnerability of all to the devils who throng the world at this time. During Carnival nobody should walk alone, whether by night or day, for they will surely be led astray or carried off by the devils. It is virtually impossible to be alone during the week of major celebration. Even sleep is more or less abandoned, and certainly nobody would sleep on their own.

The end of Carnival is signalled by the ritual dispatch of the male and female devils. Men and women in each hamlet impersonate them, wearing black goatskins over their clothes, and festooned with wild flowers and plants from the fields. The male(s) wear a cow-hide helmet, now divested of ribbons. The devils dance through the entire hamlet, visiting in turn each house; in each they are offered alcoholic drink. They are then accompanied out of inhabited space to a flat place[16] where their disguises are torn off and the 'devils' of Carnival thus sent packing. In a dramatic finale the flutes that have provided music throughout the entire season of rains are piled up together. Immediately the young men take up their *charangos* (small mandolins) and break into a radically different musical style (*kirki*) to which everybody dances round with an abandonment rarely seen on other occasions.

Only through this final rite known as Tapakayu was I able to discover the identity of the Carnival devils. I had been recording the *wayñu* melodies of the flutes, and later that evening began to play the music back. I was immediately stopped by a horrified audience: *wayñu* music belonged to the devils who were now safely dispatched on their way to the land of the dead, and would be drawn back if they heard the sound of the flutes. It thus emerged that the devils whose feast is Carnival are in some form the spirits of the dead. At this season they are personified as a source of danger – they make people ill, lead them astray and to their deaths if they remain alone instead of joining the collective celebration. But they are also celebrated as the abundance of natural increase, and are festooned with the wild and domesticated plant life they have helped to grow. It is they who make the crops flourish and reproduce the flocks. This association of danger and fertility is made in the person of spirits who are no longer individual, named ghosts but have a new identity. Nobody ever directly explained that these devils were the ancestors. Only through music did it become clear that the dead remain in the world of the living throughout the season of rains. Having understood their transformed presence, other symbolic statements became clear. For example in the temperate valleys glow-worms appear with the rains at All Saints and die at harvest time; their light in the night is that of souls, and makes known the presence of the dead in the world of the living at this season. Round mirrors, which are taboo as decoration throughout the rains, are used in neighbouring Macha to keep away the souls of the dead, for example placed at the entrance to the graveyard to prevent a death (Platt, 1978:1097). According to the Macha, mirrors are 'the enemy of the soul of the dead'. When the dead are in residence, then, there must be no hint of wishing to have them leave. Other prohibitions express the same intent; for example it is considered harmful to the growing crops to bathe oneself during the rainy season. We have already noted that water is antithetical to the souls. It is also prohibited to touch the ancient *chullpa* burial chambers through the rainy season, or the dead will send lightning or hail to destroy the crops.[17]

In the moment of death itself, explicit reference is made to the process of cultivation; at All Saints, the deceased are embraced within the agricultural cycle, and the process of bodily decay is virtually ignored in favour of that of natural increase. The feasting of individual ghosts at that time can be fully understood only in relation and in contrast to the celebration of Carnival, at which the cycle initiated at All Saints is brought to its completion.[18] The integral relationship of these two feasts was clear from the way that Laymi people talked about them. I was continually asked whether the two feasts were kept also in 'Inkiltira' (England), while nobody expressed much curiosity as to what other festivals the English might celebrate. I was told that All Saints and Carnival were *muntu intiru* (Sp. = *mundo entero*) i.e. that they were celebrated worldwide. Thus these feasts for the Laymi are universal: they unify and transcend social boundaries, while other feasts are specific to particular groups or categories, and are thus forms of individuation and differentiation.

At All Saints, the spirit is first welcomed and mourned individually, and then there is a move towards collectivity in the graveyard itself, where members of different hamlets gather to pray together for all their dead. The organisation of libations at this feast indicates a parallel movement: before the distribution of llama meat that signals the central point of feasting, libations are poured from a single bowl for the souls of the individual departed; after the meat has been distributed to the assembled hamlet and kin, libations are poured from two bowls. Here as elsewhere, duality stands for multiplicity and hence for collective fertility, both of flocks, crops and human beings.

When the property of the deceased is ritually washed during the feast of All Saints, the physical presence of death is obliterated, and the dispatch of the ghost at the end of the ritual period is a real expulsion. In another sense however the dead do not depart. As a collective presence they remain with the living. But the transformation of individual death into collectivity is not completed until the harvest. The season of rains is the time of *individual* household production; there is little movement from one place to another; each productive unit must concentrate all its energies on bringing the crops successfully to harvest and caring for the flocks. Few feasts, and no marriages are celebrated during this season.

Carnival brings seasonal reversal. Throughout the dry season collective consumption and feasting is enjoined. People travel to distant parts of Laymi territory and beyond. Through music, Carnival marks a complete discontinuity between the presence of the ghosts and their subsequent banishment to the land of the dead. While they have been there for the whole growing season, their presence is vividly dramatised during the final days before they leave. Flute music attracts rain; it is a form of dirge and thus will not cause offence to the dead whose co-operation is essential to bring the crops to fruition.[19] In stark contrast, the music of the dry season is joyful and celebratory. The *wayñu* music of the rainy season is said to weep (*q'asi*) while the *kirki* of the dry season is happy (*kusisi*).

The sharp opposition of emotions is indeed a common theme in Laymi ritual. It is found clearly in another rite celebrated for the individual soul; while the deceased is gradually caught up in the concentration of energies that produces the harvest, it is not immediately forgotten as an individual soul. In this further rite, after the first All Saints and Carnival, a life-size dummy of the deceased is made, wearing some of its former clothes. It is feasted and mourned, and then with very little respect is seized by an affine, wife-taker to the bereaved (*tullqa*); it is untied, dissolved and thrown by him out of the compound. While it is the duty of kin to weep on this occasion, it is correspondingly the duty of affines to laugh. In what is virtually an emotional division of labour, the ambivalence that all must feel toward the recently-departed is enacted, and ends with the physical dissolution of the dead person's image.[20]

When All Saints comes round a second time for the individual soul, the rites of the previous year are repeated, but on a smaller scale and with less show of grief. After this a final ritual of dispatch must be performed, known as *misa jant'aku* (Mass for laying it to rest), in which a Mass is offered for the ghost and it is finally dispatched to the land of the dead as an individual. Only after this rite is a surviving spouse allowed to remarry. The bereaved will continue to offer Masses and to pour libations for the soul as long as it survives in living memory, but it is no longer an individual threat. Its dangerous power is now harnessed to the great ceremonial cycle of production and fertility.

The fate of the soul

In the preceding account I have used indiscriminately the terms ghost, soul, and spirit to refer to the essence of a dead person which survives bodily decay. In doing this I have followed the apparent lack of consistency with which Laymi themselves think about the afterlife. Nonetheless there is a certain linguistic conformity, in that many of the terms used to talk about the recently-dead and the ceremonial addressed to them are of Spanish origin. The word used to refer to the corpse and the ever-present envious ghost of the recently-dead is the Spanish term for the non-corporeal soul (*alma*). What is in Catholic theology the aspect of the individual intended for eternal salvation is thus subverted to designate the most dangerous and repellent and also transitory, manifestation of the dead. The corpse is buried in a 'habit' (*awitu*) in a grave known by the Spanish term (*sepultura*), in a graveyard again named in Spanish (*panteón*). During the feast of the dead at All Saints, a ladder (*escalera*) is built so that the soul can ascend to heaven, aided by prayers said in Spanish or preferably Latin. As the souls are socialised into Laymi culture and their power is harnessed on the other hand, they are no longer called by Spanish terms, but by the Aymara *amaya*.[21] There is a further representation of the dead which remains within the church; this is *animasa* (Aymara: lit. = 'our souls') – a nameless human skull kept in a casket and celebrated together with the saints at the feast of the Holy Cross in the hamlet of Muruq'umarka. Beliefs and rituals concerning the dead offer a fertile ground for assessing both the separation and the fusion between Christian and pre-Hispanic cultures in the Andean world.

There are without doubt many incompatibilities in Laymi versions of what befalls the dead; rather than trying to systematise them we should perhaps heed Hertz's caution that 'the ideas relating to the fate of the soul are in their very nature vague and indefinite: we should not make them too clear cut' (Hertz, 1960:34). For example, the moment of death is when the ghost leaves the body, but one of the first ritual acts after death is intended to tie the ghost to the body. Again the ghost sets out immediately on its journey, equipped with food and other necessities; yet it also stays to haunt the living. Until the final despatching in the *misa jant'aku* it is both present and departed. One

Olivia Harris

Laymi man tried to resolve this conundrum in the same way as Tschopik (1951), by suggesting that one of the 'shades' (*ch'iwu*) goes to the land of the dead while another remains in the hamlet.[22] The shades, in tune with Laymi belief that the number three signifies ritual completeness, are conceived as tripartite; this man suggested in the interests of consistency that the third shade went after death to 'heaven', a neat solution which also resolved the ambiguities of Catholic and indigenous visions. It was nonetheless contradicted by many other people. While the spirit of the dead is tripartite, to attempt a clear-cut division of functions would be to do violence to a meaning that is intrinsically shifting and multivocal. If Laymi believe that the non-corporeal element of individuals is tripartite, it is not because the three parts go in different directions when they are liberated from the body, but more likely because they do not share Western preoccupations with the transcendent unity of the individual subject.

Concerning the land of the dead itself there is greater consistency, but also contradictory elements. This place, known as Tacna, is held to lie on the other side of the sea, which the souls of the dead must cross on the nose, or in the ear, of a black dog.[23] In reality the town of Tacna lies near the coast in the extreme south of Peru and is situated on the Laymi side of the sea. The ghosts are thought to travel the same roads as those used by living Laymi; indeed the highlanders are not freed from the dead for a while after Carnival, since all the ghosts travelling back to Tacna from the valley region must pass on their way through the highlands. As well as lying on the further side of the ocean, Tacna is said to be underneath, that is, a sort of underworld reached by crossing the water. Underneath (*manq"a*) is in some contexts synonymous with the land of the dead, and is the place where the sun goes when it is night on earth. This place is an inversion not only as regards diurnal alternation, but also of the seasons, for while the Laymi live through the rain it is dry beneath, and while on earth it is winter, the dead live through the season of agricultural growth.[24]

Descriptions of Tacna varied; there was some disagreement as to whether one could remarry there, or whether one remained for ever with one's first spouse of life on earth. But all agreed that the main occupation of the dead is the cultivation of red chilli pepper (*aji*). To say that somebody has gone to cultivate chilli pepper is a common metaphor of death.[25] This hot relish is a potent symbol in many contexts; also red as a colour is closely associated with the dead and mortuary ritual throughout the Andes. An old woman told me of how she once nearly died and went right to Tacna. It was a large town, but the buildings were very low, only a few feet high, and everything was red. The children all had flowers in their hair.

It seems that when the souls of the dead are dispatched to Tacna at the end of Carnival they go to work, to cultivate a crop whose significance to Laymi culture is paramount, both in codes of food consumption and in magic. It is however a crop that the Laymi are no longer able to cultivate since they lost control early in the colonial epoch of the hot valley-lands they had formerly worked.[26] The theme of seasonal renewal here receives an additional twist: through the rains when the living toil and cultivate in sadness, the dead among them are feasted and respected. Conversely when the living gather the harvest and rest, the dead return to work. While there is no indication in Waman Puma's account of mortuary beliefs, cited above, of a cyclical movement, his contrast between the two states enjoyed by the dead captures the stark opposition in Laymi cosmology. The world of the dead inverts not only day and night, summer and winter, but also productive activity and collective enjoyment; the dead produce a crop, that complements the subsistence-orientation of Laymi economy today – a crop which, according to the traditional patterns of Andean exploitation of the environment, the Laymi should be able to cultivate for themselves.

While I have talked of the dead as an undifferentiated category, the description applies primarily to married adults. It is they – both women and men – who have achieved full social identity; this bears emphasising since so many accounts of mortuary rites apparently assume that it is only men who die. Laymi who die single encounter similar experiences in the afterlife, but their lack of completion must be made good by burying with them a domestic fowl as companion for the future: a hen for a male and a cock for a female. Married souls, as I have said, travel on the known paths to Tacna; the unmarried go instead over the thorn bushes, and by night when human beings do not under normal circumstances travel. Since there is today no class differentiation within the ethnic group, this distinction in marital status is one of the few points of difference in how the dead are treated.

Children however experience a different fate. In general there is no mourning beyond the kin-group when a child dies, and the feast offered at All Saints is on a smaller scale, but children who die are not simply a smaller version of adults. They are called *angelitos* (Sp. = little angels); at burial little white paper wings are attached to their white 'habit' and they fly to heaven. There they are set to look after God's irrigation system and send water to earth in the form of rain. Alternatively, people say that when we weep for *angelitos* God

Olivia Harris

punishes them with his whip, and their tears of pain fall to earth as rain.[27] During the feast of All Saints there is some feeling that all souls must reach heaven; in other contexts there are assumed to be children in Tacna; certainly children are thought to be especially vulnerable to abduction by the envious ghosts of the recently-dead; still for most purposes the fate that awaits children and adults at death is recognisably distinct. The much closer connection of the *angelitos* with Christian cosmological themes perhaps reflects the Catholic doctrine that only the innocent are assured of salvation. On the other hand though they go to heaven, they too are harnessed to the needs of the agricultural economy, both directly in sending rain, and indirectly in that their work in their new home is to maintain the irrigation ditches.

One class of infants is excluded from becoming *angelitos*, namely those babies who die before being baptised. All babies are baptised by a priest on his rare visits to Laymi hamlets, or when Laymi are able to make the long journey to a parish church in the mining centre of Uncia or the old colonial town of Chayanta. Full baptism is thus often delayed many months; however immediately after birth a rite is held in order to give the child a name and thus bring it into the chain of signification that is culture. The rite itself is called 'to pour water' (*um waraña*), and a baby that dies before this rite has been performed is known as a little Moor (*muru wawa*; cf. Sp. *moro* = Moor). The Laymi definition of *muru* is 'without a name', and Bertonio's 1612 (1956) dictionary of Aymara translatees this term (*sutiuisa*) by the Spanish *infiel* (= infidel). The Italian Jesuit however also notes at length that the Aymara concept of naming is *not* the same as Christian baptiism, which is rather centred around the idea of cleansing (Bertonio, 1612 (1956):330); it is clear from the way he writes that Aymara culture in the early seventeenth century attached greater importance to the nname than to the accompanying rituals, and today too the focus of baptism is the name. A baby that dies unnamed has no place in heaven; it must be left outside inhabited space for the mountain spirits to eat. If this due is not paid the mountains punish the community by sending hail, which in the Andes can ruin an entire harvest in the space of a few minutes.

The infants who are nameless belong not to society but to the spirits who preside over the Laymi landscape – the mountains whose power is highly charged but ambiguous. To the mountains also belong those who have committed incest, known as *condenados* or condemned ones. They are extremely threatening to the living; anyone who is unfortunate enough to meet one will surely die or suffer terrible misfortune. They live out on the mountainside, or travel round the world, wearing a stone on one foot, a prickly cactus on the other.

64

Devils, fertility, ambivalence

The connections between the dead and the regeneration of fertility in Laymi culture are not immediately obvious. Human fertility is clearly affected negatively by the dead, in that women of childbearing age must be kept separate from the corpse, and if they conceive as a result of contact with spirits of the dead the result will be a monstrous birth. As was noted above, the reproduction of Laymi society is represented through the land and its fertility, rather than human fertility. But even here the connections between death and fertility cannot be immediately made. In many respects the crucial place occupied by the dead in the agricultural cycle is concealed by metaphor. Symbolic usage concentrates in many ways on the involvement of the dead in the continued fecundity of plant and animal life but these are not in the main explicit. The power vested in the collective ancestors is also indirect. Nothing in Laymi attitudes to the dead today seems to conjure up the spirit of 'adoration' and 'worship' used by early colonial writers to describe the veneration of their ancestors by Andean peoples.

An illustration of this apparent ambiguity can be found for example in the concept *niñu*. Deriving presumably from the Spanish word for child (and thus possibly from the Christ child), *niñu* when used in libation refers to the ancestors. When I inquired why the ancestors should be called children, I was told that they were the children of the sun and moon, supreme deities of the Laymi pantheon, and identified with the Christian God and Virgin Mary. *Niñu* however has also a multiplicity of other meanings that undermine this clear identification with the moral force of celestial deities. It can, for example, be used to refer variously to severe fevers, the carrion condor, the mountain spirits, bulls, and wife-taking affines. The rite performed to ward off the ravages of epidemics is known as 'taking out the *niñu*' (*niñu apsuña*); bulls are the incarnation of telluric energy, but their very power lies in their uncontrollability; wife-takers, identified in myth and ritual with the condor, are necessary for reproduction but also the source of discord and fragmentation. Many of the meanings of *niñu* are clearly sources of power which are not fully controlled. Another referent of *niñu* suggests a close connection with the representation of fertility; this is the small crosses kept in the Calvary chapel (*Calvario*) and used in the feast of Carnival to symbolise fertility and life.

The complex meanings embodied in this term are startling, particularly if it indeed derives from the unambiguous and positive power residing, according to Catholic doctrine, in the figure of the Christ child. In Laymi usage *niñu* also refers in some contexts to the mountain spirits (*kumprira*), and this meaning perhaps gives the clearest indication of its semantic parameters. The mountain peaks are the guardians of their lives; they are the source of bad weather, of hail and thunder and rain. Sacred and powerful places, they are also the source of life; they are simultaneously protectors and malevolent beings, bringers of fertility, but also disaster and illness (Martinez, 1976). The mountain spirits are classified as part of the 'evil sphere' (*saxra parti*); this is opposed to 'God's sphere' to which belong the sun, moon, and Catholic saints. The 'evil sphere' is that of the devils (in Aymara the word *saxra* means both bad, evil, and evil spirit/devil), or at least of indigenous deities who became 'evil' as Christian doctrine was imposed and Andean structures of power dismantled.[28] It will be recalled that Carnival, marking First Fruits and the new year, is called the feast of the devils; disguised with goatskins and abundant vegetation these embodiments of the ancestors celebrate fertility at the same time as they pose a serious threat to the revellers. The Laymi ancestors today do not represent a fully cultural force, embodying social morality and authority; the only unambiguous source of morality is the sun (*inti*), whose cult was central to Inka statecraft, and who is today identified with God. The sun however is remote (Tschopik, 1951); it is the spirits of the 'evil sphere' who affect more directly the daily life of the Laymi. The devils work by night, and inhabit wild places, such as gullies, waterfalls, rocks and mountain tops; graveyards are classified together with these places, feared and avoided in everyday life. The placing of the dead in the 'evil sphere' is, finally, evoked by the fact that one of the common names of the mountain spirits is precisely the term for ancestors, or grandparents (*achachawila*).

In some sense, then, the dead belong in a category of beings identified with the wild, a source both of fertility and of misfortune. An opposition between the wild and the social should however be applied with caution: the boundaries are shifting and relative. For example, while in one sense all the dead are 'devils' and categorised with other manifestations of the wild, in another sense the clear identification of unbaptised babies and of those who have committed incest with the mountains implies by contrast that other ghosts are socialised. Within this group beliefs about the journey taken, respectively, by the married and the single after death again argues that the former are closer to human society than the latter. It would however be a vain exercise to attempt to fix the significance of the dead; they are a transitive force, who move between the existences of dangerous, envious, ever-present devils, and the world of Tacna where they toil in the fields and live a life that closely parallels that on earth. While they are devils, they are more benign than some. They are a type of devil for which Masses are offered in church; with all the ambiguities of the Laymi interpretation of Christianity and the subversion of its proclaimed meanings in mortuary practice, the identification of the dead with the church renders them susceptible to the controlling power of the priest. On the other hand the close association of the dead with church buildings has the effect that these are dangerous at night and are avoided. Night is the time of devils and particularly of the spirits of the dead.

While the Laymi ancestors do not today embody social morality and authority, the feasts for the dead are the most important in the Aymara ritual calendar. This being the case, it could be argued that the dead are the major source of cosmic power from Laymi society. Why then do they pose such a threat to the living, particularly since the Laymi perceive little threat from biological processes in themselves? In part the answer to this question must lie in the fact that the processes of fertility and growth are themselves not fully controlled by the living. But there is a further dimension that concerns the exercise of political authority overall. As other papers in this volume suggest, the cult of the dead may be a way in which social and political authority is rendered eternal.

The fragmentary evidence available suggests that in Andean societies before 1532 the disposal of the dead and the cult paid to them was closely bound up with hierarchy and sources of authority. Today, too, there are some traces of a close connection between political office and the cult of the dead. The local headman (*jilanqu*) is responsible for his community's tax payments, formerly for the Spanish crown, and more recently for the Departmental coffers of the Bolivian Republic. At the same time the headman incarnates the prosperity of those he represents. It is he who ceremoniously initiates the ploughing which brings fallow land into cultivation; known as the shepherd, he must pour many libations throughout the year for collective fertility. As the person who assembles the tax payments of the community he is the critical agent mediating between State power and subsistence cultivators; he must also hear and settle disputes. His ritual importance is signalled by the fact that unlike other office-holders, he must be accompanied in all formal rites by his wife, or at least by a female partner, thus signifying the complementary duality which in Andean thought is the essence of continued reproduction (Harris, 1978*a*).

The new office-holder is installed at the beginning of Carnival; indeed it is his instalment on the Thursday before Carnival that initiates this great feast. This, in the Laymi calendar, is the time not only of First Fruits and New Year, but also the point at which the new agricultural cycle begins, with the first ploughing of the fields which will be brought into cultivation the following spring (September). In other areas of Aymara culture the connections of this office with the dead are more explicit: in Kaata for example the various secretaries of the national peasant union preside over every funeral (Bastien, 1978:178–87), and in many parts of the altiplano the office of headman is actually initiated at the feast of All Saints.[29]

Today the office of headman rotates annually. In one sense it could be argued that the rotating nature of the office eternalises it, since it is thus separated from an identification with any particular individual or individuals; however it also exemplifies the extreme limitations on power within the structures of Laymi society. All landholding adult males are expected to take their turn in office, regardless of their suitability for the post, so that in years when it is held by a weak or ineffectual person, little authority is wielded. The same holds true for the moiety authorities of the ethnic group as a whole.

Today the sources of power lie outside the reach of Laymi culture, in the army, the Church, among those who control wealth and the State apparatus. The ethnic groups of northern Potosí have not been able to forge a 'pact of reciprocity' with the Bolivian State (Platt & Molina, in press) by which the exercise of power might be clearly demarcated. The way that external power is represented suggests that for the Laymi it is ambiguous. The Catholic priest, for example, is the representative of the sun-God, but he is also a secret evil-doer who steals life-giving fat from the bodies of Indians to use for his own nefarious purposes. The townspeople who lose no opportunity to remind the Indian population of their inferior, savage status, and contrast it with their own mastery of civilisation, are called in Aymara the 'undressed' (q'ara).

For the Laymi there is thus no longer a clear source of power from which the social order is mythically derived. It is true that in some contexts Laymi talk of the sun (inti) as such a source, but the sun is a general source of morality and social life, and does not often intervene directly in human affairs. The weight of Laymi representation of the sources of good and bad fortune, of punishment and reward, is in the 'evil sphere' where the mountain spirits guard jealously over their prerogatives, and where the devils and the dead are the source of illness and death as well as fecundity and life. As power was removed from the ethnic group the veneration of their embalmed lords was forbidden; today among the Laymi, social office has ceased altogether to be incarnated in particular individuals. There are no monuments and few permanent records of the dead; those who are named receive full burial and feasting and in turn with their presence they ensure fertility. A source of ambiguous power, like the mountain tops, like the bulls who plough, they are harnessed to the service of society in an alliance which is always precarious. As long as their name lives on in someone's memory they will be offered a libation. Thereafter they become part of the crowd of 'nameless ghosts' for whom a Mass is offered at the feast of St Andrew – the end of the Inka month of the dead.

Many anthropologists have written of the victory of society over the deaths of individual members. This victory is a victory of symbolic integration, of the harnessing of the potential anarchy of death to the moral organisation of society. For the Laymi today such integration is only partial. For them it would perhaps be more accurate to talk of an uneasy truce.

NOTES

I wish to thank Javier Albó and Tristan Platt for their detailed comments on an earlier draft, and also the contributors to this volume for valuable discussion. The errors of interpretation that remain are mine alone.

1 Arriaga (1621 (1968)) and Duviols (1971) give details of the strategies employed.
2 Duviols (1973; 1978). Archaeological evidence for Qullasuyu also reveals traces of what have been assumed to be mummies and embalming cloths (Ibarra Grasso, 1965).
3 Duviols (1973:164–5) argues that mummies, known in Quechua as *mallqui*, were the equivalent of *huari* (venerated stones) which were the 'husbands' of the maize (*zarasmamas*).
4 As Cieza de León (1553 (1947)) wrote: 'There are great differences [in the mode of burying their dead], for in some parts they make holes, in others they place their dead on heights, in others on level ground, and each nation seeks some new way of making tombs.'
5 Harris (1982). Field research was conducted from 1972–4, and again in 1981. In mortuary practices I have been able to detect little systematic differentiation between the two zones. I participated in funerals and feasts of the dead in both, and accordingly my account will be a composite of observations made in both *likina* and *suni*, unless explicitly stated to the contrary.
6 Platt (1982) gives a detailed discussion of land rights in northern Potosí today, and their relation to the nineteenth-century cadastres.
7 Carter (1968) and Tschopik (1951) also stress the overwhelming authority of old men in the Titicaca region.
8 Harris (1978a; 1978b); Godoy's (n.d.) study of the neighbouring Jukumani suggests that the relative absence of authority in Laymi society may not be typical for the region as a whole.

9 Carter (1968) gives a detailed account of similar games in Irpa Chico. J. Albó (personal communication) notes that the game played with sheep knuckle bones is, like the sheep, of Spanish origin.

10 While I am not clear as to the reasons for this contrast in location of graveyards between the two ecological zones, Bastien (1978:174) suggests that in Kaata the dead return underground to the mountain top which is both point of origin and return (*uma pacha* in Quechua). Hyslop (1976:153–7) notes that in the lakeside Lupaqa kingdom, hilltop burial sites remained in use long after habitation had been moved down to the plains bordering the Lake in the Inka period.

11 While this pattern is typical of most Laymi rituals, there is no doubt that women fear the dead and prefer to stay away (Harris, 1980). This normal avoidance is occasionally breached by a powerful symbolic inversion; when illness has ravaged a community, the women, or even children if circumstances are bad enough, replace men as pall-bearers and run to the graveyard with the corpse.

12 Some of the most common icons bear the implication of mediation, e.g. ladders, birds, snakes. Bread babies in the form of a woman carrying a child are also common, and Nash (1975:150) suggests that they make a positive connection between death and human fertility.

13 Platt (personal communication) argues that water, like mirrors, is an 'enemy of the soul'.

14 Other feasts are regularly the scene of fighting between individuals as well as groups (Harris, 1978a).

15 A further message implicit in the helmets festooned with ribbons is the negation of fighting.

16 In the hamlet of Muruq'umarka this place was called the dogs' graveyard (*anupampiuna*); see note 23 (below) for the significance of dogs to the dead.

17 I owe this information to Willer Flores, regional delegate for Northern Potosí for the National Institute of Archaeology.

18 In Quechua-speaking areas of northern Potosí, according to Willer Flores, the rite at the end of All Saints is known as *misq''a Carnaval*, that is 'Carnival in advance', thus providing an explicit pointer to the feast with which All Saints is paired.

19 It may be significant that the *quena*, another form of Andean flute, was in other areas of the altiplano fashioned from human femurs taken from ancient burial grounds. The Laymi play this flute occasionally in the dry season, but the music of the quena is in the class of *wayñu*, that is, rainy season music associated with the dead.

20 The rite is known as *uruni*, 'dedicated day'. In a hamlet of the neighbouring Macha that I visited, I was told that the actual sponsors of Carnival are those obliged to perform this rite for their dead kin – another overt association between the dead and the feast of Carnival.

21 The distinction between the Spanish-derived *alma* and the Aymara word *amaya* depends on context as far as I can judge. For example *alma* is used in the feast of All Saints, and in general when libations are poured for the souls of the dead. It is *almas* again that haunt the church at night. *Amaya* on the other hand is appropriate for contexts not connected directly with Christian theology, for example the road travelled by the dead is known as *amay t''ak''i*. The degree to which these two terms are associated with a

non-corporeal essence is unclear to me. Laymi use the term *alma* to refer specifically to the corpse. Not surprisingly, Bertonio's dictionary (1612 (1956)) gives the meaning of dead body (*cuerpo muerto*) rather to the Aymara *amaya*. Today Laymi sometimes say, echoing the catechism, that after death we abandon the *saxra kurpu* (evil body) and go to heaven. There is thus no positive association for the bodies of the dead that might suggest some submerged memory of historical practices of embalming.

22 Today the terms *alma* and *amaya* refer exclusively to the dead. Shade (*ch'iwu*) and the Spanish-derived *animu* are employed to refer to the spirits of the living that survive bodily death. Duviols (1978:133–4) points out the close identity between the idea of a shadow and the *animu* as a non-corporeal element that leaves the body during certain illnesses and at death; he suggests connections with the sixteenth-century Quechua terms *camaquen* and *upani*. In Chucuito, Peru, the Aymara term *axayu* seems to correspond to the Laymi use of *animu* (Tschopik, 1951:210).

23 Dogs are associated with incest, and their bite can turn people mad. In the *suni*, graveyards were carefully sealed off not only to prevent the ghosts escaping but also to stop dogs getting in and savaging the corpses. Carter (1968:245) argues a close connection between dogs and the spirits of the dead. According to J. Albó, in the altiplano, black dogs are associated with humans (*jaqi anu*) while white dogs belong to the devils (*saxra anu*). In their journey to the land of the dead, then, ghosts are assisted by dogs that recall their human rather than 'devil' status.

24 In my innocence I frequently told people that I came from the other side of the world, from a place where it is day when night falls in the Andes, and where the seasons are reversed. They evinced no surprise, but some anxiety at my description. It was a long time before a woman confided to me in friendship that everyone had been forced to assume from what I said that I had come from the world of the dead to haunt them. In other contexts *manq"a* is better translated as below or lower.

25 This mythical use of a real place may reflect a previous epoch when the Laymi had direct economic links with that part of the Pacific coast (J. Murra, T. Platt, personal communication). Tacna is known to have been an important zone of chilli production. Thus the term *manq"a* could in this context also refer to the lower lands of the ethnic group.

26 Archivo Nacional de Bolivia: Tierras e Indios **149** (1592). Today Laymi use a wild pepper growing in the *likina*, and otherwise buy chilli from the market.

27 In this belief we can perhaps see the assertion that children, who are sinless, belong to God in a special way. God in this context is the Spanish *dios* (Aymara: *tyusa*), and heaven the Spanish *cielo* (Aymara: *silu*).

28 Platt and Molina suggest that in some contexts the best translation of *saxra* is 'secret' (in press, Ch. 3). The three 'spheres' of Laymi cosmology are discussed in Harris (1980). Taylor in a recent discussion (1980) argues that the word used commonly in the Andes to denote devils – *supay* – may well have referred in pre-Christian times to the ancestors.

29 Carter (1968), Albó (1972); the discussion of rotating offices today is only applicable for the highland *suni*: in the *likina* all indigenous offices of authority were abolished after the 1953 Agrarian Reform and replaced by a local branch of the national peasants union.

Olivia Harris

REFERENCES

Albó, J. 1972. 'Dinámica de la estructura intercomunitaria de Jesus de Machaca', *América Indígena*, **32**:773–816.
Arriaga, P.J. de, 1621 (1968). *Extirpación de la idolatria del Perú*. (trans. L. Clark Keating) Kentucky: University Press.
Bastien, J. 1978. *Mountain of the Condor. Metaphor and ritual in an Andean ayllu*. St Paul: West Publishing Co.
Bertonio, L. 1612 (1956). *Vocabulario de la lengua aymara*. Reprinted in facsimile, La Paz.
Buechler, H. 1980. *The Masked Media*. The Hague: Mouton.
Carter, W. 1968. 'Secular reinforcement in Aymara death ritual', *American Anthropologist*, **70**:238–263.
Cieza de León, P. de. 1553 (1947). *Primera parte de la crónica del Perú*. (trans. for the Hakluyt Society by C. Markham (1864)) Madrid: Biblioteca de Autores Españoles, **26**, 1947.
Duviols, P. 1971. 'La lutte contre les religions authochthones.' *Trav. Inst. Fr. des Etudes Andines*, **13**, Lima.
1973. 'Huari y Llacuaz. Agricultores y pastores. Un dualismo de oposición y complementaridad' *Revista del Museo Nacional, **39**, Lima.
1978. 'Camaquen, Upani: un concept animiste des anciens Péruviens', in *Amerikanistische Studien. Festschrift für Hermann Trimborn*. eds R. Hartmann & U. Oberem. St Augustin: Collectanea Instituti Anthropos 20.
Godoy, R. (n.d.) *From Indian to Miner and back again: Small scale mining in the Jukumani ayllu of northern Potosi, Bolivia*.
Harris, O. 1978a. 'Complementarity and conflict. An Andean view of women and men', in *Sex and age as principles of social differentiation*. ed. J. La Fontaine. ASA monograph 17. London: Academic Press.
1978b. 'De l'asymétrie au triangle. Transformations symboliques au nord de Potosí', *Annales E.S.C.*, **33** (5–6).
1980. 'The power of signs; gender culture and the wild in the Bolivian Andes', in *Nature, culture and gender*. eds. C. MacCormack & M. Strathern. Cambridge: Cambridge University Press.
1982. 'Labour and produce in an ethnic economy', in *Ecology and exchange in the Andes*. ed. D. Lehmann. Cambridge: Cambridge University Press.
Hertz, R. 1960. *Death and the right hand*. (trans. R. & C. Needham) Oxford: Oxford University Press.
Hyslop, J. 1976. *An archaeological investigation of the Lupaqa Kingdom and its origins*. Unpubl. PhD thesis, Columbia University.
Ibarra Grasso, D.E. 1965. *Prehistoria de Bolivia*. La Paz: Amigos del Libro.
La Barre, W. 1948. *The Aymara Indians of the Lake Titicaca plateau*. American Anthropologist, Memorials no. 68, Menasha.
Martinez, G. 1976. *El sistema de los uywiris en Isluga*. Isluga, Chile: Centro Isluga de Investigaciones Andinas, publ. 1.
Nash, J. 1975. *We eat the mines and the mines eat us*. Columbia: University Press.
Platt, T. 1978. 'Symetries en miroir: le concept de *yanantin* chez les macha de Bolivie', *Annales E.S.C.*, **33** (5–6).
1982. *El ayllu andino y el estado Boliviano*. Lima: Instituto de Estudios Peruanos.
(n.d.) *The Macha Ayllu*.

Platt, T. & Molina, R. (in press) *Qhuya Runa* Lima: Instituto de Estudios Peruanos.

Taylor, G. 1980. 'Supay', *Amerindia*, **5**: 47–63.

Tschopik, H. 1951. *The Aymara of Chucuito, Peru*. Anthropological Papers of the American Museum of Natural History, **44** (2), New York.

Valcarcel, L. 1948. 'The Inca calendar', *Handbook of South American Indians*, **2**, Washington.

Waman Puma de Ayala, F., 1613 (1936). *Nueva coronica y buen gobierno*. Facsimile edn, Paris.

3 Sacrificial death and the necrophagous ascetic

JONATHAN PARRY

My aim in this paper[1] is to outline two opposing ways in which the problems of temporality and man's mortality are handled within Hinduism. The first section focuses on the case of the householder. For him, I argue, the 'good' death is a sacrificial act which results not only in a re-creation of the deceased, but also in a regeneration of time and of the cosmos. In the second section I turn to a group of ascetics who are intimately associated with death, corpses and the cremation ground. By contrast with the householder, the somewhat macabre practice of the Aghori ascetic is directed at a suspension – rather than a renewal – of time, and is thus an attempt to escape from the recurrence of death implied by the endless cycle of rebirths.[2] The singularity of his means to this end lies (as Eliade (1969:296) perceived) in a peculiarly material and literal play on the common Hindu theme of the combination of opposites; but both the end itself and its theological justification are – we shall find – expressed in thoroughly conventional language.[3]

Although the life of the householder and the life of the ascetic are oriented towards two different goals, both share in the same complex of interconnected assumptions about the relationship between life and death. As Shulman (1980:90) puts it:

The Hindu universe is a closed circuit: nothing new can be produced except by destroying or transforming something else. To attain more life – such as a son, or the 'rebirth' of the sacrificial patron himself – the life of the victim must be extinguished. Life and death are two facets of a single never-ending cycle . . .

Consistent with this, we shall encounter an image of life as a limited good: thus a barren woman may conceive by causing the child of another to wither away and die. Death regenerates life: the householder sacrifices himself on his funeral pyre in order than he may be reborn; while the power derived from his intimacy with death and decay enables the Aghori ascetic to confer fertility on the householder

74

(and this despite his own disparagement of the ordinary mortal condition). What is more, the power to convert death into life is seen as intimately connected with the performance of ascetic austerities – not just in the obvious case of Aghori, but also in the case of the austerities performed by the corpse of the householder on his cremation pyre, and by the chief mourner during his regime of mourning. The cremation rituals of the householder – with their insistence on the complete elimination of the remains of the deceased – recall, moreover, the ascetic's denigration of the 'gross' physical body (a point which has been developed in more detail in the Introduction to this volume, pp. 36–8). Seen from this point of view the opposition between ascetic and householder would not appear radical. But from another perspective the difference *is* fundamental, for while the renouncer's goal is a permanent state of being unfettered by any material form, the cremation rituals of the householder hold out only the promise of a renewed existence which is itself impermanent, and in which the immortal soul is unbreakably chained to a particular transient form.

At the outset I should acknowledge that – for reasons which will become obvious – there are many gaps in my data relating to the Aghoris, and should explicitly state that I have not personally witnessed many of the secret performances with which they are most closely associated. What needs to be kept firmly in mind then is that at various points the account relates, not so much to what these ascetics actually do, as to what they say they do and what other people believe them to do.

My ethnography is from the city of Benares,[4] one of the most important centres of Hindu pilgrimage in India. Benares is sacred to Siva, the Great Ascetic, the Lord of the Cremation Ground and the Conqueror of Death; and the cornerstone of its religious identity is its association with death and its transcendence. All who die here automatically attain 'liberation' or 'salvation' (*mukti, mokṣa*) – an inducement which attracts many elderly and terminally-sick people to move to the city.[5] Each year thousands of corpses of those who have been unfortunate or undeserving enough to expire elsewhere are brought to Benares for cremation on one of the two principal burning *ghāṭs*; while vast numbers of pious pilgrims come to immerse the ashes of a deceased relative in the Ganges or to make offerings to the ancestors. Death in Benares is big business, which – as I have outlined elsewhere (Parry, 1980) – involves an elaborate division of labour between a number of different kinds of caste specialists variously associated with the disposal of the corpse, the fate of the soul and the purification of the mourners.

Jonathan Parry

Sacrificial death and the regeneration of life

Manikarnika *ghāṭ* is the best patronised of the city's two cremation grounds. It was here that at the beginning of the time Lord Visnu sat for 50000 years performing the austerities by which he created the world, and here that the corpse of the cosmos will burn at the end of time. But these events occur not only at the start and finish of each cosmic cycle. They also belong to an eternal present which is continually reactualised on the *ghāṭ* in the uninterrupted sequence of cremations performed there.[6]

A recurrent theme in Hindu religious thought is the homology which is held to exist between body and cosmos. Both are governed by the same laws, are constituted out of the same five elements and everything that exists in the one must also exist in the other (cf. Goudriaan, 1979:57). Hence all the gods and the whole of space are present within the human body – a notion which is explicitly elaborated in the *Garuda Purana* (part 15), an eschatological text to which the Benares sacred specialists continually refer. The homology is also one of the basic principles underlying the architectural theory of the Hindu temple, which is constructed on the plan of a cosmic man (Beck, 1976); while many forms of worship involve a 'cosmicisation' of the body of the worshipper (Gupta, 1979). A case in point is provided by the rituals described in the *Kalika Purana*. The worshipper begins by symbolically effecting his own death which is identified with the death of the world; and in subsequently re-creating his body he reconstitutes the universe. It is of some significance for what follows that the sacred space within which all this occurs represents 'a stylised cremation ground' (Kinsley, 1977:102).

Body and cosmos are thus equated; and this – combined with our last example – would seem to imply a further equivalence between cremation which destroys the microcosm of the physical body and the general conflagration which destroys the macrocosm at *pralaya*, the time of cosmic dissolution. (Indeed certain of the texts classify an individual death as *nityapralaya* – a regularly-enacted doomsday (Biardeau, 1971:18, 76).) But just as the world's annihilation by fire and flood is a necessary prelude to its re-creation, so the deceased is cremated and his ashes immersed in water in order that he may be restored to life. Since the body is the cosmos the last rites become the symbolic equivalent of the destruction *and rejuvenation* of the universe. Cremation is cosmogony;[7] and an individual death is assimilated to the process of cosmic regeneration. Popular thought certainly presupposes some intrinsic association between cremation and the

76

scene of original creation, for one of the reasons given for the bitter opposition to a Municipal plan to relocate the burning *ghāṭ* away from the centre of the city was that it is not possible to sever its connection with the place of the prolonged austerities (*tapas*) by which Visnu engendered the world.[8]

Now such austerities generate heat, which is in many contexts represented as the source of life and fertility. Thus Agni (the god of fire) is represented as the 'cause of sexual union' (O'Flaherty, 1973:90). Through the heat of his austerities the ascetic acquires a super-abundant sexual potency, and a creative power by which he may rival or even terrorise the gods; through the cremation pyre the seven storm-gods are born (O'Flaherty, 1973:109); and through bathing in the tank of Lolark Kund in Benares, fecundity is conferred on barren women – the tank being sacred to the sun, the source of heat. Consistent with this, Visnu is described as burning with the fire of the *tapas* by which he created the cosmos at Manikarnika *ghāṭ*. By entering the pyre here the deceased – as it were – refuels the fires of creation at the very spot where creation began. Indeed I have heard cremation described as a kind of *tapas*, and certain of the texts clearly represent it as such (Knipe, 1975:132; cf. Kaelber, 1976, who puts it in terms of Agni imparting *tapas* to the corpse).

Another way of developing the same argument would be to note that cremation is a sacrifice,[9] and that the essence of the textual conception of the sacrifice is that it is a cosmogonic act. Thus – to invoke a different account of the origins of the universe – every sacrifice may be said to replicate the primal act of Prajapati who produced creation by the sacrificial dismemberment of his own body.[10] As Heesterman (1959:245–6) puts it: 'The sacrifice may be described as a periodical quickening ritual by which the universe is recreated. . . . the pivotal place is taken up by the sacrificer; like his prototype Prajapati he incorporates the universe and performs the cosmic drama of disintegration and reintegration'. *Any* sacrifice then is, as Eliade (1965:11) affirms, a 'repetition of the act of creation' and maintains or repairs the cosmic order (Zaehner, 1962:245–6; Malamoud, 1975; Biardeau, 1976:22; Herrenschmidt, 1978 and 1979). It therefore represents a renewal of time.

What, then, is the evidence that *cremation* is a sacrifice (and hence an act of cosmic regeneration)? Here we might start by observing that the term for cremation in Sanskrit and in the Sanskritised Hindi of my more literate informants is *antyeṣṭi*, or 'last sacrifice'; and that one of the manuals of ritual practice regularly used as a guide to the mortuary rites (the *Śraddha Parijat*) explicitly equates cremation with a fire

Jonathan Parry

sacrifice. Or, to cite a different authority (though not one which my informants ever invoked), the *Śatapatha Brahmana* represents the sacrificial fire altar ritual as symbolic re-enactment of the story of Prajapati, and then goes on to lay down precisely the same rules for handling the corpse of a deceased sacrificer as for treating the sacrificial altar which represents the body of the god (Levin, 1930).

The parallels between cremation and the sacrificial procedure are, as Das points out, almost precise.

Thus the site of cremation is prepared in exactly the same way as in fire-sacrifice, i.e. the prescriptive use of ritually pure wood, the purification of the site, its consecration with holy water, and the establishment of Agni with the proper use of *mantras* . . . The dead body is prepared in the same manner as the victim of a sacrifice and is attributed with divinity. Just as the victim of a sacrifice is exhorted not to take any revenge for the pains which the sacrifice has inflicted on him (Hubert & Mauss, 1964) so the mourners pray to the *preta* to spare them from his anger at the burns he has suffered in the fire (*Garuda Purana*). (Das, 1977:122–3)

The corpse is given water to drink, is lustrated, anointed with ghee and enclosed in sacred space by being circumambulated with fire – which is precisely what Hubert & Mauss (1964:31) describe as happening to the sacrificial victim. Further, the same set of ten substances (known as *dasang*) which are offered in the pyre are also used for the fire sacrifice (*havan*); while according to the standard manual of mortuary practice – the *Preta Manjari* (p.4) – the wood used for the pyre should be that which 'pertains to a sacrifice' (*yāgyik*).

All this poses a puzzle. On the face of it there would seem to be a flat contradiction between our received wisdom that the corpse is pre-eminently polluting and dangerous, and the notion that it is a fit sacrificial offering to the gods. The situation is complex and the evidence is hard to interpret and often appears contradictory. Much of my data would certainly support the view that the corpse is contaminating (and indeed the enormous symbolic power of the association between corpses and the Aghori ascetic rests on this fact). But this is far from the whole story, for in certain respects the dead body appears to be treated as an object of great purity, even as a deity. It is said to be Siva, is greeted with salutations appropriate to Siva (cries of '*Har, Har, Mahādev*'), and continual play is made on the phonetic similarity between Siva and *śava* ('corpse'). It must be guarded against pollution, may not be touched by the impure, is wrapped in freshly-laundered cloth, is circumambulated with the auspicious right hand towards it and the pyre is ignited by the chief mourner only after he has passed through an elaborate series of purifications (cf. Stevenson,

1920:144–8). He offers the fire with his right hand; and at this time his sacred thread hangs over his left shoulder towards the right-hand side of his body, as is the rule when offerings are made to the gods (whereas it hangs from right to left when the offering is to the ancestors or to an unincorporated ghost). Or again, in the custom of certain regional communities represented in Benares, the corpse of a woman who has died in childbirth or during her monthly course must undergo special purificatory rites before she is fit for the pyre, as if only those in a state of purity are eligible for cremation (cf. Stevenson, 1920:151; Kane, 1953:231; Pandey, 1969:270–1).

I cannot confidently claim to be able to provide a definitive explanation for this apparent contradiction. I believe, however, that the most revealing place to start is with the definition of death as the instant at which the *prān*, or 'vital breath' leaves the body. Now according to the theological dogma expounded by many of my informants, this occurs – not at the cessation of physiological functioning – but at the rite of *kapāl kriyā*, which is performed mid-way through the cremation, and at which the chief mourner releases the 'vital breath' from the charred corpse of the deceased by cracking open his skull with a stave.[11] Before this stage it is commonly said to be completely inappropriate to use the term *preta* meaning 'a disembodied ghost'.

The corollary which is often derived from this is that it is precisely at the moment of breaking the skull that death pollution begins.[12] Accordingly, the *śrāddha* ceremonies which mark the end of the year of mourning are celebrated on the anniversary of the cremation rather than on the anniversary of the actual death. That on this view impurity does not emanate from the corpse itself is neatly illustrated by the case of those who have died a 'bad' death and whose corpses are not burnt but immersed in the Ganges. In such an instance, it is often claimed, no death pollution is incurred until after the *putlā vidhān* ritual at which the deceased's body is re-created in the form of an effigy, into which his soul is invoked, and which is then cremated. Since this rite may be delayed until several months after the disposal of the actual body, and since there is no impurity in the interval, it is clear that death pollution springs from the act of cremation rather than from the corpse or its physiological demise. It is, in the Benares idiom, a consequence of 'the sin of burning the body hairs of the deceased'. Hence as Pullu Maharaj explained, the chief mourner remains in a state of great purity before igniting the pyre, 'because he is performing a *mahāyugya* – a great sacrifice. It is we who pollute him by our touch and not he us.' After cremation, however, he is defiled 'for he has burnt the flesh'.

Jonathan Parry

What this definition of the point of death implies is that before the cremation the corpse is not a corpse but an *animate* oblation to the fire. As another informant spontaneously put it: 'he does not die but is killed. He dies on the pyre.' Cremation, he went on, is violence (*hatyā*) and death pollution (*sutaka*) the consequence of that violence.[13] On such a theory cremation becomes a sacrifice in the real sense of the term: it is a ritual slaughter which makes of the chief mourner a homicide, parricide or even slayer of the gods. It is hardly to be wondered at, then, that his subsequent purifications – like that of any sacrificer – resemble the expiation of a criminal (Hubert & Mauss, 1964:33). It should not be thought, however, that the victim is a reluctant one, for – as we shall see – a crucial aspect of the 'good' death is that it is a voluntary offering of the self of the gods. The corpse is thus not only alive but also a willing victim, and hence a being of extraordinary sacredness.[14]

I hasten to emphasise that all this refers only to a somewhat esoteric level of theological discourse, and that at another level it is of course universally acknowledged that a man is dead once the physical manifestations of life are extinguished. Reasoning from this starting point, other informants held that death pollution begins at the moment of physiological arrest, and that the corpse itself is a source of severe impurity. Those best versed in the texts, however, tended to steer a middle course between these two theories by distinguishing the case of the Agnihotri (by whom sacrificial fires are continuously maintained) from that of the ordinary householder. While for the former there is no death pollution before cremation, for the latter it begins when respiration ceases (cf. Abbott, 1932:177, 192, 505; Pandey, 1969:269).

What is common to both theories, then, is the view that death pollution starts when the body ceases to be animated by its 'vital breath'. The disparity arises over the point at which this happens. On the view that it occurs during the cremation, the deceased's body represents a pure oblation to the gods; while on the view that the 'vital breath' departs at physiological arrest it is merely an impure carcass.[15]

Given that the good death is a sacrifice and sacrifice is an act of regeneration, it is only to be expected that the beliefs and practices associated with cremation are pervaded by the symbolism of embryology. According to one well-known text which deals with sacrifice (the *Śatapatha Brahmana*), there are three kinds of birth: that which is had from one's parents, from sacrifice and from cremation (Lévi, 1898:106–7; Levin, 1930). Indeed the ritual techniques involved in both of the latter might be seen as a branch of obstetrics. Having dispersed

80

his own body in the sacrifice, the sacrificer reverts to an embryonic state and is then reborn (cf. Heesterman, 1959; Kaelber, 1978); while at death – as I have often been told – the body is to be taken to the cremation ground head first because that is the way a baby is born; while the corpse of a man should be laid face down on the pyre and the corpse of a woman face up,[16] for this is the position in which the two sexes enter the world. During the fifth month of pregnancy the vital breath enters the embryo through the suture at the top of the skull and it is from here that it is released during cremation. Throughout pregnancy the baby is sustained by the digestive fire which resides in its mother's belly,[17] and at death it returns to the fire from which it came and is thus reborn (cf. Knipe, 1975:1). At both parturitions an untouchable specialist acts the indispensible role of midwife – cutting the umbilical cord at birth and providing the sacred fire and super-intending the pyre at death.

At other points the symbolism of the maternity ward is replaced by that of the bridal chamber. The funeral procession of an old person is described as a second marriage party and is accompanied by erotic dancing; while a husband and wife who die within a few hours of each other are placed on a single pyre in what is explicitly represented as a position of copulation. In some texts the corpse is described as rising as smoke from the pyre, turning into clouds, rain and then vegetables, which when eaten are transformed into semen (O'Flaherty, 1973:41–2; 1976:28). The destruction of the corpse is thus converted into the source of future life.

The connection between death and sexuality is a theme which is constantly reiterated in both textual and popular traditions. In myth, for example, death enters the world as a result of sexual increase (O'Flaherty, 1976:28, 212) and childbirth is given to women as a consequence of the god Indra's brahmanicide; in folk dream-analysis a naked woman or a bride is a presentiment of impending death; and in ethno-medicine the loss of semen results in disease, old age and death, while its retention confers vitality and even immortality (cf. Briggs, 1938:324; Carstairs, 1957:84–5, 195–6; Eliade, 1969:248–9). If death regenerates life, it is equally clear that in turn the regeneration of life causes death.

It is this endless cycle which the ascetic seeks to evade. As a consequence he is not cremated. The bodies of small children, and of victims of certain diseases like leprosy and smallpox, are also immersed in the Ganges rather than burnt. Except in the case of the ascetic, however, an effigy of the deceased should later be burnt; and this also applies to one who has died a violent or accidental death

Jonathan Parry

(whose body will normally have been cremated). Unless this substitute corpse is offered to the fire the deceased will indefinitely remain as a marginal ghost (*preta*). In all cases, then, a real or surrogate cremation is a prerequisite for the proper re-creation of the departed.

While piecemeal explanations of each individual category have often been suggested, the crucial point about the list of exceptional cases given in the previous paragraph is – as Das (1977:123) has pointed out – that it constitutes a single set. It consists of those who are not fit sacrificial objects (e.g. the leper), those who have already been offered to the gods (e.g. the renouncer who has performed his own mortuary rituals at the time of his initiation and who subsequently exists on earth as a marginal ghost), and those whose death cannot be represented as an act of self-sacrifice (e.g. children and victims of sudden or violent death).

This last case ties in with the notion that the 'good' death is one to which the individual voluntarily submits his- or herself: one of the prime exemplars of such a death being the *satī-strī*, or 'true wife' who mounts her husband's funeral pyre. In the ideal case the dying man – like the sacrificer before the sacrifice (Kaelber, 1978) – forgoes all food for some days before death, and consumes only Ganges water and *charan-amrit* (the mixture in which the image of a deity has been bathed), in order to weaken his body so that the 'vital breath' may leave it more easily; and in order – as I would see it – to make himself a worthy sacrificial object free of foul faecal matter. (A similar interpretation may be placed on the bathing and occasional tonsuring of the corpse prior to cremation.) Having previously predicted the time of his going and set all his affairs in order, he gathers his sons about him[18] and – by an effort of concentrated will – abandons life. He is not said to die, but to relinquish his body.

In the case of a man of great spiritual force a kind of spontaneous combustion cracks open his skull to release the vital breath; while the vital breath of one who dies a bad death emerges through his anus in the form of excrement, through his mouth as vomit, or through one of his other orifices. Such an evacuation is a sure sign of damnation to come, a notion which is perhaps not unconnected with the idea that it is best to die on an empty stomach. An image of the way in which the soul might ideally emerge was provided by the case of an old householder, whose extraordinary spiritual development had gained him a circle of devoted disciples, and whose subsequent mortuary rituals I attended. His copybook death was said to have been consummated on his funeral pyre when his burning corpse successively manifested itself to a privileged few in the forms of the celebrated

82

religious leaders Sai Baba, Mehar Baba and Rama Krishna Param-
hamsa, as the terrifying god Bhairava (Lord Siva's *kotvāl* or 'police-
chief' in Benares) and finally as Siva himself. A rounded protuberance
was seen to move up the spine of the corpse, burst through the skull,
soar into the air and split into three parts. One fell in Benares, another
went north to the abode of Siva in the Himalayas and nobody knows
what happened to the third.

The best death occurs in Benares, or failing that in another place of
pilgrimage. But in any event death should occur on purified ground
and in the open air rather than in a bed and under or on a roof. One
would hope to die to the sound of chanting of the names of god, for
one's dying thoughts are often said to determine one's subsequent
fate, even to the extent of redeeming the most abject of sinners. There
are not only places but also times to die well – 'the fortnight of the
ancestors' (*pitri-paksha*) for example, or during the period of *uttarāyaṇa*
(the six months of the year that start with the winter solstice); while five
of the twenty seven lunar mansions (*nakṣatras*) of the Hindu almanac
are from this point of view inauspicious and require special rituals of
expiation.[19] But such inconvenience is unlikely to affect the paragon,
whose spiritual force gives him a degree of mastery over the time of his
own death.

By contrast with 'good' death, the 'bad' death is one for which the
deceased cannot be said to have prepared himself. It is said that 'he did
not die his own death'. The paradigmatic case is death by violence or as
a result of some sudden accident; the underlying notion being that the
victim has been forced to relinquish life prematurely with the result
that his embittered ghost is liable to return to afflict the survivors
unless the appropriate propitiatory rituals are scrupulously observed.
Whether these have been successful can only be judged by their
results, for the ghost that is yet to be satisfied will return to haunt the
dreams of the mourners or to vent his malevolence in other more
destructive ways. As a consequence, bad death in the family tends to
be cumulative, the victim of one causing another.

The most common expression for what I have called 'bad death' is
akāl mrityu, literally 'untimely death' (though some of the resonance of
this expression might be better captured by glossing it as 'uncontrolled
death' – by contrast with the controlled release of life which is the
ideal). Strictly speaking, it is not the age of the victim but the manner of
dying that is diagnostic of an *akāl mrityu*, and the death of an old person
may be 'untimely' if it was caused by leprosy, violence or a sudden
accident. The expression *alp mrityu* (meaning 'death in youth') is
however often used as a synonym for *akāl mrityu* – such a death being

almost *ipso facto* bad. The good death occurs after a full and complete life – the lifespan appropriate to our degenerate age being one hundred and twenty-five,[20] and this a mere fraction of that of former epochs. The fact that few attain even this modest target is a consequence of the sins of this and former lives; and the greater the burden of sin, the greater the shortfall. Those who die before the age of forty are certainly destined for hell; while the stillborn infant is probably some reprobate expiating his crimes by a succession of seven such births. There is also, however, the notion that the sins of the father may be visited on the son, and that the attenuation of this life may be a consequence of the wickedness of those with whom the individual is most closely associated. The quality of life thus determines its duration. But it also determines the quality of death. A group of Funeral Priests who – with some rancour – were regaling me with the story of the seizure of their hereditary rights by one of their rich and powerful colleagues, clinched their evidence of his iniquity with the gleeful recollection that he had died vomiting excrement. As for his son, their present employer, 'he will reap; . . . leprosy is coming out on him. He will rot as no one in our caste has ever rotted before.'

Although I cannot deal here with the extremely elaborate sequence of post-cremation rituals, there are two aspects of these rituals on which I would like to comment briefly. At death (*dehānt*, 'the end of the body') the soul becomes a disembodied ghost or *preta*, a marginal state dangerous both to itself and to the survivors. The purpose of the rituals of the first ten days is to reconstruct a physical form for this ethereal spirit – though this new form is of a less 'gross' kind than the one the deceased had formerly inhabited (see the Introduction to this volume, pp. 36–7). Each day a *piṇḍa* – a ball of rice or flour – is offered in the name of the deceased, each of which reconstitutes a specific limb of his body. By the tenth day the body is complete, and on the eleventh life is breathed into it and it is fed. On the next day a ritual is performed which enables the deceased to rejoin his ancestors. The wandering ghost (*preta*) becomes an incorporated ancestor (*pitṛ*). A ball of rice representing the departed is cut into three by the chief mourner and is merged with three other rice balls which represent the deceased's father, father's father and father's father's father. The soul then sets out on its journey to 'the abode of the ancestors' (*pitṛ lok*) where it arrives on the anniversary of its death, having endured many torments on the way – torments which the mourners seek to mitigate by thee rriittuuaallss tthey perform on its behalf. In order to cross over into 'the kingdom of the dead' (*yamlok*) at the end of its journey, the soul must negotiate the terrifying Vaitarnī river which is invariably represented as flowing with blood, excrement and other foul substances.

The first point that I want to make is that in a number of ways the symbolism of this whole phase of the mortuary rituals continues the theme of death as a parturition. The word *piṇḍa* is used not only for the rice or flour balls out of which the deceased's body is reconstructed, but also for an actual embryo (cf. O'Flaherty, 1980); and the body is completed in a ten-day period paralleling the ten (lunar) month period of gestation (cf. Knipe, 1977). What's more, there is a striking correspondence between the image of crossing the Vaitarṇī river and the birth passage of the child out of the womb, the latter also being explicitly represented as negotiating a river of blood and pollution. What we seem to have here is a case of ritual over-kill; the deceased is reborn out of the fire and then born all over again in the subsequent rituals.[21]

It is perhaps also worth noting that, in relation to the twelfth-day rituals, both the textual commentaries and the more knowledgeable ritual specialists in Benares make a rather different kind of link between death and regeneration. If the chief mourner's wife is barren, then in order to conceive a son, she should consume the rice ball used in the ritual to represent her husband's father's father (cf. Kane, 1953:346–7, 480). The *piṇḍa* identified with the ancestor thus has the quality of semen and may beget a new *piṇḍa*-embryo (cf. O'Flaherty, 1980). Though the notion is clearly inconsistent with the theory of reincarnation postulated by the doctrine of *karma*, the idea is that the great-grandfather comes back as his own great-grandson; and I would add that even those who deny the efficacy of any such procedure often assert an identity of character between the two.

My second point relates to the regime of mourning and its striking similarity to the code of the ascetic. The chief mourner must not shave, use soap or oil his hair, wear shoes or a shirt; throughout the mourning he must wear a single garment, must sleep on the ground, avoid 'hot' food and abstain from sex – all of which recalls the conduct prescribed for the renouncer. Each year tens of thousands of pilgrim-mourners go to the holy city of Gaya in order to make offerings there which will ensure the final salvation of their deceased parents. Many of them wear the ochre-coloured garments of the ascetic and it was several times explained to me that this is a symbol of their temporary assumption of the renouncer's role. Dumont (1971) and Das (1977:126) have both remarked on this parallel, and Das interprets it in terms of the liminality of both statuses. Her point is unexceptionable but, I believe, insufficient; for what she fails to note – but what some of my informants explicitly said – is that it is by taking on the role of the

Jonathan Parry

ascetic and performing austerities (*tapasya*) that the chief mourner acquires the power to re-create a body for the deceased.

I have thus returned to my starting point: the creative power of asceticism, by means of which Visnu engendered the cosmos. Austerities produce heat, the source of life – the corpse being subjected to the heat of the pyre that the departed might be reborn. Cremation is thus an act of creation, even a cosmic renewal. The paradox is that such austerities have the odour of an opportunism repudiated by the 'true' renouncer, in that they are oriented towards a regeneration of life. For the latter the value of such a goal is dubious, since the world is suffering and the corollary of rebirth is the relentless recurrence of death. The real aim of renunciation is rather an escape from this endless cycle, and it is this – I will suggest – that makes sense of the baroque excess with which the Aghori is associated.

The necrophagous ascetic and the transcendence of time

Before the creation was a void. According to the myth of Visnu's cosmogony recorded in the best-known eulogy of Benares' sanctity, the *Kaśi Khanda* (Chapter 26),[22] all that originally existed was Brahma, which cannot be apprehended by the mind or described by the speech, and which is without form, name, colour or any physical attribute. Creation proceeded by differentiation from this primal essence, duality emerging from non-duality. Much of the endeavour of the world-renouncer may be seen as an attempt to recapture the original state of non-differentiation and to re-establish the unity of opposites which existed before the world began.

The discipline of yoga is – as Eliade (1969; 1976) has shown – directed at precisely this goal. By his physical postures the yogi subjugates his body and renders it immobile; by concentrating on a single object he frees his mind from the flux of events and arrests mental process; and by slowing down and eventually stopping his breath 'he stops the activities of the senses and severs the connection between the mind and external sensory objects' (Gupta, 1979:168). Sexual intercourse may be converted into a discipline in which the semen is immobilised by the practice of *coitus reservatus*, or its normal direction of flow reversed by reabsorbing it into the penis after ejaculation. By thus controlling his body he acquires magical powers (*siddhis*) by which he may defy nature and control the world. But above all, the yogi's immobilisation of mind, body, breath and semen represents an attempt to return to what Eliade describes as a 'primordial motionless Unity'; and to attain *samādhi*, a timeless state of non-duality in which there is neither birth nor death nor any experience of differentiation.

This suspension of time and conquest of death is also, the aim of Aghori asceticism. The theological premise on which their practice is founded would appear to be a classical monism. Every soul is identical with the Absolute Being; all category distinctions are a product of illusion (*māyā*), and behind all polarities there is an ultimate unity. But what *is* peculiar to the Aghoris is a very literal working-out of this monistic doctrine through a discipline which insists on a concrete experience of the identity of opposites, and on a material realisation of the unity between them. It is a matter of a kind of externalised fulfilment of what is more orthodoxly interpreted as a purely internal quest.

Although there are many similarities of practice, and perhaps also a direct historical connection, between the Aghoris and the skull-carrying Kapalikas of certain late Sanskrit texts, they themselves trace the foundation of their order to an ascetic called Kina ('rancour') Ram, whom they claim as an incarnation (*avatār*) of Siva, and who is supposed to have died (or rather 'taken *samādhi*') in the second half of the eighteenth century when he was nearly one hundred and fifty years old. The *āśrama* (or 'monastic refuge') Kina Ram founded in Benares (which is also the site of his tomb) is one of the most important centres of the sect – though only one or two ascetics actually live there. Each of the succeeding *mahants* ('abbots') of this *āśrama* is supposed to be an *avatār* of (Siva's *avatār*) Kina Ram; the present incumbent being reckoned as the twelfth in the line.[23]

There are probably no more than fifteen Aghori ascetics permanently or semi-permanently resident in Benares and its immediate environs,[24] but others from elsewhere congregate at Kina Ram's *āśrama* during the festivals of *Lolārk Chhaṭh* and *Guru-Purnīmā*.[25] The evidence suggests that at the end of the last century their numbers were several times greater – (Barrow, 1893:215, gives an estimate of between one and two hundred) – though it is very unlikely that they were ever a numerically significant element in the ascetic population of the city.[26] Their hold on the popular imagination is, however, out of all proportion to their numbers, and some Aghoris acquire a substantial following of lay devotees. Recruitment to the sect is theoretically open to both sexes and to all castes. In practice, however, all the ascetics I knew, or knew of, were male and of clean caste origin (though some of their devotees were female).[27]

The Aghoris, wrote Sherring (1872:269), are 'a flagrantly indecent and abominable set of beggars who have rendered themselves notorious for the disgusting vileness of their habits'. Indeed the 'left-hand' discipline (*vām panthi sādhanā*) they embrace was hardly likely to commend itself to the English missionary. The Aghori performs austerities at, and probably lives on, the cremation ground – in some cases in a rough shack, into the mud-walls of which are set human skulls (Morinis, 1979:258). He may go naked or clothe himself in a shroud taken from a corpse, wear a necklace of bones around his neck and his hair in matted locks. His eyes are conventionally described as burning-red, like live coals; his whole demeanour is awesome, and in speech he is brusque, churlish and foul-mouthed.

Rumour persistently associates the Aghoris with human sacrifice, and there is said to have been a notorious case in the recent past just across the river from Benares. What is certain, however, is that during the British raj more than one Aghori was executed for the crime (Barrow, 1893:208); and only recently the *Guardian* newspaper (Thursday, 6 March 1980) reported the death in police custody of an old ascetic who was living on a south Indian cremation ground and who was suspected of the sacrifice of five children whose blood he collected in bottles for the performance of rituals by which he sought to attain immortality. The article goes on to cite a recent (unspecified) survey which claimed that there are still probably a hundred human sacrifices offered each year in India in order to avert epidemics, ensure the fertility of crops or women, or confer supernatural powers on the sacrificer.

As part of his discipline the Aghori may perform the rite of *śava-sādhanā*, in which he seats himself on the torso of a corpse to worship. By means of this worship he is able to gain an absolute control over the deceased's spirit, through which he communicates with other ghostly beings.[28] The Aghori sleeps over a model bier (made from the remnants of a real one); smears his body with ash from the pyres, cooks his food on wood pilfered from them[29] and consumes it out of the human skull which is his constant companion and alms-bowl, and which he is supposed to have acquired by some crude surgery on a putrid and bloated corpse fished out of the river. My informant Fakkar (meaning 'indigent'/'carefree') Baba, however, shamefacedly admits to having obtained his from a hospital morgue, though he claims to have taken precautions to ensure that it was a skull of the right type (see below). It belonged, he says, to a young Srivastava (Trader) who died of snake-bite. The provenance of Lal Baba's skull is reputedly more immaculate. Several of my friends at Manikarnika *ghāṭ* recall the day when he waded out into the river to retrieve the corpse to which it belonged, and one of them claims to have unwittingly lent him the knife with which he performed the operation. Before eating I have seen

Lal Baba offer the food it contains to a dog, thus converting it into the 'polluted leavings' (*jūṭhā*) of the most debased of animals, and one which is also – like the ideal Aghori – a scavenger living off the carrion of the cremation ground.[30] The 'true' Aghori is entirely indifferent to what he consumes, drinks not only liquor but urine, and eats not only meat but excrement, vomit and the putrid flesh of corpses.[31]

While I myself have been present when an Aghori drank what was said to be the urine of a dog, and swallowed what was undoubtedly ash from a cremation pyre, I cannot personally testify to their necrophagy. All I can say with complete assurance is that they readily own to the practice; that as far as my lay informants are concerned the matter is not in question, and that several of them claim to have seen an Aghori eating corpse flesh. One highly revered ascetic has hung a large portrait of himself in the leprosy hospital which he founded, in which he is shown sitting cross-legged on a corpse, a bottle of liquor in one hand while in the other is a morsel of flesh which he is raising to his lips. Apart from its very existence, the interesting thing about the painting is that the corpse which he is devouring appears to be his own (which would conform with the theology of monism I describe below). What is also relevant here is that another of my ascetic informants insisted that the crucial point about the corpse on which the Aghori sits to worship is that it is identical to his own.

Starting with the *Dabistan,* a seventeenth-century Persian source (cited by Barrow, 1893 and Crooke, 1928), the historical records treat necrophagy as an indisputable fact and provide several supposedly eye-witness accounts of the practice – though some of these are far from credible. The narrator of *The revelations of an orderly* (a semi-fictional work published in Benares in 1848) claims, for example, that: 'I once saw a wretch of this fraternity eating the head of a putrid corpse, and as I passed he howled and pointed to me; and then scooped out the eyes and ate them before me'.[32] Another nineteenth-century British account claims that 'near Benares they are not unusually seen floating down the river on a corpse, and feeding upon its flesh' (Moor quoted in Oman, 1903:166); while according to a third, the drunken Aghori 'will seize hold of corpses that drift to the banks of the river and bite off bits of its flesh . . . ' (Barrow, 1893:206). Or again, Tod (1839:84) reports that 'one of the Deora chiefs told me that . . . when conveying the body of his brother to be burnt, one of these monsters crossed the path of the funeral procession, and begged to have the corpse, saying that it "would make excellent '*chatni*', or condiment"'.

While such reports would certainly do little to allay the doubts expressed by Arens (1979) about the nature of our existing evidence for anthropophagy, what is perhaps more serious witness to its occurrence is provided by the series of prosecutions which followed the special legislation passed by the British to ban – as Crooke (1928) phrased it – 'the habit of cannibalism'. One Aghori, for example, who was tried in Ghazipur in 1862

was found carrying the remains of a putrid corpse along a road. He was throwing the brains from the skull on to the ground and the stench of the corpse greatly distracted the people. Here and there he placed the corpse on shop boards and on the ground. Separating pieces of flesh from the bones he ate them and insisted on begging. (Barrow, 1893)

The defendant later admitted that 'he ate corpses whenever he found them' (Barrow, 1893:209). Convictions were also obtained in subsequent prosecutions brought before the courts in Rohtak in 1882, and in Dehra Dun and Berhampore in 1884. In one of these cases the accused testified that 'he frequently ate human flesh when hungry' (Barrow, 1893:210); while the newspaper report of a further incident asserts that it forms 'the staple of their food' (The *Tribune* (Lahore), 29th November 1898, cited in Oman, 1903:165).

Despite the impression which such accounts may create, I am convinced that if necrophagy is indeed practised by any of the Aghoris I encountered, it has nothing whatever to do with the requirements of a balanced diet (as Harris 1977, has somewhat implausibly claimed for the Aztecs); but is an irregular – perhaps even a once-off – affair, performed in a ritualised manner at night during certain phases of the moon (associated with Siva).[33] (In view of Arens' caution, it is perhaps as well to retain an open mind on whether necrophagy ever really occurred in any but freak instances. In this context it may be worth pointing out that even the admissions of the ascetics themselves are not beyond suspicion, for – quite apart from the possibility of police duress – the hallmark of an ideal Aghori is that he consumes the flesh of corpses, and any acknowledged failure to do so is a confession of inadequacy. On balance, however, I think that the probability must remain that at least some Aghoris have always taken this aspect of their discipline seriously.) Details of the precise ritual procedure surrounding such an event are supposed to be secret; and there is a considerable discrepancy between the accounts I was given. Some said that the consumption of flesh should ideally be preceded by an act of intercourse on the cremation ground; others that having eaten of the flesh the ascetic should cremate the remains of the corpse and smear his body with the ashes. But almost everybody agrees that after eating the real Aghori will use his powers to restore the deceased to life (cf.

Barrow, 1893:221; Balfour, 1897:345–6), and that the flesh he consumes should be that of a person who has died a bad death.

This association recurs in the notion that the skull which the Aghori carries should have belonged to the victim of an 'untimely death',[34] as should the corpse on which he sits to meditate (cf. Morinis, 1979:258–9). The preference is not just a question of the practical consideration that, since such corpses are immersed, their remains are the ones most likely to be available. It is also a matter of the power that resides in such skulls, which is said to render even the most virulent of poisons innocuous. That of a Teli (Oil-presser) and of a Mahajan (Trader) who has died a bad death is especially prized. Oil-pressers, it is explained, are a proverbially stupid caste and their skulls are therefore easy to control; while Traders tend to be sharp and cunning and their skulls are particularly powerful.[35] With the proper *mantras* (sacred formulae) an Aghori can get his skull to fetch and carry for him, or cause it to fight with another. It is as if life resides in the skull itself, only waiting to be activated by one who knows the proper incantations. It is because the vital breath of a person who has died a bad death has not been released from his cranium on the cremation pyre that his skull remains a repository of potential power.

Like other sects with a close affinity to Tantrism, the Aghoris perform (or at least claim to perform) the secret rite of *cakra-pūjā* involving the ritual use of the so-called 'five Ms' (*pancañmakāra*) – *māns* (meat), *machhlī* (fish), *madya* (liquor) *mudrā* (in this context parched grain or kidney beans) and *maithuna* (sexual intercourse). A group of male adepts, accompanied by one or more female partners, sit in a circle. The woman is worshipped as a manifestation of the goddess and is offered the food and drink which is subsequently consumed by the males who feed each other. The first four Ms all possess aphrodisiac qualities and thus lead towards the fifth – in which the adept and his partner incarnate Siva and his consort unite in *coitus reservatus*. As far as my subsequent argument is concerned, the crucial point here is that the female partner should ideally be a prostitute or a woman of one of the lowest castes; and she should also be menstruating at the time and thus doubly polluted. But what is also significant is that the sexual intercourse which is supposed to occur is a calculated repudiation of procreation. (By contrast the duty to sire offspring was frequently represented by my high-caste householder informants as the only legitimate pretext for coitus.) Not only is the semen withheld, but the act takes place at a time when the female partner is infertile. Moreover, she is preferably a prostitute: the one class of women who have a 'professional hostility' to fertility and who provide the perfect 'symbol of *barren* eroticism' (Shulman's, 1980:261–2, apt phraseology; my emphasis). Consistent with the discussion of Aghori aims which follows, the act of ritual copulation thus reveals a certain disdain for the regeneration of life, and identifies the male adept with Siva locked in a union with his opposed aspect which is both without end and without issue. It is a sexual pairing rid of its normal consequences – progeny and death (the latter being commonly used in popular speech as a metaphor for ejaculation, and being caused – as we have seen – by a failure to retain the semen).

This liaison between the Aghori and the prostitute recurs in several other contexts. The prostitutes of the city not only visit the burning *ghāṭs* to worship Siva there in his form of Lord of the Cremation Ground (Smaśan-Nāth) but each year on the festival of *Lolārk Chhaṭh* they used to come to sing and dance at the tomb of Kina Ram (though the practice was abandoned in the late 'fifties after a serious disturbance among the university students). Moreover, it is said that the bed of a prostitute is equivalent to a cremation ground in that it is an equally proper place for an Aghori to perform his *sādhanā* (ritual practice).

By his various observances the Aghori acquires *siddhis*, or supernatural powers, which give him mastery over the phenomenal world and the ability to read thoughts. If he is sufficiently accomplished he can cure the sick, raise the dead and control malevolent ghosts. He can expand or contract his body to any size or weight, fly through the air, appear in two places at once, conjure up the dead and leave his body and enter into another. All this, of course, is exactly what one might predict from the Aghori's dealings with corpses and bodily emissions, for – as Douglas (1966) points out – that which is anomalous and marginal is not only the focus of pollution and danger, but also the source of extraordinary power.

While *siddhis* may, of course, be won by ascetics who follow quite different kinds of regime, it is widely believed that they are acquired more quickly and more fully by those who pursue the path of the Aghori. This path, however, is more difficult and dangerous than that which is followed by other orders; and one whose discipline is inadequate, who is overtaken by fear during his austerities, or who fails to retain his semen during *cakra-pūjā*, pays the penalty of madness and death (cf. Carstairs, 1957:232). He then becomes an *Aughar-masān*, the most recalcitrant and difficult to exorcise of malevolent ghosts.

The association between madness and the Aghori is not, however, an entirely straightforward one. The genuine Aghori, it is acknowledged, is – almost by definition – likely to seem demented to ordinary mortals, and is apt to talk in a way which they cannot comprehend. But this is merely evidence of his divine nature and of the fact that he has succeeded in homologising himself with Siva, who is himself somewhat touched, and with Lord Bhairava – one of whose manifestations in Benares is as *Unmat* ('mad') Bhairava. Moreover complete lucidity is not the best policy for one who shuns the world and does not wish to be endlessly importuned for spiritual guidance. But while there may be an element of both divine and calculated madness in an authentic ascetic, it is also recognised that some Aghoris are simply insane in the medical sense. Their affliction, however, is generally attributed to a failure of nerve or an insufficiently fastidious attention to ritual detail during the performance of such dangerously powerful rites, rather than to any notion that their attraction to these practices suggests that they were unbalanced already.

By virtue of his magical powers, the Aghori who has – in the local idiom – 'arrived' (*pahunche hue*), is likely to attract a large lay following who bring their pragmatic problems to him for solution. Baba Bhagvan Ram, for instance, has an extensive circle of committed devotees. Most of them are of high caste,[36] and many are members of the professional middle-class. (Amongst the inner circle of disciples are, for example, a retired Collector and a retired Police Inspector, a post-doctoral research fellow and an administrator from the university, a College Lecturer, a student now studying in north America, two lawyers, an engineer, a Customs and Excise officer, a factory manager, a public works contractor, and a well-to-do shopkeeper.) Two other Aghoris I knew also had a significant middle-class following. Even in the presence of an ascetic other than their acknowledged *guru*, the humility of such devotees – who would in other contexts brook no trifling with their dignity – is really remarkable. When Pagila ('mad') Baba wilfully defaecated on the string-cot on which he was reclining, a Rajput police officer and a Brahman businessman undertook the cleaning up.

Although motives are hard to be confident about, for what it is worth I record my strong impression that what attracts many of these people to the Aghori's following are the *siddhis* which he is believed to have obtained and which he may be induced to use on their behalf in an insecure and competitive world.[37] To my knowledge several of them joined Bhagvan Ram's entourage at times of grave personal crisis – the Police Inspector when he was under investigation for corruption, the contractor when his business started to fail, the Customs and Excise Officer when the prospect of providing a suitable dowry for his daughters became an immediate problem. Not of course that this is an aspect of the matter to which they themselves would publicly call attention. As at least some of these middle-class devotees were inclined to present it, the initial appeal was rather the egalitarian social ethic which Baba Bhagvan Ram preaches, and about which I shall say more later.[38] As I would somewhat cynically interpret it, however, his considerable success amongst such people is at least in part attributable to the fact that this message is one which they can identify as 'progressive' and 'modern' and which they can casuistically use to legitimise a more shamefaced and surreptitious concern to tap the source of a fabulous supernatural power.

The paradox of the situation, however, is that in order to gain and maintain a reputation as an ascetic worthy of the name, the laity require miracles as evidence of his attainments; yet the brash display of such powers is regarded with equivocation for it testifies to an incomplete spiritual development. While proof that he has taken the first step, it demonstrates that he has gone no further, for the one who has really 'arrived' is the one who scorns to indulge the laity with such trifles, who is indifferent to reputation, and who pursues his own salvation with a complete disdain for the world. In order to attain his goal of *samādhi*, a double renunciation is necessary: first a renunciation of the world and then of the powers that are thereby acquired (cf. Eliade, 1969:89; 1976:106–7).

The man-in-the-world, however, remains thirsty for miracles and his compromise is the ascetic who is seen to work wonders – as it were, under the counter and in spite of himself – while denying his capacity to do so. It is not uncommon, in my experience, for one ascetic to be disparaged by the followers of another on the grounds that he is a mere performer of supernatural tricks.[39] But at the same time the follower feels obliged to justify the claims he makes for his own *guru* by reference to a personal experience of the marvels he can accomplish. Did he not witness, or even himself benefit from, this or that miraculous cure? Was he not actually with his *guru* in Benares when the latter was unmistakably sighted in Allahabad? The fact that the ascetic himself disclaims such reports merely confirms his spiritual authenticity.

The curse of an Aghori is particularly terrible and virtually irrevocable. The food of the accursed may turn to excrement as he raises it to his lips, or his heir may die. When a filthy Aghori dressed in the rotting skin of a fresh-water porpoise was, some generations ago, refused admission to the Maharaja of Benares' palace during the performance of a magnificent *yagya*, the sacrificial offerings became immediately infested with maggots and the sacrifice had to be abandoned. As a result of this incident, the Maharaja's line has continually failed to produce heirs, and has been forced to perpetuate itself by adoption; while the curse also stipulated that any Aghori who henceforth accepted food from the palace would be afflicted by a fistula in the anus (*bhagandar*). When the late *mahant* of Kina Ram's *āśrama* was at last induced to revoke the curse and eat from the royal kitchen, the Maharani immediately conceived a son – but the *mahant* himself succumbed to the foretold disorder.

For the development of my theme the story is particularly instructive in two ways. The first is that it draws our attention to the fact that the curse of an Aghori, and – as we shall see – his blessing too, is as often as not concerned with reproduction and fertility. But what is also significant is that the exclusion of the ascetic from the Maharaja's *yagya* appears to be merely a transposition of the well-known mythological incident in which Siva is excluded from the sacrifice of his father-in-law, Daksa, on the pretext that he is a naked, skull-carrying Kapalika (O'Flaherty, 1976:278) – the sectarian precursor of the Aghori. But Siva is essential to the sacrifice if the evil it unleashes is to be mastered (Biardeau, 1976:96). Denied of his share, he spoils the whole event and precipitates a disaster of cosmic proportions. Though the scale of our story is admittedly more modest, it is not difficult to see that the Aghori is merely playing the role which was written for Siva – as well he might, for we shall find that he aspires to be Siva.

The blessing of an Aghori is as beneficent as his curse is awesome. By it he may confer inordinate riches, restore the mad, cure the incurable or bestow fertility on the barren. In order to conceive a child, both Hindu and Muslim couples go in large numbers to Kina Ram's *āśrama*, where they visit his tomb, bathe in the tank of Krimi Kund ('the tank of worms')[40] and take ash from the sacred fire which is fuelled by wood brought from the cremation pyres and which is a form of the goddess Hinglaj Devi. The tank is the one beside which Kina Ram performed his austerities – thus again making a direct link between *tapas* and the powers of creation. The same procedure should ideally be repeated on five consecutive Sundays or five consecutive Tuesdays – days of the week which are special not only to Kina Ram but also to the god Bhairava. An identical procedure will cure children of the wasting disease of *sukhaṇḍi rog* which is caused by a barren woman touching or casting her shadow on the child immediately after she has bathed at the end of her period.[41] She will then conceive, but the child will start to 'dry up' (*sukhnā*) and wither away.

An Aghori's blessing is characteristically given by violently man-handling and abusing its recipient. Bhim Baba, for example, used to live on the verandah of the City Post Office, stark naked, morosely silent, and generally surrounded by a crowd of onlookers and devotees. Every so often, as if infuriated, he would lumber to his feet (for he was massively fat) seize a small earthenware pot and hurl it with a roar into the crowd. The fortunate target of his missile could leave assured that his problem was about to be solved or his aspirations met (cf. Morinis, 1979: 244; Barrow, 1893:226).[42] It is said that on festival occasions Kina Ram would throw his urine on the crowds by way of blessing. Indeed the bodily emissions of an Aghori are charged with a special potency and have miraculous medicinal qualities. The sister of one of Bhagvan Ram's university-educated devotees, for example, was said to have been cured of a grave illness after her brother had obtained for her a phial of his *guru's* urine. A lay follower may be initiated by the *guru* by placing a drop of his semen on the disciple's tongue; while at the initiation of an ascetic the preceptor fills a skull with his urine which is then used to moisten the novitiate's head before it is tonsured (Barrow, 1893:241).

Now my informants continually stress that as a result of his *sādhanā* an Aghori does not die. He realises the state of non-duality I referred to earlier; he 'takes *samādhi*', and enters into a perpetual cataleptic condition of suspended animation of deep meditation. His body is arranged (if necessary by breaking the spine) in a meditational posture (known as *padmāśan*), sitting cross-legged with his upturned palms resting on his knees. He is then placed in a box which – in Benares – is buried in the grounds of Kina Ram's *āśrama* (and which is everywhere oriented towards the north). Unlike the householder or ascetics of most other orders his skull is not smashed in order to release the 'vital breath'. A small shrine containing the phallic emblem of Siva is erected over the site of the grave, the emblem transmitting to the worshipper the power emanating from the ascetic's subterranean meditation.

By entering *samādhi* (the term refers to his tomb as well as to his condition within it) – which he is represented as doing by conscious desire at a time of his choosing – the ascetic unequivocally escapes the normal consequences of death: the severance of the connection between body and soul, the corruption of the body and the transmigration of the soul. Provided that he has 'taken' *samādhi* while still alive (*jīvit-samādhi*), rather than being 'given' it after death, his body is immune to putrescence and decay although it remains entombed for thousands of years. It is still the occasional habitation of his soul, which wanders the three *lokas* (of heaven, earth and the netherworld) assuming any bodily form it chooses and changing from one to another at will. The real ideological stress is here, rather than on the incorruption of the particular body he inhabited before he took *samādhi*. Endless stories nevertheless testify to a conviction that the body of the model ascetic is perfectly and perpetually preserved in its tomb; and it is widely believed that this body is at times animated by his peripatetic soul which may be brought back to its former shell in an instant by the fervent prayers of the devotee.

A *samādhi* (in the sense of tomb) which is reanimated by the presence of the soul is described as a *jāgrit-samādhi* ('awakened *samādhi*). Baba Bhagvan Ram's disciples credit him with thus 'awakening' the occupants of every one of the fifty *samādhis* within the precincts of Kina Ram's *āśrama* since he took over its effective management;[43] and this makes it possible to induce them to take a more direct hand in the affairs of men. As for himself, Bhagvan Ram denies the appeal of heaven, where – as he wryly informed me – 'all the celestial nymphs (*apsaras*) are now old ladies'. His intention is rather to spend eternity 'watching and waiting' here on earth where he is within easy reach of ordinary mortals. It is out of compassion for the sufferings of humanity that such an ascetic denies himself the final bliss of complete dissolution into Brahma, for once he is finally liberated 'who will give the sermons?'.

What sense, then, can we make of the ethnography I have provided? One preliminary observation here is that Aghori ideology, if not always their practice, insists that members of the order do not solicit alms. This relates to the familiar South Asian contradiction that, while the ascetic is enjoined to remain completely independent of the material and social order, he must necessarily depend on the gifts of the householder in order to support himself, and can therefore never entirely escape from the lay world. Aghori practice may be seen as one radical solution to this dilemma. His loincloth is a shroud, his fuel the charred wood of the pyres, his food human refuse. By scavenging from the dead (who have no further use for what he takes), the Aghori escapes the clutches of the living, and in theory at least realises the ascetic ideal of complete autonomy.

We may also note that the Aghori's vigil on the cremation ground may be represented as an unblinking meditation on the classic Hindu themes of the transience of existence and the inevitability of mortal suffering. 'Surrounded by death in the place of death, those aspects of reality that end in the fires of the cremation ground become distasteful ... attachment to the world and the ego is cut and union with Siva, the conqueror of death, is sought' (Kinsley, 1977:100). Like ascetics of other orders, the Aghori aspires to die to the phenomenal world, to undergo the 'Death that conquers death' (Kinsley, 1977), and to exist on earth as an exemplar of the living dead. But what makes him different from others is that he pushes this symbolism to its logical limits.

The theological line which the Aghoris themselves most forcefully stress, however, is the notion that everything in creation partakes of *parmātmā*, the Supreme Being, and that therefore all category distinctions belong merely to the world of superficial appearances, and there is no essential difference between the divine and the human, or between the pure and the polluted. As Lal Baba represented his own spiritual quest to me, it is to become like that ideal Aghori, the sun, whose rays illuminate everything indiscriminately and yet remain undefiled by the excrement they touch.

The doctrine that the essence of all things is the same may clearly be taken to imply a radical devaluation of the caste hierarchy, since from this point of view there is no fundamental difference between the Untouchable and the Brahman. What is less obvious, however, is whether this teaching is one which relates only – as Dumont's model (1960, 1970) would suggest – to the ascetic (caste is irrelevant for *him* but not for the world at large), or whether the Aghori's devaluation of the social order is to be interpreted as a message for *all* men. My Aghori informants themselves were not altogether unequivocal on the matter – sometimes denying to caste any relevance whatsoever, while at others presenting equality as a matter of the ultimate *religious* truth of the enlightened rather than as the appropriate goal of social policy. This lack of clarity is perhaps only to be expected, since for them the central concern is with dissolving the barrier between god and man (or more precisely between Siva and the individual ascetic himself), rather than with tearing down that which divides men from each other.

It is, however, clear that the *social* implications of Aghori doctrine are far from absent from the teachings of Baba Bhagvan Ram, their most illustrious representative in Benares, who has derived from its religious truth a this-worldly ethic of equality and community service – though I concede the possibility that this may be a modern reworking of the renouncer's message. The *āśrama* Bhagvan Ram founded just across the river from Benares includes a hospice for lepers, a primary school, dispensary, post office and printing press. Amongst his circle of followers inter-caste marriage is positively encouraged. But what might also be said is that within the egalitarian order which he would have his disciples realise, a position of unquestioned privilege is nonetheless preserved for the *guru*. He drives about in a jeep, and while he sleeps over a grave, he does so in a well-appointed room under an electric fan. Even his teaching is not without its streak of ambivalence. While caste may be dismissed as a conspiracy of the powerful, the vow by which his male devotees should offer their daughters in marriage leaves considerable doubt about the equality of the sexes within marriage,[44] and the doctrine of *karma* is not in question. Lepers are paying the price of past wickedness. (I regret that I neglected to ask whether the same might not also be held to apply to the Untouchables.) What is at issue, he told me, is rather the right of others to use this fact as justification for their exclusion from society.[45]

If, however obliquely, Aghori doctrine poses questions about the ultimate legitimacy of the social order, there is a rather different way in which their practice reinforces this message of doubt. In orthodox caste society, polluting contacts between castes must be eliminated in order to preserve the boundaries of the group, for which – as Douglas (1966) argues – the boundaries of the body often serve as a metaphor. The Aghori's inversion of the same symbols of body margins implies exactly the opposite message. With the destruction of boundaries entailed by the consumption of flesh, excrement and so on, goes an affirmation of the irrelevance of caste boundaries. Coming at the issue in a more general way suggested by Turner (1969), we might also note the relationship which exists between liminal states, the suspension of the hierarchical structure of everyday life, and a stress on a vision of an unhierarchised and undifferentiated humanity. By contrast with that of the initiand in tribal society, the Aghori's liminality is permanent – and it is also of a somewhat extreme character. It is hardly surprising, then, that he should represent something of the equality which is generally associated with those liminal to the routinely ordered structure.

Perhaps the most striking aspect of the data, however, is the remarkable similarity between the character assumed by the Aghori and the person of Siva. Indeed the description of Siva given by his disapproving father-in-law perfectly fits the stereotype of the Aghori:

He roams about in dreadful cemeteries, attended by hosts of goblins and spirits, like a mad man, naked, with dishevelled hair, laughing, weeping, bathed in ashes of funeral piles, wearing a garland of skulls and ornaments of human bones, insane, beloved of the insane, the lord of beings whose nature is essentially darkness. (Briggs, 1938:153)

The epithet *aughar*, by which the Aghori is widely known and which implies an uncouth carefreeness, is one of the names of the god. Like Siva, who ingested the poison that emerged from the Churning of the Oceans and thereby allowed creation to proceed, the Aghori is a swallower of poison who liberates the blocked-up fertility of women. Like his prototype he is addicted to narcotics, is master of evil spirits, is touched with madness and his most salient characteristic is his moodiness. He is *aṛbhangi* – one who follows his whims with truculent intransigence. He adorns his body with the ornaments of Siva, plays Siva's part as spoiler of the sacrifice when denied admission to it, is greeted in a way appropriate to the god with cries of *Bom, Bom* or *Har Har Mahādev*, and indeed claims and is acknowledged to be Siva. So, for example, the *mahants* of the Kina Ram *āśrama* are explicitly said to be his *avatars*. In the rite of *cakra-pūjā*, the Aghori becomes the Lord of Forgetfulness wrapped in a deathless embrace with his consort; while his necrophagy on the cremation ground may be seen as an act of communion in which he ingests Siva (represented by the corpse), and thus re-creates his consubstantiality with him. The skull he carries associates him with Siva's manifestation as the terrifying god Bhairava who – to atone for the sin of chopping off Brahma's fifth head – was condemned to wander the earth 'as an Aghori' with a skull stuck fast to his hand. Dogs, which like the Aghori scavenge off the cremation ground, are his familiars – as they are of Bhairava in whose temples they wander freely. The special days for visiting these temples are the same as those for visiting Kina Ram's *āśrama*; the god too blesses his worshippers in the form of a (token) beating delivered by his priests, and in ritual intercourse the Aghori's female partner is often identified as his consort, Bhairavi. In short, as Lorenzen (1972:80) has noted, the ascetic homologises himself with the god and acquires some of his divine powers and attributes.[46] Above all, like Siva – the Great Ascetic and Destroyer of the Universe whose emblem is the erect phallus and whose sexual transports shake the cosmos – he transcends duality by uniting opposites within his own person, and thereby acquires Siva's role as *Mahāmritunja*, the 'Conqueror of Death', who amongst the gods is the only one who survives the dissolution of the cosmos and who is truly indestructible (*avināśī*).

This, it seems to me, is the crux of the matter. The theme of inversion and the coincidence of opposites runs throughout the material I have presented. The ascetic becomes the consort of the prostitute, the menstruating prostitute becomes the goddess, beating a blessing, the cremation ground a place of worship, a skull the food-bowl and excrement and putrid flesh food, and pollution becomes indistinguishable from purity. Duality is abolished, polarities are recombined,[47] and the Aghori thus recaptures the primordial state of non-differentiation. He passes out of the world of creation and destruction and into an existence which is beyond time.[48] He attains that state of unity with Brahma which characterised the atemporal and undifferentiated void which existed before the world began. So while I have argued in the first section of the paper that the mortuary rites of the householder represent a re-creation of the deceased, a renewal of time and a regeneration of the cosmos, I am arguing here that by embracing death and pollution, by systematically combining opposites, the Aghori aims to suspend time, to get off the roundabout and to enter an eternal state of *samādhi* in which death has no menace.

NOTES

1 I gratefully acknowledge helpful comments on an earlier draft from Maurice Bloch, Richard Burghart, Chris Fuller, Audrey Hayley, Jean La Fontaine, Edmund Leach and Penny Logan.

2 Although I try here to make some sense of the path of Aghori asceticism by contrasting it with that of the householder, it is of course clear that much of their practice might also be usefully seen in opposition to the discipline of other ascetic orders. Such an analysis is, however, beyond the scope of the present paper.

3 Cf. Bharati's observation (1976:17) that the unique contribution of Tantrism lies not so much in any philosophical novelty as in its ritual methods.

4 Fieldwork in Benares was carried out between September 1976 and November 1977 (supported by the Social Science Research Council) and in August 1978 (supported by the London School of Economics and Political Science). I am deeply obligated to Virendra Singh for his language instruction, and to him and Om Prakash Sharma for their research assistance.

5 There is however a wide variation in the meanings which different informants attach to these terms (Parry 1981).

6 This and the following paragraphs dealing with death as a cosmogonic sacrifice are borrowed with various modifications, from my paper 'Death and Cosmogony in Kashi' (1981).

7 Although I arrived at this conclusion quite independently, I now find that it is not an entirely original one. In a slightly different form it is anticipated by Biardeau's authoritative and impressive analysis of Puranic cosmogonies, and in particular by her discussion of *pralaya* as a gigantic cosmic funeral (Biardeau, 1971; also 1976:116).

8 I need hardly add that very considerable material interests are also at stake here.

9 On the conception of death as a sacrifice see Biardeau (1971:76 and 1976:38); Das (1976 and 1977:120–6); Levin (1930); Malamoud (1975); Pandey (1969:241, 253) and Knipe (1975:132–4).

10 The difference between this account of creation and the one involving Visnu's austerities at Manikarnika *ghāṭ* is perhaps only superficial. Visnu is – as Biardeau (1976:91, 96) shows – identified with the original sacrificial being (the *Puruṣa*) of the Rg-vedic hymn; while his cosmogonic austerities may be read as an act of self-sacrifice. What we appear to have, then, are not two completely different accounts of the beginnings of the world, but two versions of the same account couched in slightly different language.

101

11 For the overwhelming majority of my informants the *prān* (or 'vital breath') is synonymous with the *ātmā* (or 'soul'), and *kapāl kriyā* thus marks the separation of the soul from the body. But although most people deny that there is any distinction between them, in ordinary speech they commonly refer to the *prān* of an individual in the plural, while the *ātmā* is invariably singular. The more learned of the sacred specialists will sometimes say that the body contains five or ten *prān*, and claim that it is only the last of these – known as *dhananjay* – that is released on the cremation pyre. But there is absolutely no question of there being more than one *ātmā*. Even so, it was only a single informant – a man of formidable learning and considerable scholarly reputation – who insisted on a fundamental distinction between these concepts. The *prān*, he explained, are multiple; are located in specific parts of the body and may cause pain in their vicinity when they do not function properly, and are forms of 'air' (*vayu*) which will merge with the air at death. As opposed to the *prān* which is located and 'active' (*kriyā-vān*), the *ātmā* is 'all-pervasive' (*sarv-vyāpi*) and passive.

12 Even those who assert this theory most forcefully were, however, distinctly uncomfortable with my inference that the closest mourners might legitimately enter a temple in the period between physiological death and cremation.

13 I should note, however, that while the breaking of the skull is generally seen as a release of life from the body, most of my informants shied away from the explicit conclusion that it therefore amounts to an act of violence against the deceased.

14 In this sense, then, the deceased is himself the sacrificer; which would seem to contradict the implication that, by taking upon himself 'the sin of burning the body hairs', the chief mourner assumes this role. In fact, however, there is no incompatibility between the two, for in the Indian theory of sacrifice – as in many others – the sacrificer's offering is his own body homologised with that of the victim. Or, to put it more simply, the chief mourner is symbolically equated with the deceased. In line with this we find that throughout the mortuary rituals they are repeatedly identified, such that – for example – the chief mourner is clothed throughout in a piece of cloth torn from the shroud in which the corpse is wrapped, and is said to eat for the departed ghost during the period of mourning. But if the chief mourner is homologised with the corpse, so also is the corpse homologised with a deity, for it is a manifestation of Siva. This series of identifications between sacrificer, victim and god is characteristic not only of Indian sacrifice (as illustrated in Coomaraswamy, 1941; Long, 1977:75; Malamoud, 1976:193; Kaelber, 1978; Herrenschmidt, 1979; and Shulman, 1980:92), but also of sacrifice in many other societies (for example, Leach, 1976:88–9; Turner, 1977; and Sahlins, 1978).

15 The notion that the sacrificer is the real victim of the sacrifice (see note 14) perhaps suggests another way of looking at the ambiguity surrounding the ritual state of the corpse (i.e. whether it is pure or polluted). According to the classical theory, the sacrificer has acquired – through the initiatory rite of *dīksā* – a sacrificial body sufficiently august to be offered to the gods in sacrifice, while his profane body remains behind in the safe-keeping of the presiding priests (Malamoud, 1976:161, 193). The problem with cremation, however, is that it is impossible to disguise the fact that it is not only this

sacred entity which is dispatched by the fire, but also the sacrificer's profane and mortal being. My tentative suggestion, then, is that it might be possible to see the ambiguity over the condition of deceased as a reflection of the difficulty of retaining, in this instance, a clear conceptual distinction between the two bodies of the sacrificer. As representative of his sacrificial body, the victim is pure; but as his patently profane and incipiently putrescent corpse it is also impure.

16 Although the theory is fairly general, the practice of differentiating between the sexes in this way is – in my experience – largely confined to the Bengali community (which is quite substantial in Benares).

17 Cf. Malamoud's (1975) fascinating discussion of both cremation and gestation as a process of cooking.

18 The ideal is for a man to survive to see his son's son's son. Great importance is attached to having visited the deceased during his last hours, and deep chagrin at an unavoidable absence is a constant refrain.

19 During *pitri-paksha* the gates of heaven are said to stand open. *Uttarāyaṇa* is the day-time of the gods. Since the departed arrives, as it were, during office hours he is less likely to be kept waiting about. As calculated by Indian almanacs, the winter solstice which begins the *uttarāyana* falls on Makarasankrānti on the 14th January, and not on 21st December. The five lunar mansions during which it is particularly inauspicious to die form a consecutive block known as *panchaka*.

20 Penny Logan tells me that her Tamil informants gave one hundred and twenty years as the ideal lifespan, and justified this number by the claim that this is the period it takes for all the planets to complete their round – thus again associating the life of the individual with the cosmic cycle.

21 Were it not for the quite explicit parturition symbolism of the pyre and the funeral procession (described above), it would be tempting to interpret cremation as a mere insemination, leading to the ten-day gestation period of the subsequent rites. In this context it is interesting to note that the *Śatapatha Brahmana* refers to the fire as the womb of the sacrifice, into which the initiand at *dīkṣā* offers his being as semen (Malamoud, 1975).

22 The *Kaśi Khanda* is a portion of the *Skanda Purana*. A short summary of this myth is given in Parry (1981).

23 Siddhartha Gautam Ram was installed in February 1978, at the age of nine. He does not himself yet live in the *āśrama*, but stays with his *guru* – Baba Bhagvan Ram – in the compound of the refuge for lepers which the latter founded. He was given to Baba Bhagvan Ram to raise after Bhagvan Ram had fructified the formerly infertile union of the boy's parents. As *mahant* of the Kina Ram *āśrama* he is clearly the puppet of Bhagvan Ram, who now effectively controls the *āśrama* (having been at loggerheads with the previous *mahant*, who was his own *guru*). It is said that while the young *mahant* is an incarnation of Kina Ram, and hence of Siva himself, Bhagvan Ram is an incarnation of the god's *śakti* (his active female aspect), and more particularly of the goddess Sarveshvari (the consort of Siva as the Lord of All). The much-quoted aphorism that 'without *śakti* Siva is a *śava* (corpse)' seems particularly apposite to the present case.

24 I personally encountered twelve, but with only eight of them did I have any but the most fleeting contact. Although some Aghoris spend a significant amount of time on pilgrimage (in particular to Pryag, Pasupatinath in Nepal

and Kamakhya in Assam), most appear to have a home base, and none that I came across was rigorously peripatetic.

25 *Guru Purṇīmā* falls on the full moon day of the month of *Asāḍha* (June–July) and is a traditional time for paying formal respects to one's *guru*. The more spectacular occasion, however, is *Lolārk Chhaṭh* which is celebrated on the sixth day of the bright fortnight of *Bhādon/Bhādrapada* (August–September). An enormous fair is held at the tank of the sun, known as Lolark Kund, the waters of which provide a cure for both leprosy and human infertility. (This set of associations between the sun, leprosy and fertility recurs in a number of different contexts.) On *Lolārk Chhaṭh,* however, it is the affliction of barrenness which receives the greatest stress, and thousands of childless couples come to bathe in the tank. The festival is also said to fall on the anniversary of a well-known incident when Kina Ram gave an infertile and therefore greatly-distressed Brahman woman the blessing of the birth of three sons in the three following years by beating her three times with a stick. (I discuss the violent nature of Aghori blessings later on in the text.) According to the legend, she was a servant of Swami Tulsidas (though in reality it is not certain that the historical Kina Ram had even been born by the time of Tulsidas' death). After consulting with Lord Rama, Tulsidas had told her that it was not in her fate to conceive. As we shall see, fertility may also be procured by bathing in the tank of Krimi Kund, which is situated inside the compound of Kina Ram's *āśrama*, and by subsequently visiting his tomb. Hedging their bets, many couples undergo both remedies on the day of *Lolārk Chhaṭh*. It was also then that the prostitutes of the city used to come to sing and dance at the *āśrama* in honour of Kina Ram (see below).

26 For a general account of the ascetic sects represented in Benares, and some idea of their relative strengths, see Sinha & Saraswati (1978). They estimate (p.50) that there is roughly one ascetic for every hundred and fifty lay Hindus in the city's population.

27 A female ascetic who lived in Benares until her death some twelve years ago is said to have been an Aghori, and is certainly described as performing the ritual practices which are the hallmark of the order. Vidyarthi, Saraswati & Makhan (1979:220–4) contains an interview with a householder–ascetic who lives with his wife and who claims to be an Aghori; while Sinha & Saraswati (1978:145–6) provide a brief account of an Aghori couple who live together as Siva and Parvati. All those I knew had completely renounced family life, though the *guru* of one of my ascetic informants was a householder. (See also Barrow, 1893:224.)

28 According to the descriptions I was given, the corpse is held fast during *śava-sādhanā* by a silken thread, which binds its wrist or ankle to a stake in the ground. It is then surrounded by a protective circle, within which the evil spirits of the cremation ground cannot penetrate, and outside of which are placed meat and liquor for them to consume. These spirits will try to engage the adept in a dialogue which he must at all costs resist. Provided that he is sufficiently resolute, they will eventually tire and accept the offerings he has left for them. This is a sign that his austerities will be rewarded. The corpse's mouth will relax, allowing the Aghori to feed it a tiny quantity of *khir* (rice pudding). He will subsequently decapitate it in order to acquire the skull, or cut a bone from the spine; and finally immerse its remains in the river. This is followed by a period of severe ascetic

restraint which completes his mastery over the deceased's spirit. The *ojhā*, who is a specialist in the control over the malevolent dead, is also said to perform *śava-sādhanā* for similar ends. But while the Aghori sits on the corpse's chest, the *ojhā* sits on the stomach.

29 In theory Kina Ram's *āśrama* has the right to claim five unburnt logs and five *paisa* for every pyre lit at the nearby cremation ground at Harish Chandra *ghāṭ*. It is alleged that in practice the Dom funeral attendants appropriate this perquisite, though every day somebody goes from the *āśrama* to collect charred wood from the pyres. This is not only used for cooking but also for maintaining the sacred fire which is the embodiment of the goddess Hinglaj Devi (a manifestation of Agni) who came to dwell with Kina Ram in Benares after he had visited her shrine in Baluchistan.

30 Dogs are also the attendants (*gan*) of Siva in his form as the terrifying Lord Bhairava (see below).

31 In the ritual language of the Aghori, liquor is known as *dāru* or more commonly as *dudhvā*, urine as *amarī pān*, and excrement as *bajrī*. *Dāru* means medicine or simply liquor; *dudhvā* would seem to relate to the standard Hindi *dudh*, 'milk'; and *amarī pān* to *amrit*, 'nectar of immortality'. I do not know what, if anything, *bajrī* means outside this context and the word is not given in the standard dictionaries I have consulted. I speculate that it is derived from the Sanskrit *vajr*, which is the weapon of Vishnu (and Indra), but which also has the connotation of 'hard' or 'strengthening'.

32 Although the account is written in fictional form, it was clearly intended to be – and was – read as an exposé of the reality confronting an impotent and corrupt local administration. The selection from, and commentary on, the orderly's revelations which was published in the *Calcutta Review* (1849, **11**, 318–96) claims that 'the whole is essentially true, the form only is that of a work of fiction'.

33 The night most closely associated with such practices is *chaturdaśi*, which is also known as *Mahākāl rātri* – the night of Siva as the destructive Lord of Time. *Chaturdaśi* is the penultimate (lunar) day of the dark fortnight of Hindu month, and is an inauspicious time during which Vedic study is proscribed (cf. Kane, 1941:II:395). It immediately precedes the even more inauspicious new-moon day of *āmāvasyā* when ghosts are abroad and easy to contact (cf. Stanley, 1977). The *chaturdaśi* which falls in the month of *Phalguna* (February–March) is the day of the festival of *Sivarātri*, which celebrates Siva's marriage and is one of the most important days for visiting his temples.

34 My evidence thus contradicts Crooke's (1928) implication that the Aghori is indifferent about the kind of skull he uses.

35 Other informants had a completely contradictory notion of the Oil-pressers, claiming that they are particularly intelligent. But whichever view they favour, everybody is agreed that there is something special about their intellects which creates a special demand for their skulls.

36 The magnetism of the Aghori ascetic for many high-caste householders was reported as early as the first half of the nineteenth century. 'In the holy city (of Benares), many Brahmans, Kshatris, and high Sudras, take instruction from this sage (the *mahant* of Kina Ram *āśrama*); but do not venture to imitate his manners' (Martin, 1838:II:492). The same source notes that 'the

Rajas and their chief relations have a strong hankering after their doctrine'.
37 If he should fail them, however, they are likely to go elsewhere. Until his son died, the Raja of one of the small states in the region was a devotee of Baba Bhagvan Ram. He subsequently transferred his allegiance to Ram Lochan Baba, another Benares Aghori.
38 One or two frankly acknowledged that membership of his following provided them with a ready-made network of social contacts with other like-minded professional people, not only in Benares, but throughout northern India.
39 More damning still is the accusation that he uses his *siddhis* for material gain. Whether the magical powers in question are those of the Aghori, or those of the old woman who knows a charm for curing piles, in the long term they are completely incompatible with the accumulation of profit, which leads to their inexorable decline.
40 Some informants claim that Krimi Kund is a bastardisation of the correct name Krin Kund. *Krīn* is the 'seed' *mantra* of the goddess Kali.
41 *Sukhaṇḍi rog* is also cured by visiting Aughar Nath ka Takhiya, which is in another part of the city and which contains the tombs of several Aghoris.
42 A photograph of Bhim Baba (who died before my fieldwork started) and a light-hearted account of a brief encounter with him and another Aghori are given in Newby (1966:228–34). A special edition of the popular Hindi magazine *Nūtan Kahaniyān* (Allahabad, June 1977) was devoted to stories of miraculous encounters with Aghoris. One of the articles is a profile of Bhim Baba and provides a vivid description of his method of blessing (which was also retailed by several of my own informants). This source also contains an account of Bhim Baba's origins which has extremely wide currency in the city. According to this account he was a Judge who renounced the world and became an Aghori after having to deal with a case in which he was obliged to administer a manifestly unjust law. On a brief visit to Kathmandu I was able to track down Bhim Baba's younger brother (an architect with a poultry business on the side). The family are Maharashtrian Karade Brahmans who settled in Nepal when their father obtained an appointment at the Pasupatinath temple through the good offices of the *raj-purohit*. Bhim Baba was apparently in continual conflict with his somewhat disciplinarian father, refused to study, and finally left home (completely naked) after a quarrel in which his father reproached him with ingratitude for years of parental support. He was never employed, far less a Judge.
43 On Baba Bhagvan Ram's control of the *āśrama* see note 23 above.
44 'Oh Shiva this daughter in the form of energy, I am offering to you to be used for the satisfaction of your holy desires and for the benefit of society – that is for breeding to such a progeny (*sic*) as may be useful for humanity, without any restriction of caste, creed or nationality' (cited in a pamphlet entitled *An introduction to Shri Sarveshwari Samooh*, published by the Awadhoot Bhagwan Ram Kust Sewa Ashram).
45 I encountered a very similar ambivalence in the case of another Aghori whose public pronouncements continually stress the brotherhood of all men and the meaningless character of the social hierarchy. It was clear that he regarded himself as a member of a small spiritual elite karmically qualified for the attainment of *samādhi*.
What is also striking is that both of these ascetics not only repudiate caste

but also the divisions between Hindus and others; and both are prepared to appropriate Christian symbols to make this point. Bhagvan Ram's leprosy hospice is surmounted by a Christian Cross; while Sadhak Basudeb showed me a pictorial autobiography he had made for the instruction of his devotees which contains a drawing in which he is receiving the stigmata from Christ who appeared to him during his wanderings in the Himalayas. This element of religious syncretism is also apparent at the shrine of Aughar Nath ka Takhiya, which contains several Aghori *samādhis* and which is said to belong equally to Hindus and Muslims. The influence of a devotional *bhakti* ideology is also particularly clear in much of the Aghoris' discourse.

46 The Aghoris' identification with Siva does not, of course, make them unique. The same might, I think, be said of many other Saiva ascetics and even of Saiva priests. What is again unusual about the present case is the means rather than the end, and perhaps also the aspect of Siva with which they choose to identify.

47 One obvious symbol of this merging of opposites is the androgyne; and it is perhaps significant that Baba Bhagvan Ram – despite his unambiguously masculine physique – has assumed a somewhat androgynous character. He is said to be an incarnation of a female deity (see note 23 above); is represented as a swollen-breasted goddess in a picture kept in a shrine within the *āśrama* he founded, and is said to appear sometimes before his followers in a *sāṛī*.

48 In a number of respects all this invites parallels with the annual pilgrimage of the Huichol Indians to the Wirikuta desert, where all the separations of profane life are obliterated and everything is done backwards in order to effect a return to the time of creation (Myerhoff, 1978). One crucial difference, of course, is that the Aghori's reversal is a life-long commitment rather than a temporary phase in the annual round. Unlike Rigby's (1968) Gogo rituals of purification, his inversions are not merely aimed at going back to the beginning of things so that time may start again, but rather at arresting time altogether.

REFERENCES

Abbot, J. 1932 *The keys of power: a study of Indian ritual and belief*. London: Methuen and Co.
Arens, W. 1979. *The man-eating myth: anthropology and anthropophagy*. New York: Oxford University Press.
Balfour, H. 1897. 'The life-history of an Aghori Fakir', *Journal of the Anthropological Institute* (London), **26**, 340–57.
Barrow, H.W. 1893. 'On Aghoris and Aghoripanthis', *Journal of the Anthropological Society of Bombay*, **3**, 197–251.
Beck, B.E.F. 1976. 'The symbolic merger of body, space and cosmos in Hindu Tamil Nadu', *Contributions to Indian Sociology*, (n.s.), **10**, 213–43.
Bharati, Agehananda 1976. *The trantric tradition*. Delhi: B.I. Publications.
Biardeau, M. 1971. 'Etudes de mythologie hindoue (III): 1. Cosmogonies Puraniques', *Bulletin de l'école française d'extrême-orient*, **58**, 17–89.

Jonathan Parry

1976. 'Le sacrifice dans l'hindouisme', in *Le sacrifice dans l'Inde ancienne*. M. Biardeau and C. Malamoud, pp.7–154. Paris: Presses Universitaires de France (Bibliothèque de l'école des hautes études, sciences religieuses, vol.79).

Briggs, G.W. 1938. *Gorakhnath and the Kanphata Yogis*. Calcutta: YMCA Publishing House.

Carstairs, G.M. 1957. *The twice-born: a study of a community of high caste Hindus*. London: Hogarth Press.

Coomaraswamy, A.K. 1941. 'Atmayajna: self-sacrifice', *Harvard Journal of Asiatic Studies*, **6**, 358–98

Crooke, W. 1928. 'Aghori', in *Encyclopedia of Religion and Ethics*. ed. J. Hastings. **1**: 210–3. New York.

Das, Veena 1976. 'The uses of liminality: society and cosmos in Hinduism', *Contributions to Indian sociology*, (n.s.), **10** (2), 245–63.

1977. *Structure and cognition: aspects of Hindu caste and ritual*. Delhi: Oxford University Press.

Douglas, M. 1966. *Purity and danger: an analysis of concepts of pollution and taboo*. London: Routledge and Kegan Paul.

Dumont, L. 1960. 'World renunciation in Indian religions', *Contributions to Indian Sociology*, **4**, 33–62.

1970. *Homo Hierarchicus: the caste system and its implications*. London: Weidenfeld and Nicolson.

1971. 'On putative hierarchy and some allergies to it', *Contributions to Indian Sociology*, (n.s.), **5**, 58–78.

Eliade, M. 1965. *The myth of the external return*. Princeton: University Press (Bollingen series 46).

1969. *Yoga: immortality and freedom*. Princeton: University Press (Bollingen series 61).

1976. *Patanjali and Yoga*. New York: Schocken Books.

Garuda Purana (n.d.) (With Hindi commentary by Sudama Misr Shastri.) Varanasi: Bombay Pustak Bhandar.

Goudriaan, T. 1979. 'Introduction: history and philosophy', in *Hindu tantrism*. S. Gupta, D.J. Hoens & T. Goudriaan, pp.3–67. Leiden: E.J. Brill (Handbuch der Orientalistik).

Gupta, S. 1979. 'Modes of worship and meditation,' in *Hindu tantrism*, S. Gupta, D.J. Hoens & T. Goudriaan. pp.121–85. Leiden: E.J. Brill (Handbuch der Orientalistik).

Harris, M. 1977. *Cannibals and kings*. New York: Random House.

Heesterman, J. 1959. 'Reflections on the significance of the Daksina', *Indo-Iranian Journal*, **3**, 241–58.

Herrenschmidt, O. 1978. 'A qui profite le crime? Cherchez le sacrifiant', *L'Homme*, **18** (1–2), 7–18.

1979. 'Sacrifice symbolique ou sacrifice efficace', in *La fonction symbolique*. eds M. Izard and P. Smith. Paris: Editions Gallimard.

Hubert, H. & Mauss, M. 1964. *Sacrifice: its nature and function*. London: Cohen & West.

Kaelber, W.O. 1976. '"Tapas", birth and spiritual rebirth in the Veda', *History of Religions*, **15**, 343–86.

1978. 'The "dramatic" element in Brahmanic initiation: symbols of death, danger and difficult passage', *History of Religions*, **18** 54–76.

Kane, P.V. 1941 & 1953. *History of Dharmasastra*. vols 2 & 4. Poona: Bhandarkar Oriental Research Institute.

(Sri) *Kaśi Khanda* (n.d.) (Compiled and rendered into Hindi by Baikunthnath Upardhyay.) Varanasi: Shri Bhragu Prakashan.

Kinsley, D.R. 1977. '"The death that conquers death": dying to the world in Medieval Hinduism', in *Religious encounters with death: insights from the history and anthropology of religions*. eds E. Reynolds & E.H. Waugh. pp.97–108, University Park & London: Pennsylvania State University Press.

Knipe, D.M. 1975. *In the image of fire: Vedic experiences of heat*. Delhi & Varanasi: Motilal Banarasidass.

1977. 'Sapiṇḍīkāraṇa: the Hindu rite of entry into heaven', in *Religious encounters with death: insights from the history and anthropology of religions*. eds E. Reynolds & E.H. Waugh. pp.111–124. University Park & London: Pennsylvania State University Press.

Leach, E.R. 1976. *Culture and communication: the logic by which symbols are connected*. Cambridge: Cambridge University Press.

Lévi, S. 1898. *La doctrine du sacrifice dans les Brahmanas*. Paris: Bibliothèque de l'école des hautes etudes, sciences religieuses, **11**.

Levin, M. 1930. 'Mummification and cremation in India', *Man*, **30**, 29–34, 44–8, 64–6.

Long, B. 1977. 'Death as a necessity and a gift in Hindu mythology' in *Religious encounters with death: insights from the history and anthropology of religions*. eds F.E. Reynolds & E.H. Waugh, pp.73–96. University Park & London: Pennsylvania State University Press.

Lorenzen, D.N. 1972. *The Kapalikas and Kalamukhas: two lost Saivite sects*. Berkeley and Los Angeles: University of California Press.

Malamoud, C. 1975. 'Cuire le monde', *Puruśartha: Recherches de Sciences sociales sur l'Asie du sud*, **1**, 91–135.

1976. 'Terminer le sacrifice: remarques sur les honoraires rituels dans le brahmanisme', in *Le sacrifice dans l'Inde ancienne*. M. Biardeau & C. Malamoud, pp.155–204. Paris: Presses Universitaires de France (Bibliothèque de l'école des hautes études, sciences religieuses, vol. 79).

Martin, M. 1838. *The history, topography, and statistics of Eastern India*. London: W.H. Allen & Co.

Morinis, A. 1979. *Hindu pilgrimage with particular reference to West Bengal, India*. Unpubl. D.Phil, thesis, University of Oxford.

Myerhoff, B.G. 1978. 'Return to Wirikuta: ritual reversal and symbolic continuity on the Peyote hunt of the Huichol Indians' in *The reversible world: symbolic inversion in art and society*. ed. B.A. Babcock, pp.225–39. Ithaca and London: Cornell University Press.

Newby, E. 1966. *Slowly down the Ganges*. London: Hodder & Stoughton.

O'Flaherty, W.D. 1973. *Asceticism and eroticism in the mythology of Siva*. London: Oxford University Press.

1976. *The origins of evil in Hindu mythology*. Berkeley, Los Angeles & London: University of California Press.

1980. 'Karma and rebirth in the Vedas and Puranas', in *Karma and rebirth in classical Indian traditions*. ed. W.D. O'Flaherty. pp.3–37. Berkeley, Los Angeles & London: University of California Press.

Jonathan Parry

Oman, J.C. 1903. *The Mystics, ascetics, and saints of India: a study of sadhuism, with an account of the Yogis, Sanyasis, Bairagis, and other strange Hindu sectarians.* London: T. Fisher Unwin.

Pandey, Raj Bali 1969. *Hindu samskaras: socio-religious study of the Hindu sacraments.* Delhi & Varanasi: Motilal Banarasidass.

Parry, J.P. 1980. 'Ghosts, greed and sin: the occupational identity of the Benares funeral priests', *Man*, (n.s.), **15** (1), 88–111.

1981. 'Death and cosmogony in Kashi', *Contributions to Indian Sociology*, **15**:337–65.

Preta Manjari. (Samvat 2032. Compiled by Sudama Misr Shastri and revised by Mannilal Abhimanyu.) Varanasi: Bombay Pustak Bhandar.

(The) Revelations of an orderly. (by Paunchkouri Khan (pseudonym) 1848.) Benares: Recorder Press (Selections reprinted in *Calcutta Review* 1849, **11**, 348–96).

Rigby, P. 1968. 'Some Gogo rituals of "purification": an essay on social and moral categories', in *Dialectic in Practical Religion*, ed. E.R. Leach, pp.153–78. Cambridge: Cambridge University Press (Cambridge papers in social anthropology, no 5).

Sahlins, M. 1978. 'Culture as protein and profit', *The New York Review of Books*, November 23, pp.45–53.

Sherring, M.A. 1872. *Hindu tribes and castes as represented in Benares.* London: Trubner & Co.

Shulman, D.D. 1980. *Tamil temple myths: sacrifice and divine marriage in the South Indian Saiva tradition.* Princeton: University Press.

Sinha, S. & Saraswati, B. 1978. *Ascetics of Kashi: an anthropological exploration.* Varanasi: N.K. Bose Memorial Foundation.

Sraddha Parijat (n.d.) (Compiled by Rudradatt Pathak). Gaya: Shri Vishnu Prakashan.

Stanley, J.M. 1977. 'Special time, special power: the fluidity of power in a popular Hindu festival', *Journal of Asian Studies*, **37** (1), 27–43.

Stevenson, S. 1920. *The rites of the twice-born.* London: Oxford University Press.

Tod, Lt. Col. J. 1839. *Travels in Western India.* London: W.H. Allen.

Turner, V. 1969. *The ritual process: structure and anti-structure.* Chicago: Aldine Publishing Co.

1977. 'Sacrifice as quintessential process, prophylaxis or abandonment', *History of Religions*, **16** (3), 189–215.

Vidyarthi, L.P., Saraswati, B.N. & Makhan, J.H.A. 1979. *The sacred complex of Kashi.* Delhi: Concept Publishing Company.

Zaehner, R.C. 1962. *Hinduism.* London: Clarendon Press.

4 Witchcraft, greed, cannibalism and death: some related themes from the New Guinea Highlands

ANDREW STRATHERN

Introduction

New Guinea Highlands and Fringe Highlands societies show a range of variation in terms of ideas about witchcraft, on the one hand, and cannibalism on the other. Can we make a sense of this variation? In what follows, I propose to discuss this problem by drawing attention to further patterns of ideas which run across several of the Highlands societies.

At the outset, I must make it clear that in concentrating on ideas I do not mean to suggest that these are in themselves determinant. To the contrary, if we look at the Highlands area in geographical terms, it is evident that the practice of cannibalism is (according to reports) associated most clearly with sparsely-populated fringe regions where large herds of domestic pigs are absent. Although we cannot argue from this that protein-hungry people become anthropophagous, there is obviously a material correlation of some interest here. The reasons why the argument cannot be made in a simple manner are that, first, the fringe peoples have alternative sources of protein in wild game, including feral pigs themselves, so that they are not necessarily or universally protein-hungry at all; and second, cannibalism as an approved practice has been reported from the Gimi and Fore Areas of the Eastern Highlands, where herds of domestic pigs are certainly kept. Overall, however, there is sufficient evidence to enable us to speculate that in the areas where agricultural intensification has proceeded to its greatest lengths, cannibalism is absent, and a classic complex of symbolic associations between witchcraft, greed, incest and cannibalism emerges.[1]

It is with this complex of associations that I am mostly concerned here. I begin with some data on a rumour of cannibalism which developed, with apparent suddenness, in the Melpa area of the Western Highlands Province during 1977. By mid-1979 it had died down and was still quiescent in 1980 and April 1981. As an event, the

111

Andrew Strathern

rumour remains rather obscure. It is difficult to say where and how it began and why interest in it lapsed. As a symbol of themes to do with production and consumption and the proper forms of cyclicity between life and death, it becomes more amenable to analysis.

The rumour

In 1964–5, when I first worked with the Melpa, I had learned that a few people, chiefly certain women, were secret cannibals, who obtained human flesh by robbing graves of newly-buried corpses. They would assume the appearance of dogs[2] to evade attention or recognition while on their necrophagous raids, and because of this magical power and their greed for flesh their actions were described as *kum kondor-omen*, 'they make *kum*'. The 1977 rumour built on this established theme by suggesting that many more people were now becoming cannibals and that the habit was being deliberately spread. Converted cannibals were said to be placing pieces of human flesh at the heads of streams so that juice or 'grease' (*kopong*) from the flesh would mingle with the water, and people downstream who drank from it would feel how sweet it was and would also acquire a taste for human flesh. The implication was that the cannibals would also use sorcery to kill their victims so that they could consume their bodies.

Cannibalism as a general practice is feared and abhorred among the Melpa, though it is also associated with a category of Sky-Beings (*Tei-Wamb*) who often figure in the origin stories of particular groups. When Europeans first entered their area in the early 1930s, the Melpa thought these pale-skinned intruders, who came from the sky in light planes, belonged to this category of cannibal beings from their folk-tales, and were terrified of them until the explorers produced valuable shells and showed that they were human by exchanging these for goods and services. Aeroplanes themselves were sometimes described as a kind of *kum* or witchcraft, since they could fly just as *kum* is said to fly through the air. *Kum* is obviously associated with power and mobility as well as with desire. But actions motivated or instigated by *kum* are morally reprehensible. *Kum* takes, consumes and kills: it does not behave reciprocally.

The 'true home' of *kum* is the hot, low-altitude Jimi Valley to the north of the main Melpa area. There *kum* may be seen by night in the form of lights flitting from tree to tree. Or it may enter human beings and give them the power to turn themselves into birds, which fly out and attack victims, entering them by the anus, eating their insides and emerging via the mouth.

112

These more distant *kum* are seen as controlled by males; closer to home it is in-married females who are the suspects. Although it is not said that body-stealing is exclusive to women, in practice both men and women name other women most frequently as suspected canni-bals. In each clan group at most one, two or three women are named. There are three, for example, married into the clan group with which I am associated. The clansmen claim also that women of two particular neighbouring clans have a tendency towards cannibalism; that daugh-ters learn the practice from their mothers; and that in one case the husband has recently decided to shun his wife altogether, since she has caused his jaw and windpipe to close up, making it difficult for him to speak or to swallow food. (Perhaps a bad attack of viral pharyngitis precipitated this.) The implication is that over the years she has eaten parts of his insides and that she has moved her attention to his throat, which he himself uses to eat, so it was time to break with her. The idea of the incoming witch who eats one's insides is an exaggerated version of anxiety concerning the ordinary in-marrying wife who shares the husband's resources and 'eats' his semen; but whereas the ordinary wife 'consumes' semen in order to bear children, the witch-wife attacks the inner parts of the husband himself in order to destroy him.

The traditional symbolism of the witch, then, follows two lines: that of the distant, dangerous male witches who come from the Jimi, and that of the nearby female witches who come from intermarrying clans. In either case, however, the witch is pictured as a cannibal, who kills by eating the internal parts of the victim's body and/or practises necro-phagy as a means of obtaining human meat as such. Destruction from within and the robbing of graves are the themes involved.

The ideas, which are clearly paralleled by similar notions among the Kuma (Reay, 1976:1–20) and the Chimbu (Brown 1977:26–29), exist in a kind of 'steady state'. They were present in 1964–5 and are also present now (1981). They form the background against which the 1977 rumour developed. The effect of the rumour was to make people very circumspect about drinking water from any source outside of their own sub-clan territory, where they could check the headwaters of streams thoroughly for any chunks of flesh planted there. There was thus a tightening of clan boundaries and a renewed feeling of danger in travelling outside of one's home area.

Another effect was that people felt they had to guard dead bodies with great vigilance. People said that witches were now appearing in cemeteries not just as dogs, but also as cows and horses (animals introduced into the Hagen area by Europeans). Relatives took turn to stand guard over graves of the recently-dead. In order to put the

113

witch-cannibals off, a death might be dissembled, the body buried secretly, and the public funeral held only later. By that time, the corpse would no longer be fresh and would not attract the cannibals' interest. At funerals themselves, and on other public occasions, as well as when travelling on pathways between settlements, mothers were careful to hide from view any especially healthy children, since the growing number of witches would prefer these as succulent victims and might kill them by staring at them with their greedy red eyes. The lust of witches for human children's flesh may be compared here to the pleasure which men express in eating the sweet flesh of young piglets as against that of grown pigs. Both themes are expressions of the desire for premature and incorrect consumption which runs against the dominant ethic of production for exchange. It is this question, concerning the place of consumption in the ideological system, which is also crucial in the interpretation of cannibalism across the range of Highlands societies.

Before starting comparisons, however, we must look again at Melpa ethnography in order to answer two questions. First, why should the rumour of cannibalism have sprung up when it did? And second, why was the practice of grave-robbing seen as constituting so severe a threat that men armed with bows and arrows would stand in vigilance at night-time over the graves of their kinsfolk?

The historical context

The rumour began in 1977, was powerful by the time of the wet season (around Christmas) in that year, flourished in 1978, and died away in 1979. To date (1981), it has remained quiescent, though all the associated ideas are still present in people's minds. Why this brief span of prominence?

My argument is that the story coincided with an increase in the consumption of introduced goods in the particular local clan areas where the rumour spread most strongly (the Møka Valley, Dei Council). Unfortunately, I cannot document this point quantitatively. The interpretation is *post-hoc*, and my fieldwork over these three years consisted only of short visits, oriented towards further recording of ceremonial exchanges rather than overall patterns of consumption. However, some support can be given for the argument, as follows. 1977 marked a time when prices paid in cash for coffee beans, grown extensively by the Melpa, had been at a peak, and were just beginning to fall. The effect of some four years of high prices had been to increase gradually consumer demand for canned fish, meat and rice sold in local tradestores and also for large cartons of frozen beef, imported from Queensland in Australia, and costing about K50 (fifty Kina, or *c*. £40.00) each. Like cartons of beer, these were becoming standard items of purchase for use in ceremonial activities. The beef contained in them was defrozen and then cooked in earth-ovens in the same way as pork.[3] Prestigious purchases of large pigs, reared for sale by commercial companies, were also becoming common. From 1977 onwards, a large pig might cost anything between K500 and K1000. Beef, beer and purchased pigs thus accounted for some of the cash surplus generated by the boom in coffee prices. Much of the rest was absorbed in massive prestations of money made in *moka*, and in the acquisition of four-wheel-drive vehicles. The Kawelka Kundmbo clansmen, with whom I live, were vigorously involved in all of these trends during 1977 and 1978.

It is particularly the consumption side of these activities which is of importance here. Consumption, like production, is associated with the female gender by Hagen men. They say that women want to eat pork, while they themselves would rather give it away. The big-man, who represents male ideals, should not be a consumer but an investor of goods. Hence, witchcraft that is close at home is seen largely as a product of female greed. Such 'female' values can invade those spheres controlled by men and disrupt them; men themselves can become 'unmanned'. And indeed they had, in a sense, unmanned themselves, by their own excessive consumption of beer, which they monopolised to women's exclusion. This combination of beef and beer, I suggest, is mirrored in the ideas: (1) that now both women and men were becoming cannibals, (2) that cannibals were appearing in graveyards in the shape of cows (female) or horses (male), and (3) that the cannibal habit was being picked up from *drinking* polluted water, which nevertheless had an irresistibly attractive taste. (This last idea parallels the established notion that *kum* stones may jump up from the stream-beds where people stop to drink before attending a pig-killing festival: they then become inordinately hungry for pork.)[4]

Such trends towards dangerous consumption were vigorously opposed by big-men. Beer-drinking was branded as a 'rubbish' activity, although the derogatory label seems to have had little or no effect in curbing actual consumption by young men. The big-men stressed that they were distributing beef and pork for the benefit of the women, and that men should concern themselves rather with *raising* money and thus increasing clan prestige. This would be threatened by a collapse into self-indulgent and ultimately self-destructive patterns of consumption. The habits of young men in chasing after prostitute girls were also a target for criticism by big-men, and it is interesting that, in one anecdote told to me by a young woman in 1979, the themes of illicit sex and cannibalism were brought together. She told me that she knew of a man who lived in the eastern part of our council area (near to the Kuma) and who allowed his house to be used as a venue for prostitutes. Customers reported, she said, that the house had a peculiar stench because its owner stored pieces of human flesh in it for later consumption. It is a male stereotype that the genitals of prostitutes are also malodorous, and prostitutes are 'prime consumers' of cash and semen while at the same time avoiding the obligations of wives to labour in gardens and produce food and children for their husbands.

There is another feature of these data which is relevant. Cash, frozen beef, prostitution and live cows were all introduced by Europeans since the 1960s. In common with other Highlanders, the Melpa have adopted cash as another kind of 'valuable', replacing the pearl shells which they used to esteem so highly. They grow coffee to obtain cash, and devote an ever-increasing amount of time and energy to this end. They are aware nowadays of the potential conflict between the use of cash for ceremonial economics and its use for domestic consumption. Europeans, who are seen as the 'creators' of money, are thus regarded with some ambivalence. They are the 'wealth people', yet they have also introduced a new 'consumption' mentality, since money can be used to obtain a range of goods and services which pearl shells could not. It is not irrelevant to recall here that these same Europeans were originally seen by the Melpa as cannibal creatures, *Tei wamb-nui wamb*, and hence even their forms of wealth, which at first were pearl shells and other goods such as axes and cloth, are still latently tinged with that suspicion. Cash, which enables consumption to take place on an unprecedented scale by making it possible to exchange food directly for wealth, might itself then, be said to stand for potentially cannibalistic values.

In terms of local history, I see a connection here, too, between the 'cannibals' rumour and the cargo cult of 1968–71 (A.J. Strathern, 1979a, 1980). Money disappears in consumption: it goes back to its 'makers', the Europeans. The Europeans first give it in exchange for something which they consume, coffee, but they take it back in return for rice, meat, and so on. The cargo cult was a determined effort to overcome this problem by finding a way actually to 'produce' money on the spot. The cult managers used up a great deal of pork, food, and cash supplied by their extensive web of supporters in an effort to make this production successful. Hugely inflated returns were promised, enough to enable people to survive in the foreshadowed time of Independence, when the Europeans would leave. In the event, the cultists and their supporters lost everything: the cult flopped. A supreme engine of production was revealed as its opposite. The cult and its leaders had 'eaten' all their investments and given nothing back. The wish for cargo had been an inordinately strong desire, a *kum*, and had brought its own destruction. The 'cannibals' rumour was, I think, an echo of the earlier trauma. The people had learnt the dangers of too much consumption. Just as the cult leaders had spread their gospel of production with great rapidity, so now there was a fear that the cannibals were covertly spreading their habits of inordinate consumption. The underlying fear was that of internal self-destruction. The last act of *kum* is to eat the body of the person in which it has lodged, after driving the person to immoderate acts of consumption in order to feed it.

By mid-1979, the vogue for imported beef and for purchased pigs was on the wane. People were saying that beef was unpleasant to the taste, and that their own home-grown pigs were better than European-reared stock. They refused to pay inflated prices for meat, and turned to purchasing frozen chickens for minor ceremonies, reserving their home stock of pigs for major occasions.[5] Such pigs were also the best vehicles for sacrifices to the ghosts. This brings me to the second question: why did the Melpa fear the actions of cannibals in robbing flesh from the cemeteries?

Death and sacrifice

The Melpa have not developed an elaborate cosmology to deal with what happens to a person's spirit after death. Nevertheless, ghosts are of considerable importance to the living, and the relationship between the living and the dead has continually to be reaffirmed by sacrifices of pigs. Major versions of such sacrifices are made at stages after a death, culminating in the largest, and final, killing known as 'the head-hair pigs' (*peng ndi kng*).

At death, the flesh of the person is expected to rot, and in the past, prior to the influence of Christian missions, the skull of an important man and some of his limb bones might also be taken as relics and established in a *peng manga* ('head house'). In accordance with a structure of ideas which is common in the Highlands, flesh is thought of as associated with 'female' values, whereas bone is linked with 'maleness'. The enduring 'male' part was thus preserved and made a focus for continuing communication; while the flesh rotted back into

117

the earth. From one perspective, then, flesh may be seen as impermanent, that which is lost at death; and this helps to explain why
payments of permanent wealth items or sacrifices of pork had to be
made to maternal kin (A.J. Strathern, 1981), as a compensation for this
loss. Yet, in another sense, the flesh is not lost. It goes down into the
earth and contributes to the earth's 'grease' or 'fertility' (*kopong*). In
turn plants grow from the soil, people eat these, and the cycles are
continued. There is thus a 'grease-cycle' which passes through people,
plants, and the earth, and which contrasts with the creation and
deposition of bone: bones represent individual claims to soil or claims
to power as a means of access to a ghost, they are associated with the
jural and political world, while flesh is associated with the cycle of
fertility, reproduction, consumption and rot.[6]

Some caveats need to be entered here. First, the idea of a grease-
cycle is *not* explicitly stated by the Melpa: I have constructed it from
their general remarks about *kopong*, and from stories which they tell of
'strange places', such as the Southern Highlands, where corpses were
traditionally placed on trestles and the putrefying liquids from them
allowed to drip on to garden plots below as a means of fertilisation.
Significantly, such 'stranger' peoples are also imaged as cannibals. The
image indicates why the idea of a grease-cycle is suppressed in Melpa:
it borders on cannibalism. As one might expect, then, since cannibalism is regarded as a heinous act, cemeteries are cut off from gardens,
and one should not make a garden where a cemetery has been
established in the past. And yet, bodies must be buried, and protected
against interference, particularly the overt cannibalistic interference of
witches. Why? I argue that at a deep level it is because a body's grease
should go back into the earth and restore fertility.

It would be possible to argue that a different reason is that, unless
the body remains buried in local soil, the spirit will be angry and
wander about, causing destruction. But I do not know of any instances
to support this idea. There is one story I heard which is perhaps
relevant, however. A Kundmbo clansman, Rongnda, was confronted
one evening by a throng of singing men and women, on the way to his
lavatory hut down from his house. These were ghosts, who told him
that they (the living clansfolk) must stop burying people on top of
other people buried earlier, since this was throwing dirt in their eyes.
As a result of this encounter, the Kundmbo moved a recently-buried
corpse, and they had no more complaints from the ghostly throng.
This story does suggest that ghosts care about where their old body is,
and by implication that they would be distinctly put out to find it had
been eaten by a witch. If this is correct, I would regard it as

supplementary, rather than alternative to the argument on grease which I have made.

Pork sacrifices themselves are said to 'make grease' in the earth. It will be remembered that pork is steamed in ovens dug in the earth, lined with banana leaves and heated stones.[7] At the bottom of the normal conical pit which is dug for this purpose, liquid fat from the meat is expected to collect, and the amount of fat is taken as an index of the quality of the meat and its preparation. This in turn is a sign of ghostly goodwill towards the cookers. On April 12th, 1981, Ndamba, a Kundmbo big-man, made an invocation over two pigs cooked to celebrate the building of a new house at Kiltkayake settlement. In calling to several ghosts, he said that such pork sacrifices were good because they ensured that 'grease will go' (*kopong mba*) into the earth around every house in the clan area. Each house must be 'blessed' in this way, both as a sign of ghostly favour and to ensure its continuation; and jawbones of pigs are hung up on nearby fences to commemorate the sacrifice.

Sacrifices gain favour with the ghosts, and also 'make grease' in the earth, as well as providing food for people. As I have noted, no explicit cosmology surrounds the act of killing pigs at and for a person's death, but it is not hard to construct the general logic of sacrifice involved. For a child which has newly entered life, similar sacrifices are made as payment to its maternal kin, including payments later for the cutting of its head hair. The death sacrifices are analogous to those after birth, and culminate with pigs killed 'for the head hair' also. It is plain that they ease the entry of the new ghost into the realm of the dead. The ghost then stays in the cemetery, or comes back to its old settlement; or else it goes to a place far off in the Jimi Valley, *Mötambo Tilip Pana*, where it feeds on fruits and leaves, and may take the form of a forest creature, (bird, snake, marsupial or wild pig). The souls (*min*) of the living also visit *Mötamb* while their bodies lie asleep at night, so souls of the living and ghosts (*tipu* or *kor*) of the dead mingle there. In dreams, therefore, people may see the dead. The ghost, or spirit, of a dead person is mobile all the time. It acquires a certain universal ambience: ghostly displeasure may be shown by an untimely shower of rain at a *moka* festival, as well as by sickness sent to the ghost's living kin.

The person, as an amalgam of body (*king*), mind (*noman*) and soul (*min*), has to be rooted in a particular locality, just as the body has to be buried there. This idea of 'rooting' the person is expressed in the cordyline ritual, performed soon after a child's birth. At this the child's navel-string and the mother's placenta are buried together, and a cordyline or a banana tree is planted on the spot. The father is

119

supposed to do the planting and to construct a fence around the cordyline. The fence is called the 'child faeces fence' (*kangambokla te pakla*), since ideally faeces which the child produces while still of an age to be drinking from the breast (up to three years old) should be thrown inside it. As the plant grows, so the child will grow. Interpreting this custom, I argue that the child's *min* in a sense derives from this planted assemblage (cf. Rappaport, 1968:149 and Schwimmer, 1973:93 for parallels). The navel-string, which once connected the child to the mother in her womb, now connects it to the earth, and this link is represented by the cordyline, which in several Melanesian cultures is a plant that marks the boundary between life and death. For the Kawelka people, it also happens to be their sacred divination-substance (*mi*), intimately bound up with their own origins as a group. The 'cordyline shoot' is also planted in a special raised tub, constructed at the head of each ceremonial ground, and here too it is expected to harbour the *min* of dead clansmen, as well as having magical packets, designed to induce fertility and wealth, planted at its roots. The 'child faeces fence' and the 'cordyline shoot' are both 'soul-traps' or lodging places for soul-stuff to congregate in, and both serve to anchor persons, living or dead, to particular pieces of earth, and so infuse the earth with their vitality and link them to the earth's own power of fertility (cf. A.J. Strathern, 1977).

When a child is weaned and its hair is first cut, the father is expected to make a payment to his wife's kin. Up to that point, its faeces, composed largely of residues from the mother's milk, have been returned to the navel-string site. From this time on, however, the child eats a wider range of foods and also knows how to deposit its own faeces in lavatory-places. The payment which the father makes is in recognition of the mother's prolonged breast-feeding. She has given the child the 'grease' of her breasts; now it will take its own grease from plants and pork.

My point in citing this information on customs to do with early stages of a child's life is to indicate the parallels with the early stages of a ghost's 'career' after the person's death. The soul at death escapes through the fontanelle, the gap which in early childhood takes some time to close. It finds its own food in the forest by assuming the guise of a wild creature, and this shows that there is a danger that it might turn 'wild' altogether and not return to help protect its kinsfolk. The body has accordingly to be 'planted' like the child's navel-string so as to 'anchor' the ghost; and just as in life payments must be made to maternal kin, so sacrifices must be made on behalf of a new ghost to ensure its proper acceptance into the world of the dead. Pigs are killed and eaten in order to produce 'grease' as a sign of the proper reproduction of the cycles of fertility between the dead and the living; for although fertility is realised by the living, it is essentially a gift to them from the dead.

Death and cannibalism

The Melpa concern with death is to ensure that it takes its ordered place in the overall scheme of things. Corpses are neither particularly polluting nor particularly dangerous in themselves. Their tendency to rot is seen as entirely correct, for by this means flesh returns to earth and bone is separated from flesh. What is particularly disturbing is that this ordered process of decomposition, paralleled by the process of establishing the soul among the ghosts of the dead, might be interrupted by an act of necrophagy. This type of cannibalism would disrupt and short-circuit the correct cycles of exchange, just as incest short-circuits the exchanges generated out of marriage. For the Melpa, necrophagy is horrific because it negates exchange. That is why, when they discovered that Europeans carried valuables and were willing to exchange them for other goods, they accepted them provisionally as humans and not just cannibal Sky-Spirits after all.

If this is true for the Melpa, how can we understand societies in which, the ethnographers tell us, cannibalism actually is, or was, practised? Surely, their symbolic universe, and their ideas of witchcraft, must be strikingly different from those of the Melpa? In fact, however, common symbolic themes run through all of the Highlands societies, while their evaluation in terms of social practices and norms varies.

The association between witchcraft and cannibalism is very marked in a number of Highlands societies. For example, Steadman writes of the Hewa that, 'the one critical trait of a witch is that she eats humans, either openly or surreptitiously' (Steadman, 1975:117). Hewa men generally accuse women of this crime, and Steadman notes that Hewa women are vulnerable to male violence and are also objectively short of protein. Old men are in a rather similar situation, and they too may be accused.

The Hewa do not appear to practise cannibalism as a legitimate activity (Steadman, 1975:118), and in this respect they are like the Melpa and their eastern neighbours the Kuma and Chimbu.[8] In these latter two areas the complex of ideas is almost exactly the same as among the Melpa. Paula Brown writes of Chimbu that: '*Kumo* (witchcraft) was very often blamed for deaths ... Dead bodies, and new graves, especially those of important men, were guarded at night to prevent witches from taking flesh and liquids from the corpse to consume and develop *kumo* power' (Brown, 1977:26).

The last point is a valuable one: witches eat human flesh in order to increase their own powers of witchcraft. Here we see an indication that a corpse may be considered powerful, and a source of dangerous strength. I was not told this among the Melpa, but it would certainly make good sense as an addition to what I was told.

The Kuma case adds some further points. Reay says that witches may be of either sex and that they operate only within their own local community. A witch is, in a sense, a traitor to his or her community and as such is received with sympathy by that community's enemy if publicly accused and forced out. Most frequently, the witch is a male, but one of low status, a 'rubbish-man'. Witchcraft is to some extent 'involuntary', because:

The term for witchcraft *kum*, refers to a thing ... like the foetus of a small marsupial. This being lives inside the host's abdomen. The *kum* has an insatiable appetite for meat which pork ... cannot satisfy ... The hapless witch, having no will of his own apart from that of the hungry *kum* within him, exhumes corpses and cooks and eats them ... Then ... he takes to killing people ... in order to maintain a supply of human meat'. (Reay, 1976:2)

An important matter here is that *kum* replaces *numan* (or *noman* in Melpa) as the seat of motivation, will, and judgment. *Noman* is always influenced by the ghosts, the repositories of morality, so that when *kum* takes over the proper link with the ghosts is snapped. The Kuma also picture *kum* as 'like a small foetus'. Perhaps it seeks food in order to grow, and eventually it would eat its host. The somewhat greater preoccupation with *kum* which the Kuma and Chimbu have, by comparison with the Melpa, may also be related to the fact that they practise periodic pig-killing festivals rather than *moka* exchange, and so are more concerned with matters to do with consumption of pork.[9]

The next set of societies I turn to are those of the 'fringe Southern Highlands', South of the main belt of large, settled agriculturalist populations such as the Melpa. As examples we may take the Etoro, Kaluli, and Daribi. In these very small-scale societies, enemies killed in warfare were eaten as an aggressive act of exo-cannibalism, but also people from within the community might be eaten. The data are not very explicit, perhaps partly because of the ethnographer's diffidence about discussing the topic, and because all of these people had been affected by Christian mission teaching at the time when anthropologists worked with them. But it is also possible that there was in any case some ambivalence about the act, as Fredrik Barth reports also for the Baktaman (Barth, 1975:152). Schieffelin tells us this was the case for the Kaluli (Schieffelin, 1976:156). If so, this is not very surprising, because these societies display also the association between cannibalism and witchcraft which is found in the Melpa case.

Kaluli witches (*sei*) were thought to be cannibals, and retaliatory raids were mounted to kill suspects. When a witch was killed his heart was cut out and thrown on the ground till it ceased twitching, when it was thought that the *sei* creature in it had moved off to the forest. The killers might then take the body and distribute parts of it for consumption to men of other longhouses who had helped them in raids. They would not eat it themselves for fear of attracting an attack by a brother *sei* of the victim.

The specific idea of witchcraft seems here to have become attached to the category of enemy males. Women, however, possess debilitating powers which are at least analogous to men's witchcraft and in the case of the Etoro the analogy between witchcraft and sexuality is made quite explicit (Kelly, 1976). For the Etoro, female witches are in part responsible for the break-up of small patrilineages, since they may be suspected of killing one of their husband's brothers. The husband and the witch's own brother are then expected jointly to contribute to a compensation payment, and the effect of this alignment of loyalties is often to split the lineage. Witchcraft is a force which attacks and weakens people; analogously, heterosexual intercourse is thought to be severely depleting and to lead to men's death. A strong value is placed, by contrast, on homosexual intercourse between senior and junior males, and semen is thought to assist young boys to grow.

The female witch among Etoro, then, does not seem to personify the greed for flesh which is evident in the Melpa stereotype, but rather the power to deplete men and break up their fragile lineages. It is this which most concerns Etoro men, rather than the focus on exchange of wealth which is found in the Melpa case. The Etoro female witch 'eats' men's semen, as well as mystically attacking them, and she causes disruption in male-based groups. Yet it is quite obvious that the 'eating' of semen is a prerequisite for actual reproduction, and Etoro men are well aware of this, even though they severely limit, by various taboos, the occasions on which heterosexual intercourse can occur.

The paradox underlying Etoro male attitudes is a classic one, and the theme is certainly shared by other Highlands peoples, including the Melpa. Women are the source of reproduction, yet that source is also closely linked to death, and men are continually attempting to circumvent the implications of this 'fact'. The Melpa Female Spirit Cult can be interpreted as a response to this same problem for example

123

Andrew Strathern

(A.J. Strathern, 1979*b*). The Daribi, who live to the east of the Etoro but show some structural similarities to them, exhibit this connection between women and death in an explicit form. In the Daribi long-house: 'Men live in the direction of sunrise, trees, and *sezemabidi* (wood sprites); women live (at the back of the longhouse) in the direction of sunset, water, the *izara-we* (subterranean female spirits), and the dead' (Wagner, 1972:123).

Men also live on the top storey and women in the lower one. Wagner further points out that the central passageway, along which food is taken, mirrors the 'direction of life'. Food is brought in and prepared at the men's end; it is consumed and excreted at the back, the women's end. The house is a macrocosm of the body, and the body recapitulates its own life-cycle.

Women are thus linked by the Daribi very clearly to the fact of death. At the same time, as we might expect, they are seen as vital for the re-creation of substance. Mother's milk makes the child's body. Men lose their 'juice' through the ejaculation of semen, women through breast-feeding their babies. Daribi say that this 'juice' (clearly the same as Melpa 'grease') can be replenished only by eating meat. Hence, in life-cycle payments, it is meat which is exchanged against the vital substance of persons. Further, there is a latent identification between the consumption of meat (pork) and sexuality. If a man who has recently eaten pork strays beside a river where the *izara-we* female spirits live, they will smell the odour of the meat and be sexually attracted. They remove his soul from him and invite him into their subterranean home. The man then goes with them and dies. Inter-course, meat-consumption, and death are thus linked; yet the first two are also needed for reproduction and health.

The Daribi, like the Etoro and Kaluli, did practise both exo- and endo-cannibalism. Wagner tells us how the meat was removed from the body for steam-cooking, but he says nothing about the relation-ships of the consumers to the consumed, nor does he report that women were especially the ones who ate the flesh or indeed that women were especially feared as witches. The association of women with reproduction and death is made at a *general* level by the Daribi, and is not especially linked with the practice or the idea of cannibalism. Cannibalism itself is not seen as an interference with the proper cycles of life and death; it is apparently a 'normal' way of supplementing one's vital juices.

The one case in which cannibalism is both said to be practised traditionally and to be uniquely linked to the question of the cycle of reproduction comes from the Eastern Highlands. This is the case of the

Gimi, recently analysed by Gillian Gillison (1980). The Gimi show a symbolic contrast also found among the Melpa: they oppose the forest as a male domain of purity and power, to the hamlet, an area polluted by women's sexuality. Men's decorations and initiations are all founded on the attempt to identify themselves with the forest world of birds and flowers. Women, on the other hand, are recognised as uniquely nurturant and able to make children, plants, and pigs grow, through an intense projection of themselves. Yet this incorporation has to be broken: hence the need for male initiation, Gimi men say. Women's powers can be dangerous, because they deny this male need to separate from the female. Like most Highlands men, the Gimi express a fear of women's menstrual blood, linking it to the destructive side of their reproductive capacities. Gillison discusses the logic of the Gimi version of this fear in striking terms. If a man eats menstrual blood, then: 'his body (by implication equivalent to his penis) symbolically retraces the path travelled by what he ate, is taken back inside the female and devoured ... The eater "places himself back inside the female" where he becomes the "child", her ingested "food"' (Gillison, 1980:150).

To this powerful female negativity is linked an important positive function in the cycle of male regeneration itself. Women eat the dead bodies of men in order to release their individual spirits (*auna*) so that they can rejoin the collective body of ancestral spirits (*kore*) in the forest. Men originally stole the initiation flutes from women, and these flutes are like an original hollow penis which the women possessed. In revenge the women cannibalistically eat men's bodies, regaining the penis; but only so as to release the men's spirits. Originally, men say, they used to allow men's bodies to decompose in their gardens, after which they collected the bones in which the *auna* resided and placed them in the forest. However, the women subverted this by stealing the bodies from the gardens and eating them along with wild greens shoved into bamboo containers. Women sang to men's bodies brought home from battle 'Come to me lest your body rot on the ground. Better it should dissolve inside me!' They thus represent their cannibalism as an act of compassion. The wild greens are eaten so as to ensure that the man's spirit will escape to the forest. Prior to 1950, when the Gimi area was pacified and missionisation began, women did consume men's bodies in the men's house, and men then gathered the bones and placed them in old fallow gardens expected to revert to forest.

This death ritual has to be seen in relation to the initiation of brides, at their first menses (girls were betrothed while young). The girl's husband's male kin make her drink water taken from a river belonging to them, and give her a 'spirit child' (a marsupial shot in the husband's clan forest). The water is regarded as ancestral semen. In this manner the way is prepared for the 'return' into her of *auna* which has been released in the cannibal death feast held by the earlier married wives. So the cycle is completed, and cannibalism is a required element in it. The equation between sexual intercourse and 'eating' the partner's essence is also clear (i.e. the eating of blood, eating of semen).

These very striking Gimi data and Gillison's perceptive interpretation of them stand in a definite relationship to the Melpa data with which I began. Gimi values and practices appear to reverse those of the Melpa, yet common symbolic themes clearly emerge. In both cases, for example, the male/female opposition is paralleled by that of the wild versus the domestic (cf. M.Strathern, 1980:191ff); and in both there is a strong dogma about the dangers of menstrual blood. The basic fear that the female will consume the male seems to underlie this idea. Female consumption, however, has been given a 'transcendental' role among the Gimi, since cannibalism is held to release men's spirits and to enable them to escape to the forest which is their true realm. For Melpa men, such an idea would be anathema: in their system, cannibalism has become entirely associated with the 'bad' refusal of exchange, with incest, greed and witchcraft. Is it possible to suggest why the outcomes are different in the two cases? In the final section of this paper I will briefly sketch a possible approach to this problem, although I cannot offer firm conclusions.

Death and exchange

The discussion which follows is built around a set of propositions:
1 Exchange is a dominant theme and a matter of primary concern in all the societies I have looked at.
2 The ideas of cannibalism and the idea of witchcraft associated with it are also very prominent and call for explanation.
3 Male/female oppositions are basic and connected with 1 and 2.
4 The marriage and overall exchange system of these societies, however, differ in definite ways; further male initiation occurs in the Eastern Highlands, but is not practised by the Melpa.
5 The societies also differ in ecological terms; the main contrast is between those societies with large populations, intensive agricultural practices, and large herds of domesticated pigs, and those without these features (= Highlands versus Fringe Highlands).

My question is: are variations in 2 and 3 connected with the variations referred to under 4 and 5? Relying on point 1, I take it that matters to do with exchange ought to provide the clue here, but that 'exchange' has to be conceived in very broad terms, to include exchanges of substance in sexual intercourse and transactions of exchange with spirits through sacrifice, as well as tangible exchanges of wealth goods between social groups and categories of persons.

The societies in which cannibalism definitely appears to have been practised share another characteristic: they were all ones in which very small-scale local groups, of just a few individuals, engaged in marriage patterns which were variants of sister-exchange, appearing often in its 'delayed' form of patrilateral cross-cousin marriage. Although in no case does a fully-developed 'elementary' type of marriage prescription appear, marriage nevertheless tends towards an elementary form: marriage ties are reduplicated and turn back on themselves. The results of this tendency are shown most clearly in the smallest of the societies I have examined here, the Etoro, who number about 400. The Etoro keep some 85% of their marriages within their own population, allowing the remaining 15% with two small neighbouring peoples, the Petamini and the Onabasulu. It is true that the Etoro population has probably declined by more than 50% since 1935, as a result of new epidemic diseases such as measles and influenza strains brought by Europeans into Papua; but, even so, the pre-contact population was a small one, and endogamy had to be 'managed' carefully so as to enable marriageable categories of persons to be continually available.

I am not arguing that there is a direct link between such marriage rules and cannibalism: in other words, I am not trying to explain cannibalism *itself*. But it is notable that cannibalism is not stigmatised in these societies in the same way as it is in my 'type-cases' of large, central Highland societies, the Melpa, Kuma and Chimbu. I suggest that this is because of two factors: (1) the idea of 'turning back' or of repeating marriages is not seen as wrong, and similarly the idea of 'turning back' to eat one's own kind is not regarded as wrong;[10] (2) in the Fringe societies herds of domestic pigs, which could be used as substitutes for the exchange and consumption of persons, are less prominent. This does not mean that pigs are entirely absent. The Daribi, for example, keep pigs and have obviously developed an idea of pork as the equivalent of the human body and its capacities; but they have not exempted the human body itself from the category of things which may be eaten.

It is possible that I am forcing the argument on to a comparative scale here, when in fact it was developed originally to fit the Melpa themselves. For them, it is clear that there are elaborate rules against marrying kin, against repeating marriages between small groups, and against direct sister-exchange. And these elaborate prohibitions also go with an obvious stress on proliferating exchange ties, on facing outwards to an expanding network, and on a continuous substitution of wealth items, pork and shell valuables (or nowadays cash), for the person. In this context, cannibalism stands for an unacceptable 'turning back', and is thus symbolically equated with incest. Further, it represents greed for consumption, a tendency which must be held in check in favour of a stress on production, conservation and exchange, according to the big-men.

This imagery is taken further in relation to death itself. Death requires the transfer of the spirit into the world of ghosts, and such a transfer, like any other, can be effected only by means of an exchange, in this case, a sacrifice of pigs. The sacrifice is designed to ensure the goodwill both of the new ghost and of the already constituted community of ghosts. It is analogous to the payment of pigs in bridewealth which men also make, except that in this case the pigs are killed, whereas in bridewealth, they are given live: live pigs for a live bride, dead pigs for a dead soul. The funeral mourners, of course, in fact eat the pigs' flesh and this coincides with the release of the deceased's soul. It is hard to avoid the conclusion that the pork is eaten *instead of* the deceased; just as in bridewealth pigs and shells are given *instead of* another bride. The bride's kin are said to 'eat' the bride-wealth, while the husband 'eats' (i.e. has sexual intercourse with) the bride. In compensation payments for killings, also a 'man-bone' gift is made by the bereaved side to the killers, and is said to be 'because you did not really eat him'.[11] The killers 'eat' this wealth, and then make a much bigger payment 'for the victim's head'. In all of these cases wealth substitutes directly for the person and particularly for the person's body. In sacrifices at funerals, pigs are slaughtered and presented both to the ghosts, in order to persuade them to accept a new ghost, and to the deceased's maternal kin, in substitution for the flesh which will rot and return to the earth. The bones are, or were, kept by the paternal kin, and placed in special houses where further sacrifices were made.

What is fascinating to note here is that the Gimi people say that this is what they also used to do, before women invented cannibalism. They therefore explicitly see cannibalism as a kind of short-circuiting by women of what men would otherwise have managed differently; but this is allowed, because (a) it is in revenge for men's theft of the flutes used in initiations, and (b) cannibalism in any case releases men's souls; it therefore obviates the need for pigs. The initiation theme, with its stress on the requirement of ritual to separate males from females, is precisely, of course, what is so marked in all of the Eastern Highlands societies, by contrast with those of the Western Highlands and Chimbu, as Michael Allen remarked (Allen, 1967). In some ways this stress on initiation is a structural focus just as *moka* exchange is for the Melpa. It seems to go with a very strong conceptualisation of the male life-cycle and its phases of growth, maturation, destruction and return as spirit, and with the necessity to regenerate, by ritual, this male cycle. The important, male-organised exchanges among the Gimi have to do with this rather than with exchanges between affines, as among Melpa, and so they must all be seen as falling directly within the realm of initiation and sacrifice. Women intervene in that cycle as a threat to men and yet as important agents for the release of male spirits. As such, their cannibalism is in the end redeemed; whereas, for the Melpa, the practice of substitution of wealth for the person makes cannibalism both unnecessary and unacceptable and thus ensures that it is classified directly with witchcraft.[12]

The common elements which run through these cases have to do with basic models of sexuality. In sexual intercourse, the sexes 'eat' each other. More particularly, females consume male semen, but do so in order to achieve reproduction through a combination of semen and their own blood. Menstrual blood is dangerous because it is 'dead' and rotten; so it can threaten men with death rather than promising them children. Loss of semen also means depletion and thus decrepitude for males. Women lose their 'grease' in breast-milk fed to children. The overall process of reproduction, symbolised in the passage of semen from male to female, and the passage of milk from female to child, is associated with the death of the body, overcome only by the survival of the spirit of life-force, identified ideologically with the paternal or male side. In this way, women and death become closely linked. (The argument here bears a resemblance to Bachofen's early speculations, cf. Bachofen, 1967.)

These ideas seem to me to be present clearly or implicitly, in both the 'central' and the 'fringe' societies which I have discussed. If this is so, they should be seen as a cultural substratum or baseline. The variations, in terms of ideas of witchcraft and cannibalism, which I have tried to explore, have therefore to be linked with concomitant social, and perhaps ecological, variation. Hence I have argued for the relevance of marriage rules and also the presence or absence of large herds of domestic pigs, plus attitudes towards their consumption and exchange. The discussion has been far from systematic, and the argument itself is tentative. But unless we attempt to look across a range of cases in this way, we shall be confined to artificially narrow and bounded explanations for symbolic ideas and institutions in single societies. This paper has been written in the belief that a proper understanding of the Highlands societies and their fringe congeners will only come through making comparisons (cf. also Rubel & Rosman, 1978), and that such a form of analysis must face the question of whether there are or are not institutional correlates of variations in symbolic themes – such as the themes considered here, of death, reproduction, incest, male–female oppositions, greed, witchcraft and cannibalism.

NOTES

1 I am not suggesting that cannibalism actually represents an 'earlier stage' of society. The Gimi people of the Eastern Highlands actually argue that cannibalism was a fairly recent invention by Gimi women (Gillison, 1980:157). A similar idea is reported from the nearby Fore (Lindenbaum, 1979:22), and Lindenbaum further suggests that the Fore may have adopted cannibalism following the removal, through agricultural activity, of forest resources in their territory (1979:24). She points out that the eating of human flesh was mostly a practice of women (as it is with the Gimi), and that men at one place, Awarosa, argued that where men could get forest products still by hunting they avoided cannibalism. Also, traditional male curers never practised cannibalism. Lindenbaum's data and ideas can profitably be read in conjunction with Gillison's.

2 The significance of dogs in this context would merit a separate investigation. Dogs among the Melpa (as among the English) are thought of as partially identified with their human owners, and as themselves partially 'human'. Hence not everyone will eat dogs, and dog appears in mythology as the bringer of fire to man (fire = the power to cook food in an approved manner). Yet the dog will eat its own food raw, and it will also steal meat if it can. Witches thus assume a form which is a debased but 'supernaturally' powerful version of humanity.

3 Note that this beef is therefore 'cow', and that witches were said now to be appearing at graveyards in the guise of cows. On the analogy of dogs and their ambiguous edibility, one can conjecture that this part of the rumour signalled the problem of whether beef was properly edible or not. (I am grateful to Mr Richard Seel for a suggestion along these lines.)

4 The symbol of polluted water carries another association also. Water running in streams is comparable to male semen or *noimb kopong* ('penis grease'). Bespelled water is drunk as a medicine against menstrual contamination. The pollution of water by flesh is thus comparable to such menstrual contamination, and a link between cannibalism and female death-dealing powers can again be perceived. In one settlement among the Melpa during the time of the rumour a crisis arose when people drank cool water from a saucepan left out overnight and then found a curious piece of flesh at the bottom of the pan. They decided to cover the matter up, because one of their own women was a suspected cannibal.

5 Why chickens? Chickens are birds, and although they are in fact domesticated creatures, they perhaps belong in category terms to creatures which are hunted in the forest, and in that sense are pure. Forest marsupials, at any rate, are in many cults alternatives to pigs as forms of sacrifice. The chicken is also sold as a 'whole creature', and thus may be carved in a recognisable manner as is pork, whereas frozen beef cannot be 'reconstituted' in this way.

6 The same symbolic structure is apparent among the Maring (Buchbinder and Rappaport, 1976). Maring women especially look after corpses while they rot in gardens. They are not, however, particularly associated with witchcraft. Rather, they help to guard dead bodies against possible attacks by male witches.

7 In a Melpa 'cannibal story', Tet-Penge, an ogre, carries off a human head and cooks it in just this position, at the bottom of an oven, so as to conceal it. See Vicedom (1977:9b – myth no. 71, trans. A. Strathern) and Schild (1977:97 – story no. 37). The Melpa myths contain frequent references to cannibalism, and a separate study of them in the light of the themes discussed here would be worthwhile.

8 The Hewa belong to the 'Fringe Highlands' category, and are an exception to the tendency in societies of the fringe area to practise limited forms of both exo- and endo-cannibalism. It is possible, of course, that Steadman missed the occurrence of exo-cannibalism, although this is made less likely by the fact that his fieldwork spanned two years and was done before the Hewa were effectively pacified.

9 It would be feasible to argue the reverse, however, i.e. that since the Melpa deny consumption more than the Kuma it is they who should be the more concerned. This argument would turn on the issue of whether the Melpa *do* deny consumption in this way, and data are not at hand to assess that question. Irrespective of this point, I argue that Kuma and Chimbu, as pig-killers, are more concerned about pork as a focus of interest for consumption than are the Melpa. Pigs are defined as creatures destined for eventual consumption rather than for giving away alive. The idea of *kum* as a small creature is known to the Melpa, who tell stories about court cases in which the creature comes out of the body joints of an accused witch and steals flesh. The witch may then, they say, be absolved of responsibility for the creature's acts.

10 The Hewa case is interesting here because their marriage rules involve quite extensive prohibitions, for example, on marriage into the patriclans of one's four grandparents, and sister-exchange is also precluded. Hewa may however, marry into the clan of their MBS (Steadman, 1971:172ff). It will be recalled (note 8) that Hewa ideas on witchcraft and cannibalism also parallel those of the Melpa; although their methods of dealing with witches (by direct accusation and killing) are quite different. Hewa dependence on female labour is probably much less than for the Melpa as pig-rearing is considerably less extensive (Steadman, 1971:54).

11 In Melpa statements about compensation we see a kind of 'refusal' of cannibalism, and a substitution of pork for human flesh. When an enemy has died, men kill a pig in exultation and eat its liver, saying that they are eating the liver of the victim. In fact, several men may share the parts of the pig, naming them as parts of the dead man's body. 'Of course they were

Andrew Strathern

actually only eating the pigs' livers', as Ongka notes (A.J. Strathern, 1979c:76).
12 Cf. note 1. The overall problem of understanding differences between the 'fringe' and the 'central' Highlands societies in terms of their marriage rules and systems of production remains.

REFERENCES

Allen, M. 1967. *Male cults and secret initiations in Melanesia*. London and New York: Melbourne University Press.

Bachofen, J.J. 1967. *Myth, religion and mother right*. (*trans*. R. Mannheim). Princeton: University Press (German original published in 1926).

Barth, F. 1975. *Ritual and knowledge among the Baktaman of New Guinea*. Oslo: Universitetsforlaget.

Brown, P. 1977. '*Kumo* witchcraft at Mintima, Chimbu Province, Papua New Guinea', *Oceania*, **48**:26–9.

Buchbinder, G. & Rappaport, R. 1976. 'Fertility and death among the Maring', in *Man and woman in the New Guinea Highlands*. eds P. Brown & G. Buchbinder. Washington, DC: Special publication No. 8, American Anthropological Association.

Gillison, G. 1980. 'Images of nature in Gimi thought', in *Nature, culture and gender*. eds C. MacCormack & M. Strathern. pp.143–73. Cambridge: Cambridge University Press.

Kelly, R. 1976. 'Witchcraft and sexual relations', in *Man and woman in the New Guinea Highlands*. eds P. Brown and G. Buchbinder. Washington, DC: Special publication no. 8, American Anthropological Association.

1977. *Etoro social structure: a study in structural contradiction*. Ann Arbor: University of Michigan Press.

Lindenbaum, S. 1979. *Kuru sorcery. Disease and danger in the New Guinea Highlands*. Palo Alto: Mayfield Publishing Company.

Rappaport, R.A. 1968. *Pigs for the ancestors. Ritual in the ecology of a New Guinea People*. New Haven: Yale University Press.

Reay, M. 1976. 'The politics of a witch-killing', *Oceania*, **47**:1–20.

Rubel, P.G. & Rosman, A. 1978. *Your own pigs you may not eat: a comparative study of New Guinea societies*. Chicago: University of Chicago press.

Schieffelin, E.L. 1976. *The sorrow of the lonely and the burning of the dancers*. New York: St Martin's Press.

Schild, V. 1977. *Märchen aus Papua – Neuguinea*. Düsseldorf: Eugen Diederichs Verlag.

Schwimmer, E. 1973. *Exchange in the social structure of the Orokaiva*. London: Hurst & Co.

Steadman, L. 1971. *Neighbours and killers. Residence and dominance among the Hewa of New Guinea*. Ph.D.thesis, Australian National University, Canberra.

1975. 'Cannibal witches in the Hewa', *Oceania*, **46**:114–21.

Strathern, A.J. 1977. 'Melpa food-names as an expression of ideas on identity and substance', *Journal of the Polynesian Society*, **86**:503–11.

1979a. 'The red box money-cult in Mount Hagen, 1968–71 (Part 1)', *Oceania*, **50**:88–102.

1979*b*. 'Men's house, women's house: the efficacy of opposition, reversal and pairing in the Melpa *Amb Kor* cult', *Journal of the Polynesian Society*, **88**:37–51.

1979*c*. *Ongka: a self-account by a New Guinea big-man*. London: Gerald Duckworth & Co.

1980. 'The red box money-cult in Mount Hagen, 1968–71 (Part 2)', *Oceania*, **50**:161–75.

1981. 'Death as exchange: two Melanesian cases' in *Mortality and immortality*. eds S. Humphreys and H. King. London: Academic Press.

Strathern, M. 1980. 'No nature, no culture: the Hagen case', in *Nature, culture and gender*. eds C. MacCormack and M. Strathern, pp.174–222. Cambridge: Cambridge University Press.

Vicedom, G.F. 1977. *Myths and legends from Mount Hagen*. (trans. Andrew Strathern) (German original published at Hamburg in 1943) Port Moresby: Institute of Papua New Guinea Studies.

Wagner, R. 1972. *Habu. The innovation of meaning in Daribi religion*. Chicago: University of Chicago Press.

5 Lugbara death

JOHN MIDDLETON

The Lugbara view of death

For the Lugbara of Uganda death is a frequent and important event. It is frequent in the sense that as the Lugbara live at a very high density of population the incidence of ordinary deaths within a small neighbourhood is high; they occur almost daily within a relatively small area and people are constantly aware of the deaths of kin, neighbours and friends. It is reported for many peoples living in small settlements at a low density that one is hardly aware of death, but in Lugbara it is an everyday occurrence. It is also normally an event that takes place publicly, in the sense that its occurrence is known, even if not actually witnessed, by all members of a local community; and the mortuary rites that follow it are attended by many people whether related to the deceased or not. The Lugbara have few rites to do with birth, puberty or marriage. But the rites of death are important, elaborate, and often longlasting, and lead to the reorganisation of local social relations of many kinds. A death is more than that of an individual family member: the dead person has also been a member of a lineage which is assumed to be perpetual and a constellation of ties of many kinds was centred upon him. A death disturbs the continuity of the lineage and mortuary rites are performed in order to restore this continuity. The aim of this paper is to assess what are the function and meaning of these rites and why it is that such emphasis is placed on them. As might be expected, the Lugbara see this situation as 'normal' and commonsensical, and regard rites of neighbouring peoples, where there may be a different balance between funerary and other rites, with scorn and ridicule. Behind this reaction lies the particular view that the people hold of their own society, its structure and its history, and it is essentially this view that I try to elucidate in this essay.[1]

The Lugbara live in north-western Uganda and north-eastern Zaire, and number about a quarter of a million. They are peasant farmers, growing mainly grains, with some livestock. There is great

134

pressure on the available land, as the density of population in most of their country is high, some 250 persons to the square mile. Traditionally they lacked chiefs, but chiefs were appointed during colonial rule, and in more recent years they have been elected. The basis of their political system has been and still is a structure of patrilineal lineages, and the scale of political relations is small. With the exception of rain-makers, very occasional prophets, and locally influential men known as 'men whose names are known', the traditional holders of political and domestic authority are the elders of family clusters only a few generations in depth. Above the elders authority is considered to be held by the dead of the lineage; the living elders are regarded as the temporary stewards of the lineages, their principal role being to ensure the continuity of a system of social order that was established long ago by the two Hero-ancestors of myth. Elders should not innovate change but protect this order and much of the significance of Lugbara mortuary ritual hinges on this view of their role.

It is convenient here to set out some Lugbara views as to the basic features of death and the rites associated with it. Death is an individual experience or condition that is unknowable and therefore indescribable. It is definable only in a negative sense, as the opposite of living on the surface of the world as a human being. The dead continue to exist, in a mysterious sense, and the nature and experience that are theirs may be described only by metaphor. Other than birth and ageing, death is the only human event or process that is common to all people, yet it takes many forms, the number of which is beyond counting. The time of death is the least predictable event in a human's lifetime, yet it is the most certain of all to occur. It is also paradoxical in another sense, as being both final and also a transition from one condition to another. Being an event of transition, the living must recognise the change in the status and moral condition of a once-living person and at the same time ensure the perpetuation of that status or social personality and thereby of the group to which it belongs. Death is marked – indeed, it is thought to be caused – by the unforeseeable and unavoidable intrusion into society of an external and suprahuman power, that of Divinity. This is beyond ordinary human comprehension but nonetheless the living must somehow control it lest they become overwhelmed by it. Without this intrusion men might have a chance of running their lives in permanent order and predictability. They cannot do this, but must attempt to do so if they are to ensure the perpetuity of their own society, by ensuring the continuing fertility of its members living with a sense of order and authority. Death thus leads to some kind and degree of confusion of social and moral categories. There is confusion between the sphere of the small local community and that of the wilderness that surrounds it. There is confusion at death between lineage and family order, continuity, authority and fertility, on the one hand, and disorder, discontinuity, uncontrolled power and sexuality, on the other. Finally, people must perform ritual so as to ensure the renewal of order and continuity, even though as mere humans they cannot understand the means by which ritual actually brings this about.[2]

These views about death provide a beginning for an enquiry into the function and meaning of Lugbara mortuary rites. These rites essentially act out the relationship between men and Divinity. Since men and Divinity are entities of different quality or order, rather than being merely different in degree, men see themselves as ignorant of the true nature of divine power. Divinity is omnipotent and everlasting, men are weak and live only short and helpless lives the time of whose end on earth cannot be predicted. Lugbara have no notion of individual destiny of the kind reported for many other African peoples: as they say when asked about their expectations in and from life, 'Who can know these things?'.

The person and Divinity

In this context there are first two questions that must be asked of the Lugbara: What is a human being? That is, what is the composition of a man or woman? And what is a definition of the event and the condition of death? These questions are closely related and I attempt to give definitions as the Lugbara see them, not necessarily in their own words but nonetheless using their own notions and concepts.

Like all peoples, the Lugbara are interested in the nature of a living member of society, in the differences in the nature of persons whether male, female, adult or child, and in the relationship of persons with Divinity who creates them and in one way or another, and in one form or another, destroys them or allows them to be destroyed. Their notions of a living and bounded person and a timeless and unbounded Divinity are complementary.

In Lugbara thought there are certain elements that compose a person.[3] Not every human being is attributed all of them, and humans may pass through phases in which they temporarily lack one or two of them, such as phases of possession, trance or dream. An individual has first a body (*rua*) composed of limbs, organs and so on. At death this becomes a corpse (*avu*), is placed in a grave or in some cases thrown into the bushland and then rots away and becomes dust: *de'bo*, 'it is finished'. The body contains blood (*ari*), movement of which is a sign of life.

There are also several immaterial or psychical elements. Perhaps the most important is that known as *orindi*, which I translate as 'soul'. This element endows its possessor with a sense of lineage, family and neighbourhood responsibility (but particularly the first), which increases with age. Men have souls but the position with regard to women is uncertain. Those who are first-born and so genealogically ambivalent are thought to possess souls if they live long but other women are thought not to do so. After death the soul is treated in various ways that I mention below and becomes what I call a ghost, *ori*. The word *orindi* means something like 'the essence of the ghost'; that is to say, a ghost is a responsible member of the lineage.[4] Besides the soul there is the element known as *adro*, the word used for Divinity and for spirits of many kinds. Every individual carries *adro*, which we may translate as 'spirit', a sign of his or her divine creation. It is associated particularly with individual or idiosyncratic behaviour and in various ways is opposed to the soul. Women may have powerful spirits and so do witches: the spirit is the seat of behaviour that is unconcerned with lineage responsibility and so is associated with irresponsibility and anti-social behaviour. After death a spirit leaves the body to dwell in the bushland away from the inhabited compounds in the form of a diminutive man or woman. The third element is that called *tali*, which might, not very satisfactorily, be translated as 'personality' or 'influence'. *Tali* may also develop in strength during a person's lifetime and enables him or her to influence other people. After death it joins a collectivity of lineage *tali*.[5] Lastly, an individual possesses breath (*ava*), a sign of life that vanishes into the air or wind at death, and a shadow (*endrilendri*) that also vanishes at death. These are not very important notions.

These Lugbara notions must be set in the context of their views about moral space, the 'home' and the 'outside'. The Lugbara distinguish three levels of existence or experience: that of the sky or universe, that of the surface of the world, and that of the individual bounded by his body. In the sky dwells Divinity, *Adroa* the Creator; on the surface of the world dwells *Adro*, the immanent aspect of Divinity, and the spirits of dead people, also called *adro* or *adroanzi* (literally, 'spirit children'); within the individual is his or her spirit, *adro*.[6] The Creator Divinity, *Adroa*, created the world and set human beings on it; after several generations these human beings became social beings and society was formed by them as it is today, or at least as it should be were no changes to threaten or destroy it.[7] Throughout the myths of creation and the formation of society runs the distinction between the 'home', *akua* (literally 'in the compound'), and the 'outside', *amve* ('outside') or *asea* ('in the grass'). On the surface of the world are the compounds and settlements, occupied by social beings living in lineage groups and bound by proper authority; outside them are the areas of bushland or wilderness, places of divine power and lacking social or moral authority. Between lie the cultivated fields and the areas of grazing land. A similar *schema* is found within the person: the soul is inside, as it were central and fixed; the spirit is volatile and not central in a moral sense. Good is 'inside', evil is 'outside'; stability is 'inside', change is 'outside'.[8] Above and apart from all is the sky, where dwells the Creator Divinity. Lugbara say that Divinity is all-good or comprises both good and evil: these statements express the belief that *Adroa* is omnipotent.

Besides doubts as to whether women have souls, there are other differences in Lugbara thought between men and women. Men are said to be 'inside', as *'ba akua*, 'people of the home', and women to be 'outside', as *afa asea*, 'things of the bushland': women are not considered to be full 'persons'. But their moral position is more complex than this simple dichotomy suggests. They are ambiguous, belonging both to the bushland and also to the home. They are born as daughters and sisters in the home but they move elsewhere as wives and mothers. They are both 'good', *onyiru*, when they accept the authority of fathers and husbands, but are said also to be 'evil', *onzi*, a complex notion that refers basically to being mystically associated with power that comes from Divinity, as contrasted to authority, an attribute of men. The essential point here is that women, as possessors of a divine or divinity-like power of procreation (also called *adro*), are dangerous to society unless this power is controlled by men. Their sexuality, if uncontrolled, is destructive of ordered social life. If it is controlled by those who are given authority over them – their fathers and husbands – then it provides part of the basis for lineage continuity: it is transformed into fertility, a very different notion. At marriage the bride is formally blessed with his spittle by her father before she goes to her husband: if he does not do this or does so with a 'bad heart' then she will not become pregnant; and divorced women and young widows are said (by both men and women) to be likely to behave in a sexually promiscuous way with many men, but not to conceive until they remarry or are properly inherited. This distinction and complementarity of men and women is seen in the Lugbara myth of creation,[9] in which the two Hero-ancestors come from the wilderness into Lugbaraland; with each of them is a sister's son and a bull. Each has buffalo meat that he has killed but no fire. The sister's son espies smoke in the distance, seeks out its source and finds a leper woman with a fire. They cook the buffalo meat and share it; the Hero cures the woman with his magic, and by restoring her missing nose, fingers and toes makes her complete; he impregnates her; her brothers appear and threaten him with spears; he calls up his bull and other cattle and pays bridewealth; the leper woman becomes the mother of one of the clan-founders. Thus are instituted marriage, the legitimate use of force, and legitimate sexuality and fertility on behalf of clan and lineage. The theme of the uncontrolled and 'wild' female sexuality contrasted to legitimate fertility controlled by men is obvious, and the former is associated with incompleteness and barrenness. The widely occurring link between sexuality and fire is also clearly made: like sexuality, once tamed, fire is also at the centre of ordered social life.[10] There are certain occasions when this aspect of women's moral status is manifest publicly, and these are considered by men to be dangerous to them and are feared by them. They include certain women's dances known as *nyambi*, when women dance aggressively singing obscene songs that ridicule men, and occasions when women behave promiscuously when they are referred to as *azazaa*; this word is also used for those girls who at puberty run naked in the bushland as a sign that they are called by Divinity to become diviners.

The nature of death

I wrote above that the Lugbara regard death as the consequence of the intrusion of Divinity into the sphere of men and the 'home'. They say that death can only be decided upon and brought about by Divinity: witches and sorcerers can in mysterious ways invite Divinity to cause a person's death but they cannot by their own actions actually bring it about. This is done only by Divinity, whose motives and reasons cannot be known by ordinary people.

To define death in a few words cannot very meaningfully be done in Lugbara other than by the use of metaphor. The word *dra* is both verb and substantive, meaning both to 'die' and 'death': a dead person is *'ba drapiri*, 'a person who dies'. So we must look at what the Lugbara say actually happens at death, at different kinds and occasions of death, and at what they themselves do when someone dies. At death the various elements that make up a person are thought to be dispersed and some of them are then relocated by the performance of certain rites. The body becomes a corpse, is placed in the ground and then

139

dissolves into dust in the soil. After the physical death of a man the body is washed and shaved, the hair being take to be buried somewhere in the bushland, like all body hair removed at various occasions, whether ritual or not. This is done by the widows' co-wives or those of the deceased's brothers. It is said that as they gave birth to children for the living men of their husbands' lineage so they do for the dead of that lineage. The corpse is then wrapped in an ox hide or, more usually today (unless the deceased is an elder whose position is likened to that of a bull in a herd), in white calico. It is placed in the grave by sisters' sons, where it lies in a recess and protected by granite slabs. The bodies of women are also washed and shaved but apart from being dressed in fresh pubic leaves 'from respect' they need not be wrapped in cloth although this is often done, again 'for respect'. The body is placed on its right or left side according to whether a man or a woman; the head points to one of the two 'sacred' mountains in the centre of the plateau according to its clan.[11] Certain objects that symbolise its status as a man or woman are placed with it,[12] and properly its hut broken and no longer occupied. The grave is marked with stones but soon hoed over and forgotten, except for that of an elder which is traditionally planted with a fig tree that stands for many years and is named for the dead man. There is no notion of a journey to the land of the dead, and when the corpse is buried the agnatic kin spit on it and curse and mock it as no longer having status or authority: but they place the corpse correctly to show 'respect', *ru*. The spitting removes the individuality from the corpse: it is now nothing but a former vehicle for the soul spirit, and *tali* that have given it identity while alive. Not all corpses are buried: those of infants, lepers and people killed by lightning are traditionally merely thrown into the bushland – I return to a consideration of these cases below.

The dispersal of the various elements of a dead person is all-important, and there are significant differences in this regard between them. The breath goes from the body into the air or wind (*oli*), where it remains, above the surface of the earth, invisible and of no further importance. The soul goes to the sky where it joins, or rejoins, Divinity in a way that living people say they do not understand. At some time afterwards, up to a year, when the succession to the deceased's lineage status has been decided (this should include the inheritance of widows, which may take some time), and when it is clear that the soul is not trying to contact the living by appearing as a spectre (*atri*) or in dreams, a diviner performs the rite of *orindi ti zizu*, 'contacting the mouth of the soul'. This is also known as *agu drapi'bori en azu*, 'raising the man who has died'. The diviner, using a divining gourd to put herself into a trance, contacts the soul, slaughters a ram (a beast associated in sacrifice with Divinity, because the soul is at that time with Divinity in the sky) and anoints with its blood members of the deceased's family. A shrine is then built for the soul and placed under the granary of the first wife of the deceased's son, where sacrifices will later be made to the ghost. By this rite the soul is redomesticated and transformed into a ghost, a responsible member of the lineage and able to know what lineage members are doing and thinking and to control them through sending them sickness.[13]

The spirit, *adro*, is an aspect of the collective power that is Divinity, outside the home in the wilderness and the sky. At death, this power is thought to enter the 'inside' sphere of social life. The individual spirit then wanders into the bush where it remains with the immanent aspect of Divinity, *Adro*, and is merged into a collectivity of the spirits of all the dead, known as *adroanzi* (literally 'spirit-children', a collective plural form), the little figures formed like men and women that live near river beds and protect raingroves. They are not named individually and they do not resemble in appearance any actual dead people. The *tali* goes to the sky and then joins a collectivity of lineage *tali*, and shrines are placed for this collectivity in the lineage compounds where they may be contacted by offerings. The degree and kind of contact that may be made with these elements by the living differ in one important respect. Men may talk with the ghosts, by actual speech used in invoking them both at sacrifice of blood and meat or in the case of a senior man without sacrifice. The *tali* may be given bloodless offerings without actual invocation in words. The spirits may be given bloodless offerings, but only by individuals who have been possessed by them,[14] and without words being spoken. There is also a difference in their spatial positions after they are dispersed. The elements that are concerned with responsibility, the soul and the *tali*, remain on the surface of the world and the space immediately beneath it, although they first visit the sky, the place of Divinity. The spirit goes to the bushland outside the compounds.

The occasions of death

I turn now to the kinds and occasions of death. First we must distinguish between what may be called physical and social death. Physical death, for the Lugbara, occurs when the body stops drawing breath and the blood stops circulating and begins to coagulate. The body grows cold to the touch and soon begins to smell. The breath goes

141

immediately, and at some time about which Lugbara are uncertain the psychical elements disperse from being together within the living body. However, since they cannot be seen it is thought that they may often hang about the place of death for some time, and the soul may then be seen as a spectre, something greatly feared. As in all situations of transition, they pass through a stage of seclusion and of non-belonging to any proper sphere. But the Lugbara say that this is all they know about how this process actually happens.

Social death is more complex. It refers to the extinguishing of the present social identity of the deceased and its transformation into another. We come here to the transition from a living member of a lineage and neighbourhood into a dead member of these groupings. While alive an adult man is the centre of a cluster of ties, of duties and of obligations. If the elder of a minimal lineage he is the link between the living and the dead members, and the ties of authority and obedience within the lineage group centre upon him; he is the focus of a network of kin and neighbourhood ties of many kinds, including those with the dead. Even if he is not a lineage elder, once he acquires a wife and children he may also enter into direct relations with the dead through the process of ghost invocation and sacrifice.

The mortuary rites, which I describe below, form a set of transition rites. To undergo a rite of transition one must be in the right place and have the right status to begin with or one cannot change it into a new one. Ideally a man should die at the correct time, in the correct place, and in the correct manner. If these conditions are satisfied then the process of his transformation into an ancestor and ghost can start immediately and be carried out peacefully and without rancour or disagreement on his part (as evidenced by his appearing in dreams or as a spectre) or on that of his living kin (as evidenced by their quarrelling over his property or offices).

A man should die in his hut, lying on his bed, with his brothers and sons around him to hear his last words; he should die with his mind still alert and should be able to speak clearly even if only softly; he should die peacefully and with dignity, without bodily discomfort or disturbance; he should die at the time that he has for some days foreseen as the time of his death so that his sons and brothers will be present; he should die loved and respected by his family. He should die physically when all these conditions have been or can be fulfilled and when he is expected to do so because he has said his last words and had them accepted by his kin and especially by his successor to his lineage status. The successor then steps outside the deceased's hut and

calls the latter's *cere*. The *cere* is a falsetto whooping cry whose 'melody'
is that of certain words that make a phrase 'belonging' to the 'owner'
and which is unique to a particular man or woman. It may never be
called by anyone else other than his successor on this single occasion. It
then marks the death, physical and social, and the actual moment of
succession. All this does often happen in the proper way, and even if it
does not in a strict sense it is perhaps usually thought to have
happened. Often all has been done to ensure a proper social death and
then the dying man refuses to die and lingers on. This is not serious
and provided that the lingering is not too prolonged no one worries
about it unless the deceased comes later in dreams or as a spectre. The
mortuary rites are performed as though he were physically dead.
When the physical and social deaths are reasonably proper and
congruent, then it is said that the person dies a good death, *dra onyiru*,
one that Divinity the Creator in the sky has decided. When they are
not so then it is said that he dies a bad death, *dra onzi*, which is
associated rather with *Adro*, the evil and immanent aspect of Divinity
that dwells in the bushland.

Let us look at the occasions of bad death. Essentially a bad death
takes place when the psychical elements of the person do not disperse
properly and at the same time, or they do so at a wrong time or in a
wrong place. The Lugbara word that I here translate as 'wrong' is *onzi*,
'evil' or 'dangerous', a complex notion. The occasions for a bad death
are many but they have two characteristics in common. They occur in
some way 'outside', *amve*, and they are unforeseen and unexpected:
even though the time of death is unforeseen in general, some forms of
death are less expected than others. For a man they include death
when outside the home, *aku*, when in the bushland when hunting or
when killed (in the past) in feud or warfare; when killed in homicide
away from one's compound and before one's proper time; when killed
suddenly by witchcraft or sorcery and when dying outside Lugbaraland as a labour migrant. As I have mentioned above, the actual death
is believed to be caused by Divinity, who is 'reminded' or encouraged
to do so by a witch, sorcerer, or other human agent. When one of these
deaths takes place the elements cannot disperse or do so improperly,
in the sense that they are not in the right place to begin the
transformation they are to undergo. The body is in the wrong place to
be buried; the soul and *tali* may not easily be able to find their way to
the sky or to the compound from which their journey should start, and
more importantly they may not wish to do so as they have been
insulted. The spirit also may get lost in finding its way back to the

compound from which there is a proper path to the bushland for it to take. A man dying a bad death cannot speak his last words to his successor who therefore cannot utter the *cere* call to mark the orderly succession. There is uncertainty about the proper beginning of mourning and of mortuary rites.

The actions and beliefs associated with the death of a woman are similar to those for a man, except that having little lineage property and usually no lineage office her last words are unimportant and need not be made; however, a senior woman may make them to her sisters and daughters to show that she is dying contentedly. The death is followed, as in the case of a man, by a series of mortuary rites; an important woman such as the elder sister of a lineage elder will become a 'woman-ghost', *oku-ori*, and so the rite of 'contacting the mouth of the soul' will be made at the appropriate time by a diviner. For a woman the most common form of bad death is to die in childbirth. She is at the time surrounded by taboos that symbolically remove her hut from the remainder of the settlement in which it stands, and so she dies in the 'bushland' just as though she were killed fighting outside in the bushland (indeed, I have been told that for a woman to give birth is 'like' a man going to fight enemies: both are central to their 'duty' or 'work' (*azi*), that is, to their socially approved roles). She is also herself in a condition of transition and so not a 'normal' person at that moment. Birth is part of the process of procreation and her power to give birth is known as *adro*. Also for her to die in childbirth means that there is a break in the orderly process from sexuality to fertility, so that control over lineage fertility has been lost, a point that I consider below. The other common bad death for a woman is to be killed by witchcraft or sorcery.

A bad death is defined, at least on most occasions, by taking place in the 'outside'. Lugbara also consider that a person dies a bad death if in some way he or she is in a state of physical reversal. The example that I know is that of a person dying of leprosy or of some other disease that involves a change of skin colour from black to white, or death from burning, which does the same. One woman who died of some such skin disease was described to me as having been turned inside out. To be killed by lightning usually involves both being outside in a spatial sense and also being burned, as well as being struck directly by the overt power of Divinity. Drowning is seen as a bad death, since it takes place in the wrong medium of human existence and also in water which is associated with the power of Divinity.[15] Accidental burial is also considered bad, since death should take place on the surface of the world.

Death and purification

The deaths that are considered as bad lead to a condition of confusion and disorder but without the means for removing and resolving them. These kinds of death are followed by rites of purification. These have as their main function to remove the impropriety of the death and to produce the situation which enables the deceased and his living kin to start the various processes of transition and transformation properly. I need not here give a detailed description of the purification rites that are made for the victims of bad deaths. They are known generally as *rua edezu*, 'to cleanse the body' and *angu edezu*, 'to cleanse the territory'.[16] By removing the impropriety of the death they bring together the physical and social deaths. The main problem is that the deceased has not spoken his last words so that no one can formally take over his status. When he has died away from the settlements in the bushland, or in a battle far away from inhabited areas, something that he has had on his body is brought back; or if possible the corpse will be carried home, but normally this cannot be done. If it can be done then it is buried; in the former case the object brought back, which is imbued with the personality of the deceased, is abandoned in his hut which is then burnt. The expected successor touches it or the corpse and then calls the deceased's *cere*. Some of the earth where the body fell is also brought back, as it contains the blood that has fallen on it and also something of the spirit or essence of the 'bad' place; it is then made harmless by a diviner who performs the rite of 'cleansing the territory'.

There are two obvious questions that arise with regard to these rites as well as to those performed for someone who has in any case died a good death. One is the notion of pollution that is involved and the other is the mechanism by which they are thought to be effective. Pollution is not a very important notion among the Lugbara, but certain things and occasions are dangerous to living people, and we may refer to them as polluting. In the situation of death there are two kinds of pollution, that of the corpse and that brought about by the act of dying. The corpse is not regarded as particularly unclean (unless the death is from a physically disgusting disease). It should be put into the grave by sisters' sons and not by lineage kin; but the former also dig the grave, an arduous task but hardly an unclean one as such. In a good death the corpse loses its identity and becomes as 'nothing' by being insulted by the lineage kin. But in the case of a bad death there may be no corpse, though if it is brought back for burial then it is very polluting in the sense of being mystically dangerous as it still contains the identity of the deceased. This danger is removed by the diviner's rite of 'cleansing the territory'. As I mention below, the corpse of a rain-maker is dangerous in that it is thought to be able to turn suddenly into a leopard that leaps from the grave to wound or kill the close kin who are standing there. The leopard is considered the most powerful and dangerous of all animals and is mystically associated with rain and the wilderness. The notion of the danger of the corpse – of an adult man or senior woman, at any rate – is that it is, until its identity is removed, an object containing the divine power that has brought about the death. The other aspect of pollution here is that it is due to the confusion in time that is involved when the physical and social deaths may take place at different times or in different places. Even where these are congruent there is always the idea that the dead man has, merely by dying, confused time. He has stopped the orderly passing of ordinary time in his own case; this is anomalous and leads to pollution. Pollution is also thought to be due to the fact that the deceased may have died with grudges in his heart or while quarrelling with a kinsman. The rite of 'cleansing the body' is then performed by a diviner to remove this pollution; it takes the danger away from the kin and places it in the bushland or in the wind, the places of divine power.

So far I have discussed only the deaths, whether good or bad, of ordinary men and women. It is useful at this point briefly to consider the cases of two extraordinary persons, the rain-maker and the prophet. Both are human beings but are given attributes that make them very different from ordinary men.[17] The Lugbara hold views about their deaths that make them significant here.

There is one rain-maker in each sub-clan, the senior man of the senior descent line. He is closely linked with Divinity as being able to control weather and the fertility of men, women, animals, and crops. He knows part of the ultimate secret truth (*a'da*) about the structure of moral and cosmic categories that lie at the basis of all social order and history, that is only fully known by Divinity who allows rain-makers and prophets to know or to give out parts of it.[18] When a rain-maker inherits his position he is initiated by 'brother' rain-makers at a rite that properly includes a symbolic burial and a digging-up of the new rain-maker. His initiation is a rite of transformation to make him into the successor to a long line of rain-makers that has come from the clan-founder at the beginning of society's history. By his initiation he undergoes symbolically his social death. When he does in time actually undergo physical death he is buried differently from ordinary men. They are buried near their compounds; he is buried some way outside; they are buried in the day-time, with singing, dancing and drumming; he is buried at night, in total silence lest he turn into a leopard. He is both the senior man of the sub-clan and also, of course, an ordinary elder of his own little family cluster. When he undergoes physical death his ordinary lineage position has to be filled by a successor; but his status of custodian of truth and the powers of rain-making is not transmitted at the funerary rites but at a later rite of initiation of the new rain-maker. Since he is already a repository of divine power and truth and since he is buried near, or even in, the bushland, there is not the need for rites (that I describe below) that drive divine power back to the wild.

The death of a prophet is simple to discuss: he is said not to die at all. Prophets come from outside Lugbaraland, or at least the greatest of all prophets, Rembe, did so. He was in historical fact taken to Yei in the Sudan in 1916 and there hanged, but Lugbara maintain that he never died and they still await his return even after a lapse of well over half a century. Rembe was the emissary of Divinity and as such was timeless, omnipotent on earth, knowing the secret truth, given all kinds of symbolic attributes to demonstrate his near-divine position. Since he did not die he underwent neither physical nor social death (he had no kin or lineage to be affected by either) and in the minds of the people he has maintained his timelessness and other qualities ever since they last saw him and heard him speak in 1916.

The rites of mourning

Let us return to a consideration of the series of mortuary rites that follow the deaths of ordinary men and women. They restore the state of order and continuity in the lineage that has been disrupted and that is based on the proper control of authority and fertility within the lineage. They are performed during a period of mourning and of formal categorical disorder, in which 'the words are finished', *e'yo de'bo*. The rites comprise certain elements and phases that bring this period to an ordered end at any time up to a year after the death: the actual period depends mainly on the status of the deceased, the more important it is the longer the period of mourning and the more important the proper performance of the rites. The elements include the burial, the death dances, the expression of symbolic chaos, the transition from living to dead person, purification, and the control of fertility and speech. I have already mentioned some of these and here briefly consider the others.

After the burial, or even with it, there are held various death dances, which are the main component in the process of restoring order. They are more than mere 'dances'; rather they are rituals that by acting out

John Middleton

certain mystical processes and events bring about desired relationships between the living, the dead, and Divinity.[19] The dances have
two main functions. One is to re-form the relationships between
lineages, both those related patrilineally and those related affinally,
that have been temporarily broken by the death of the person who was
at the centre of the constellation of these ties. By the performance of
competitive dances and the exchange of arrows a new constellation of
ties is recognised. The other, on a more mystical plane, is to
re-establish the continuity of the lineage, as expressed particularly in
authority (dependent on the recognition of proper relations of hierarchy) and fertility (dependent on the proper control of the complementary sexuality of women and men). This takes place on two levels,
one visible in action and the other invisible to ordinary people who
cannot themselves comprehend the mystical process by which it takes
place. The latter is represented in terms of the former, the representation by the performance of rites and dances providing a means of
bringing about this mystical process.

I have mentioned the invisible process that consists essentially of the
dispersal of the elements of the person and their being placed in their
proper areas of moral space and their proper relationships to men and
Divinity. The visible level involves different but complementary
behaviour by men and women in which their respective relationships
to power and authority are expressed. Briefly, men dance, act
aggressively as members of their own lineages in competition with
others, drink heavily, utter mutual threats and sometimes fight with
weapons. The men sing and speak words that refer to sub-clan and
lineage origins, ancestors, and moral and physical prowess.[20] They
portray the ideal role of warriors and protectors of the home. Women
weep and mourn publicly, wailing with no meaningful words and
rolling in the ashes of the courtyard fire that has been extinguished;
they shave their heads and cover their faces and bodies with white
chalk and ashes as a sign of pollution and association with the 'outside'
sphere of death and barrenness. They demonstrate their inherent
nature as morally beings of the 'outside', the sphere of divine power.

Certain acts, however, are performed together by men and women.
Young men and women use the occasions of death dances to have
sexual intercourse, but in a form of reversal. It takes place in the fields
just outside the compounds (where it would normally pollute the
crops) and it is said that clan siblings may have intercourse together, at
other times a strictly forbidden act. It is an occasion of moral confusion,
in which women may openly express their sexuality, associated with
the wild, a reversal of controlled sexuality that takes place only within

148

the homestead between married couples.[21] It is said that girls who do this at death dances will not conceive from that particular act of intercourse. They bring the expression of this sexuality into the cultivated fields, which although not as 'inside' as the compounds themselves, are extensions of them and quite distinct from the real bushland that lies beyond them. Compounds are the place of fertility of people, the fields of fertility of crops and livestock; beyond is the bushland, the place of non-fertility except of wild animals whose breeding is uncontrolled and so the expression of pure sexuality. The people engaging in illicit intercourse are not, after all, animals, but liminal at this occasion; so that the fields, which are also liminal, provide the proper place for this activity.

During the dances men and women, ideally lineage siblings, run out from the dance arena and mimic the shooting of arrows into the surrounding fields and bushland, while they call their respective *cere* and so demonstrate their particular social identities. To utter the *cere* in this situation is said to threaten revenge on the powers of the wild that have caused the death, to show defiance and lack of fear of them, and to show that kinsmen and women stand together to protect the homesteads. They are driving back the powers of the wild that have come near to the sphere of the home by bringing about the death. These two acts (shooting arrows and sexual intercourse) performed by men and women together are in a sense mirror images of one another: the 'inside', protecting the home and observing rules of exogamy, facing uncontrolled sexuality brought by kin dangerously close to the home.

These death dances are known as *ongo* ('dance') or *auwuongo* ('wailing dance'). At a later time, after the soul has been redomesticated by the rite of 'contacting the mouth of the soul' and given shrines, a second series of death dances are performed, known as *abi*. Whereas the *ongo* are performed by groups of lineage kin, *abi* are performed by visiting groups each of which represents a lineage into which one of the deceased's daughters has married. They come as 'sisters' sons', 'sisters' husbands' and 'fathers' sisters' sons'. They dance, are given arrows by the host lineage, and restore the temporarily-broken or weakened affinal tie. If they fail to do this, the daughters may not bear children in future. Their power of procreation was transferred to their husbands by their fathers when the latter blessed them with spittle at the time of their marriages. This transfer is not really considered a final one, in the sense that it can be withdrawn at any time until the bridewealth has been fully transferred, which may take many years and even last into the next generation. The point is

John Middleton

that the ordered continuity of lineages depends on the controlled fertility of the women married into them. In this case the lineages concerned are those related affinally to the deceased, and not the deceased's own group: the death affects many groups besides that of the deceased himself. The groups related affinally of course compose a wide constellation of kin ties, and it is the fertility of this network that is affected. There is also the notion that by showing that the bride-giving group gives arrows (it received them at the original marriages), the deceased's successor continues to honour the original transfer of fertility and by so doing shows that the sexuality of its daughters is again controlled by their fathers and husbands.

Throughout this account runs the significance of the Lugbara notion *e'yo*, which is in its literal usage translated as 'word'. But it means much more than that. It frequently also means a 'deed', as in the phrase 'the "words" of our ancestors were great'. A 'word' is an expression of acts and relationships based on order and the proper recognition of hierarchy within lineage and neighbourhood. When a dying man speaks his 'last words' on his deathbed he is thereby exercising, for the last time, the formal authority of his position within a situation of formal order; he is behaving as a man; after his death it is said that 'the words are finished' when order and hierarchy vanish in the face of confusion and disorder entering the 'home' from the sphere of divine power 'outside'; the 'mouth of the soul' is contacted by a diviner so as to restore communication by speech between dead and living whereby the latter accept the proper authority of the former.

Divinity, the living, and the dead

Let me turn now to the way in which Lugbara conceive the world of the dead. It lies somewhere beneath the surface of the world. The ancestors of a particular lineage live beneath its compounds and close fields and come to the surface at sacrifices made at shrines erected for them. A single ghost may have many shrines distributed among his descendants' compounds, and ancestors who are not ghosts are regarded as a collectivity for which shrines are also set. The existence of the dead is said to be something like that of the living, but they do not procreate, although they may engage in sexual intercourse. They do not engage in warfare nor do they kill one another or die. They speak with one another, although it is not known whether they speak in Lugbara, and they know what their living kin are saying and even what they are thinking if they sit deliberately in the compounds while doing so and project their thoughts to the dead. In short, the world of the dead has no death, no fertility, and neither the passing of time as among the living nor any particular location in space except that they are beneath the ground near the homesteads of their living kin. However, there is one situation of change, that of the continual entry of newly-dead people (there is no notion of reincarnation, so people do not move out back into the world of the living). The distinction between living and dead is not absolute. There is continuous communication and entry into the category of the dead. The distinction is one between the poles of a continuum along which move the living and the dead, a progress that is one-way. What happens to a particular person who after his death is made into a ghost is that he becomes more senior in generation; he is depersonalised in the sense that his individual characteristics fade away so that he is no longer considered to be good- or bad-tempered as he was when alive; and his appearance is forgotten and irrelevant. But his name is remembered, since his shrine is given his name or it is known who is the incumbent of a particular shrine; and an elder is commemorated in the fig tree that is planted at the head of his grave, which is nourished by his corpse and which is given his actual name. In time he becomes a senior ghost who does not himself listen to living kin but who takes messages from his juniors who consult him about what should be done to keep the living in order. He moves from being underneath the compounds to living under the surrounding fields and then he later moves farther away under the bushland. This is shown by his being given more important and more powerful shrines, the 'external' shrines that are set away from the compounds and visited only by elders and not by junior men. When very senior he is thought to merge with Divinity and he loses any particular location.[22] On another level this process is that of acquiring a greater knowledge of the secret truth held only by Divinity and those few whom Divinity permits to know a part.

The notion of time is significant here. The Lugbara accept two kinds of duration. Ordinary men and women pass through time in the sense of growing older year by year until they die. The seasons come and go, and although they are not repeated in the sense of there being a cycle, there is the notion of a pendulum-like swing in such matters as the rotation of crops and fields. Outside, in the wilderness and the sky, there is no duration and there are neither change nor growth. The whole is linked in Lugbara thought with the notion that living communities are bound and controlled by order and by hierarchy: there are recognised, clearly-defined differences in proper authority and obligations of respect and obedience, which develop for the individual as he or she grows older. Order, hierarchy and authority

John Middleton

are associated with and sanctioned by differences in genealogical generation and by age, and depend on the passing of time. Lineage continuity depends also on these factors and on the control of fertility by the older men and women (both can bestow it by blessing and destroy it by cursing). 'Outside' the sphere of the 'home' there is only power, and that is neither ordered nor hierarchical but merely confused and anarchic. The timelessness of the 'outside' and the wilderness is associated with lack of order, lack of fertility, and lack of hierarchical authority. True, Divinity is man's creator but is not higher in any sense of social hierarchy. He is above all social hierarchy altogether.

According to a Lugbara myth men once lived in the sky with Divinity with whom they could converse and share in the divine knowledge of the structure of moral and cosmic categories. Men could descend to earth by means of a rope or a tree. This was cut by a woman hoeing at a time when the people were on earth and so they could no longer return to converse with Divinity. Since then they have lived on earth, each people speaking its own language, ignorant of divine knowledge and liable to death. Once dead they return partly to Divinity, but only partly so. They are both partly outside the earthly system of hierarchy (yet they exercise authority over the living) and they are linked with Divinity in the sense that, as they pass beyond the process of becoming senior and so move slowly outside time, they become merged with Divinity and cease to exercise direct authority over the living. The continuum is between men and Divinity and the dead are along its centre reaches. In various senses they are ambiguous and so dangerous to the living, who must maintain a careful and difficult balance with them by the regular performance of rites of sacrifice. The dead are always moving slowly along the continuum, and the rites of sacrifice and of death ensure that each dead person remains on his or her appropriate point on it.

NOTES

1 Fieldwork among the Lugbara was carried out between 1949 and 1953 with assistance from the Worshipful Company of Goldsmiths and the Colonial Social Science Research Council, London. The material was initially written up with aid from the Wenner–Gren Foundation for Anthropological Research, New York.

   A general ethnographic account of the Lugbara is given in Middleton (1965).
2 General accounts of Lugbara religion are given in Middleton (1960) and (1977).

3 See Middleton (1973a).
4 I use the word 'ghost' in this particular sense only and 'ancestor' for any of the collectivity of the ancestors of a particular person. Thus all ghosts are ancestors but only certain ancestors are ghosts, those for whom individual shrines are placed. See Middleton (1960:Ch.2).
5 The word *tali* is also used for a place where divine power has been made manifest to men, such as a rock that has been struck by lightning; or where a wondrous event has taken place that was due to the immediate impact of divine power. It further refers to the mystical power of blessing that is in the spittle of senior men.
6 I use capitals to begin the words used for Divinity or God, whether in the sky or immanent, and the lower case for other forms of spirits or refractions of Divinity.
7 See Middleton (1960:Ch.5).
8 See Middleton (1968).
9 See Middleton (1960:Ch.5).
10 Traditionally a new village was established by the elder having sexual intercourse with his wife and making fire on a central hearth, a widespread custom found in many African societies.
11 See Middleton (1955).
12 A man is typically buried with his quiver, his drinking-gourd and his stool; a woman with her beads, the firestones of her hearth, and one of the grinding stones she has used for grinding flour. These represent his or her status while alive; there is no belief that they are to accompany him or her on a journey to the world of the dead.
13 See Middleton (1960:205ff).
14 See Middleton (1969).
15 See Middleton (1963).
16 See Middleton (1960:101ff).
17 See Middleton (1963; 1971; 1978).
18 See Middleton (1973b).
19 See my article 'The dance among the Lugbara', in *The dance in society*. ed. Paul Spencer. (in press)
20 This occurs between lineage segments that are related patrilineally. The same hostility is expressed between unrelated groups when in warfare the body of a killed enemy was taken and its head and penis placed in a tree facing the enemy.
21 Sexual relations between unmarried couples were traditionally permitted in special 'girls' houses', but without physical penetration only: the sexuality was carefully controlled.
22 Such an ancestor is typically one who existed when the particular lineage lived elsewhere before migrating to its present location, so that the site of his grave and shrines are in any case far away in a different part of the country.

REFERENCES

Middleton, J. 1955. 'Myth, history and mourning taboos in Lugbara', *Uganda Journal*, **14**(2):194–203.

John Middleton

1960. *Lugbara religion*. London: Oxford University Press.

1963. 'The Yakan or Allah water cult among the Lugbara', *Journal of the Royal Anthropological Institute*, **93**(1):80–108.

1965. *The Lugbara of Uganda*. New York: Holt, Rinehart & Winston.

1968. 'Some categories of dual classification among the Lugbara of Uganda', *History of Religions*, **7**(3):187–208.

1969. 'Spirit possession among the Lugbara', in *Spirit mediumship and society in Africa*. eds J. Beattie & J. Middleton, pp.220–31. London: Routledge & Kegan Paul.

1971. 'Prophets and rainmakers: the agents of social change among the Lugbara', in *The translation of culture*. ed. T.O. Beidelman. pp.179–201. London: Tavistock Press.

1973*a*. 'The concept of the person among the Lugbara of Uganda', in *La notion de la personne en Afrique noire*. ed. G. Dieterlen, pp.491–506. Paris: CNRS.

1973*b*. 'Secrecy in Lugbara religion', *History of Religions*, **12**(4):299–316.

1977. 'Ritual and ambiguity in Lugbara society', in *Secular ritual*. eds S. Moore & B. Myerhoff. pp.73–90. Assen: Van Gorcum.

1978. 'The rainmaker among the Lugbara of Uganda', in *Systèmes de signes: textes réunis en hommage à Germaine Dieterlen*. pp. 377–88. Paris: Hermann.

6 Of flesh and bones: the management of death pollution in Cantonese society

JAMES L. WATSON

The ritual repertoire associated with death in Chinese society is so complex that it confounds those who would attempt to 'make sense of it all' as a uniform set of symbolic representations. This very challenge, no doubt, is precisely the reason why the subject has preoccupied three generations of sinological anthropologists. One of the most puzzling aspects of Chinese mortuary ritual is the extreme ambivalence shown toward the physical remains of the deceased. This seems to be particularly true for the rural Cantonese. Few who have witnessed a funeral among the Cantonese can fail to be impressed by the fear and apprehension that pervade the ritual. The general aversion to death, and anything associated with the corpse, is so overpowering that ordinary villagers hesitate to become involved, and yet the bones of the ancestors must be preserved at all costs as they are essential to the wellbeing of the descendants. The living gain some control over the natural environment by planting, as it were, the bones of their predecessors in auspicious locations. The bones then transmit the good geomantic influences of the cosmos to the living by means of a pig sacrifice ritual. These geomantic forces, known as 'wind and water' (*feng shui* in Chinese), can thus be harnessed for the benefit of descendants, provided the bones are located properly and preserved from decay.

For many centuries the Cantonese have followed a system of double burial whereby the corpse is first buried in a coffin and left for approximately seven years. The bones are then exhumed and stored in a ceramic urn. Finally, when an auspicious location has been acquired, the urn is reburied in an elaborate, horseshoe-shaped tomb. The final stage may not occur until decades or even generations after death, depending on family circumstances.[1] The bones begin to function for the benefit of descendants only after the final stage in the burial sequence has been completed. Space does not permit a full discussion of the Chinese double burial system in this paper; it is a vastly complex topic (see for example Wilson, 1961; Freedman, 1966:118–54; Potter, 1970; Ahern, 1973; Pasternak, 1973).

Before the living can use the bones of their ancestors the flesh of the corpse must disintegrate completely. This liminal phase is the most critical – and dangerous – in the whole sequence. My main concern in this essay is to explore the social implications of death pollution during the earliest phase of mortuary rites. An analysis of the ritual sequence helps us to unravel many aspects of Cantonese social organisation and shows that the pollution of death must be taken on, or managed in some way, by the descendants before the deceased can be transformed from a dangerous corpse into a settled ancestor. This taking on of pollution must be understood as the first transaction in a relationship of exchange between the living and dead that stretches over many generations – up to 30 and 40 in the cases described below. The ancestral cult is built on ideas of reciprocity but the balance of power in the relationship shifts gradually over time. During the early phase of mortuary ritual the deceased is extremely powerful and unpredictable. However, by the time the bones have been deposited in the final tomb, the ancestor is totally dependent on living descendants. This theme will be explored elsewhere. The following discussion covers the ritual sequence from the moment of death to the cessation of mourning, which normally occurs seven days after the initial burial.

In Cantonese society strict rules dictate those who are obligated to take on a portion of the pollution of death. These rules reveal a great deal about the Cantonese system of inheritance. From one point of view it can be argued that male mourners must earn the worldly goods they inherit by absorbing a major share of the deceased's pollution. Following J. Goody's (1962) lead in *Death, property and the ancestors*, an analysis which focuses on the inheritance of property helps us to make sense of male participation in Cantonese funerary ritual. For women, another approach seems more suitable and I shall argue that the ritual actions of women at Cantonese funerals are more directly related to the concerns of fertility and physical continuity than to the inheritance of property. Bloch (1971) has shown, in a number of passages, how in Merina society it is thought essential for women to handle the corpses of their predecessors in order to ensure the fertility of the living generation (Bloch, 1971:159ff). As outlined in this paper, a similar set of ritual actions is found in South China among Cantonese peasants.

It may not be a coincidence that this parallel between Merina and Cantonese mortuary rites should be so striking. Both Merina and Cantonese place great weight on the preservation of physical remains and they are both preoccupied with the construction and maintenance of elaborate tombs. The Merina and Cantonese, I would argue, stand near one end of a continuum of cultures that stress the preservation of physical remains. The Hindu tradition, described elsewhere in this volume by J. Parry would seem to occupy the opposite end of such a continuum. In Hindu culture the object of mortuary ritual is the total obliteration of the deceased in a physical sense. Nothing of the corpse is preserved and monuments are rarely erected. Among the Cantonese, on the other hand (as with the Merina), the world order and the social structure of the living have meaning only through the manipulation and preservation of the dead.

Although the Hindu and the Chinese systems could hardly be further removed in terms of treating the remains of the dead, there are some intriguing similarities in the management of death pollution in the two cultures. Both societies, for instance, have a hierarchy of funeral specialists based on relative exposure to the contaminating aspects of death (cf. Parry, 1980). Among the Cantonese, a proper[2] funeral cannot take place unless the bereaved are willing to pay for the services of professionals who specialise in 'white affairs', *pai shih*, (white being the colour of mourning). A complex division of labour operates among funeral specialists and, not surprisingly, they are ranked according to the extent of physical contact with the corpse. Geomancers, whose tasks do not require attendance at the funeral, rank highest. Lowest in the hierarchy are menial labourers employed to handle the corpse and dispose of clothing, bedding, and other materials most directly associated with death. These corpse handlers are so contaminated by their work that villagers will not even speak to them; their very glance is thought to bring misfortune. Between the two extremes there is a whole range of professionals who earn all or most of their income from 'white affairs': priests, nuns, musicians, coffin makers, fortune tellers, exhumation specialists and others. Many carry the pollution of death with them wherever they go; others are unaffected by regular attendance at funerals. Like the Hindus, therefore, the Cantonese draw a clear distinction between permanent and temporary pollution (cf. Dumont and Pocock, 1959; on Hindu ideas regarding death pollution see especially Das, 1977:120–6).

Death pollution is not an easy topic to investigate in Chinese society. Among the more traditional of the Cantonese, including those who live in rural Hong Kong, it is considered bad luck even to mention the subject of death (see also Chen, 1939:175). What follows, therefore, is an account based largely on personal observation. I witnessed 16 funerals, in part or in full, during 29 months of field research in the Hong Kong New Territories. Most of the data were gathered while the funerals were actually in progress. Only on these occasions were people prepared to offer opinions about the meaning of various rituals and the role of specialists.

Observations were made in the villages of San Tin and Ha Tsuen (see J. Watson, 1975*b* on San Tin and R. Watson 1982 on Ha Tsuen). These communities are inhabited by powerful lineages of the type that once dominated the agrarian economy of South-eastern China. There are no significant differences in the funeral ritual as practised in the two villages. People from San Tin and Ha Tsuen have intermarried for centuries and speak the same sub-dialect of Pao An Cantonese. As the data are drawn from such a limited area, few claims can be made for the general applicability of the model presented in this paper. There are, of course, parallels in other parts of China (to which the reader's attention will be drawn) but it is not my intention to make a general survey of Chinese mortuary customs. Rather, this study deals with ideas concerning death pollution in one local system: the hinterland surrounding the market town of Yuen Long in the Hong Kong New Territories. Many of the funeral specialists live in Yuen Long and provide services to approximately 50 Cantonese villages in the town's catchment area.

'Killing airs': two aspects of death pollution

News of an imminent death spreads rapidly in Cantonese villages. Residents usually have enough warning to protect those who are most at risk. Pregnant women and children are advised to stay well away from the house in question; neighbours close their doors and find an excuse to be away for a few hours. Farmers make sure that sows with piglets are removed from sheds nearby and calves are taken out of the village. These precautions are necessary, it was explained, because newborn creatures of all types are extremely vulnerable to the 'killing airs', *sat hei*, that emanate from the corpse at the moment of death. The killing airs permeate the house of the deceased and cling to the mourners 'like an invisible cloud' (to quote one informant in Ha Tsuen). There is general agreement that the *sat hei* associated with untimely or inauspicious death are particularly virulent. Worst of all are the killing airs that accompany suicide. In San Tin and Ha Tsuen, houses that were once the sites of suicides are usually abandoned; no one dares live in them. Older villagers hesitate to visit hospitals because they fear the overpowering presence of multiple deaths (see Topley, 1952:151–2 on death houses among the Cantonese in Singapore).

In the area under study there appear to be two aspects of death pollution: one associated with the release of the spirit and the other relating to the decay of the flesh. This distinction is not made in everyday speech; villagers use the Cantonese term *sat hei* (Mandarin *sha ch'i*) to describe any adverse effect caused by exposure to death. Nonetheless, the dual nature of pollution is very evident when one pays close attention to the actions of mourners, spectators, and specialists during critical transitions in the funeral ritual. These are marked by what I call *aversion points* which occur when the corpse is physically moved and the spirit is thought to be undergoing a transition. At such points most people in the assemblage avert their eyes because, as informants explained, 'we do not want to offend the spirit'. To look on the corpse during these transitions invites terrible retribution – described as *sat hei* – from the disembodied, and hence, unpredictable spirit. Funeral specialists, as demonstrated in the following account, are relatively immune to this aspect of death pollution.

The *sat hei* associated with decaying flesh is quite another matter. Everyone, including the specialist, is in danger when she or he handles anything that has been in direct contact with the corpse. This aspect of pollution is thus *passive*; it has no volition and affects everyone equally. The aspect associated with the spirit, however, is *active* and extremely unpredictable. In effect, the lowest ranks of funeral specialists are paid to manage the passive pollution of the flesh. Higher ranking professionals, especially priests, are hired to cope with the spirit but they are rarely affected by the active *sat hei* of death (assuming, of course, that they perform the rituals correctly and do not offend the spirit).

The ritual sequence, I: From death to burial

Before proceeding with the discussion of inheritance and fertility it seems appropriate to provide some background information on Cantonese funeral ritual. The sequence outlined below covers the main elements of the ritual from the moment of death to the formal cessation of mourning. It is during this liminal period (cf. Hertz, 1960) prior to the settling of the soul that the pollution of death is most virulent. The ritual sequence has been distilled, as it were, from 16 funerals. Some were more elaborate than others, depending largely on the age of the deceased and the wealth of the bereaved, but, in general, all funerals share a basic structure. Furthermore, every funeral must be serviced by a minimal set of specialists which includes at least two corpse handlers, a priest, and a musician. The ritual cannot proceed without these men in attendance. Wealthy families sometimes hire

James L. Watson

up to a dozen additional specialists to complement the minimal set.

The following account puts special emphasis on the problem of death pollution which means that other aspects of the ritual have been deleted.

The early stages of ritual have the effect of warning the community that a death has occurred and that members of the household in question have entered a mandatory period of mourning. The moment of death (and, hence, the release of killing airs) is formally announced by women of the household who burst into high-pitched, stereotyped wailing. The wailing is sometimes accompanied by funeral laments that women learn when they are young, often while living in maiden houses prior to marriage (on laments see Blake, 1978). Women of the household continue wailing in shifts until the corpse has been encoffined; this usually takes place on the day of death or, in the event of death during the evening, on the following afternoon. The wailing is soon augmented by the sound of a reed instrument (akin to an oboe or shawm) renowned for its haunting, lyrical melodies. The message conveyed by this pipe is unmistakable – on hearing it strangers turn in their tracks, workmen disappear, villagers drop whatever they are doing and take children indoors. The sounds associated with death are marked by a clear sexual division: women wail, men play musical instruments. The pipers who perform at funerals are always male. I have never seen a Cantonese village woman play a musical instrument (nuns sometimes do but they are not part of the community and villagers do not perceive them as 'women'). Conversely, men never wail or use their voices to express grief in public (chanting, however, is a different matter – see below).

The house of the deceased is physically marked off from all others in the community. A blue mourning lantern is hung from the eaves and the red door charms, put up every New Year festival for good luck, are covered with white paper. Members of the household change into white mourning garb made of sack cloth, hemp, and coarse cotton. As in other parts of China (see particularly Wolf, 1970), mourners dress according to a complex code that symbolises their relationship to the deceased.

Unless the death is completely unexpected this initial phase of the ritual, which signals the onset of mourning, is accomplished in a matter of hours. The stage is then set for the funeral ceremony itself which takes place in a public arena reserved for this purpose. In most cases the coffin has already been ordered from a shop in the nearby market town. It is brought to the village by a contingent of corpse handlers and placed, lid open, on stools in the designated arena. The sight of an open coffin near the entrance of a village is enough to discourage the most determined of intruders. (One elder said that this ploy was once used to ward off bandits in the 1920s.)

The arrival of the coffin is also the cue for those who are not members of the deceased's household to prepare themselves for their part in the ritual. As noted above, Cantonese villagers are reluctant to become involved in funerals; they participate only to the extent that obligation defines. In some close-knit communities, such as the hamlet of Shek Gong Wai in Ha Tsuen, every household is expected to send at least one representative to each funeral. Failure to comply is punished by ostracism and a poor turn-out when someone dies in the offending household. In Fan Tin, San Tin's largest hamlet, a number of 'old people societies' (*lao jen hui*) have been formed to ensure a large attendance at funerals. Organised much like rotating credit associations, these funeral societies charge an entrance fee and pay benefits upon death (cf. Wong, 1939; Gallin, 1966:121–2; Pasternak, 1972:64–6). According to villagers, however, an equally important feature of these societies is the obligation of surviving members to participate in the funerals of their less fortunate peers. The obligation passes to members' descendants and, in fact, doubles upon death: when a member dies she or he is replaced by two representatives. During my most recent field trip one sprightly woman of 96 who had survived to be the last member of a particularly large society in Fan Tin took sardonic pleasure in reminding fellow villagers of their obligation. As she put it, 'I have beaten them all [the other members] and now their children and grandchildren will have to be there when I go'.

The public ceremony begins with a procession from the house of the deceased to a stream or well outside the village. Led by a priest and musicians, the chief mourner (ordinarily the senior son or nearest agnatic equivalent) pays homage to the guardian spirit of the stream and 'buys water' (*mai shui*) by leaving a few coppers. This water is taken back to the house and used to bathe the corpse, the last act before encoffining. The water-buying procession is the point at which the focus of the ritual begins to shift from the household to the public arena. As soon as the procession has returned to the house, members of the community begin to assemble near the coffin. One of the most critical aversion points in the ritual occurs soon after: at a time chosen by a fortune teller, the corpse handlers wrap the body in a reed mat and carry it with deliberate speed to the coffin. Their approach is announced with a particularly loud burst of piping. This is the cue for people in the assemblage to avert their eyes. Most women turn to the nearest wall and hold both hands over their faces; men generally turn their heads and look at their feet. Meanwhile the corpse handlers adjust the deceased and pack the coffin with stacks of funeral paper. They work rapidly under the watchful eyes of the priest and the chief mourner. The assemblage does not turn until the priest raps on a table, signalling that the corpse is settled in the coffin. After making offerings to the spirit of the deceased and checking to see that all is well the priest orders the handlers to place the lid on the coffin. Again all except the chief mourner and the specialists avert their eyes and do not look on the proceedings until the lid is firmly hammered into position. The chief mourner, or a representative of the family, sets the first nail with a few taps and the handlers finish the job. The most critical transition is complete at this point. The corpse is safely encoffined and the community phase of the ritual begins in earnest.

Representatives of every household obligated to attend step forward and make offerings to the spirit. They pour out cups of wine, in sets of three, according to their relationship to the deceased: three cups for ordinary neighbours, nine cups for close agnates (*shu pai hsiung ti*, descendants of common grandfather), and on up to 33 cups for the chief mourner. Significantly it is usually a woman from each household who fulfils this obligation, often pouring out cups for her husband or son. Women ordinarily outnumber men at funerals by three to one. Informants claimed that the sexual imbalance was unavoidable because 'our men are too busy to attend'. This seems unlikely, however, considering the fact that the teashops and gambling houses in both villages were crowded with local men on most funeral days. Men usually attend only important funerals in the village, namely those for leaders and popular old people. It is, as I shall show, women rather than men who are expected to intercede for their families in 'white affairs' and thus assume the burdens associated with death pollution.

When everyone in the assemblage has offered wine to the spirit, the priest calls for another phase of the ritual to begin. Members of the group gather at the head of the coffin and bow three times; they are then led in a large circle three times, clockwise, around the coffin. Meanwhile the younger women of the deceased's family (daughters-in-law and married daughters) kneel in the centre of the circle and sing funeral laments while rubbing their unbraided hair against the coffin.

In San Tin the circling of the coffin is sometimes followed by a cord-cutting ceremony, especially if the deceased has many descendants. A white cord attached to a coffin nail is stretched out such that everyone in the assemblage, beginning with the chief mourner and ending with unrelated neighbours, holds a bit of it. As he progresses down the line the priest cuts off small pieces of cord, again in sets of three, directly into the (left) hand of each mourner. The bits of cord are then burned before the recipient returns home (see Ahern, 1973:171 on cord cutting in Taiwan). Although local people are familiar with the custom, I did not witness a cord-cutting ceremony in Ha Tsuen. Instead, the household of the deceased distributes coins, often in white envelopes, to everyone who participates in the funeral. The coins are kept in a box under the coffin and are distributed toward the end of the public ceremony. The coin is treated very gingerly: it is held in the (left) hand or inserted in the (left) ear; it must never be put in one's pocket (to do so, I was told, would bring bad luck). As soon as the funeral is over the coin must be spent on a sweet or, better still, given to a beggar. The people of San Tin sometimes combine this custom with the cord cutting at important funerals.

The final act of the public funeral ceremony is the removal of the coffin from the village to the burial site. After the coins and/or bits of cord have been distributed, the priest calls the corpse handlers to attention and stands before the coffin in a final homage to the spirit. At an auspicious moment, chosen in advance by a fortune teller, the priest abruptly ends the ceremony by striking the coffin with a pair of scissors, producing a loud, resonant sound (note that the priest uses percussion to mark transitions (see Needham, 1967) many times during the ritual sequence). At this signal members of the assemblage again avert their eyes as the handlers hoist the heavy coffin onto a carrying frame or, following recent innovations, onto a specially constructed cart. After the chief mourner has checked to see that the coffin is secure, the priest raps the coffin a second time and the handlers charge out of the village at a fast trot, chanting rhythmically as they go (in San Tin they often chant 'out, out, out'). The path is cleared by a youth, or a man hired for the purpose, who scatters white funeral paper as offerings to appease any ghosts that might lurk in waiting. Nothing can be allowed to impede the steady progress of the entourage as it winds its way through the hills to the grave (which has been prepared by men from the same company that supplied the coffin). Once the coffin has passed the notional boundaries of the village the bearers slow down to allow the mourners to catch up. Only the male descendants of the deceased, a few close agnates (descendants of common grandfather), and community leaders accompany the coffin

163

all the way to the grave. Village women stay behind as do most members of the assemblage. If nuns are in attendance they follow the procession and chant Buddhist sutras next to the coffin right up to the moment of burial; this is thought to have a calming influence on the spirit. The priest does not join the march to the grave. His role ends as soon as the coffin leaves the village.

At the grave only the closest agnates, together with the nuns and bearers, gather to witness the actual burial. Other men fall back just before reaching the site and wait, out of sight, for the mourners to reappear. As the coffin is settled into its final resting place the chief mourner and the specialists who dug the grave watch carefully – all others avert their eyes. For the descendants this is a particularly critical point in the proceedings. The prosperity of the living depends, according to local views, on the physical condition of the ancestors. A 'peaceful burial' (*an tsang*) is essential if the spirit is to rest properly and be transformed into a benevolent ancestor.

As soon as the chief mourner is satisfied that the coffin is properly aligned (this can take up to an hour) a final offering is made to the spirit and the grave is quickly filled in by the specialists. The procession of mourners then winds its way back to the village by a different route 'so the spirit will not be able to follow us', according to most informants. The nuns and other specialists return to their homes in yet another direction. They are not allowed to re-enter the village until they are summoned for a funeral. Specialists are instructed to arrive from the east and leave in a westerly direction whenever possible, thus completing a circle 'to take the *sat hei* out with them.' The east-west dichotomy corresponds to *yang* (life, light, sunrise) and *yin* (death, dark, sunset); similarly the land of the dead is called the Western Paradise. Members of the community and guests do not have to make this circle but they are careful not to bring any bad influences of death with them back into the village. Upon leaving the vicinity of the grave everyone steps over a small fire (except the handlers and nuns who do not bother). As the villagers approach the gates of the community they wash their hands, necks, and faces in bowls of fresh water containing pomelo leaves, a purificatory agent. Older women prepare water and watch carefully to make certain that each man who has accompanied the coffin is thoroughly cleaned before he proceeds into the village (on occasion I have seen these women halt men and order them to scrub with more vigour). When all have washed the community returns to normal: doors are flung open, children run through the narrow lanes once again, and farmers retrieve their livestock. The danger has passed.

The ritual sequence, II: The cessation of mourning

After the burial, the descendants of the deceased begin a seven-day period of mourning during which, ideally, they do not emerge from their houses or do any work. Except for the wealthy, however, a total retreat is rarely possible. Most mourners in San Tin and Ha Tsuen compromise by withdrawing from non-essential activities. They do not attend weddings or banquets and do not enter temples or ancestral halls. Their presence, in fact, would not be welcomed because they are thought to carry the aura of death with them until they have been purified at the cessation of mourning ceremony (see below). Mourning is reckoned in multiples of seven days with the full 'seven sevens' (49 days) marked by a meal to honour the dead. At this point mourning is officially ended and members of the household are free to participate in community activities. For most families, however, the period of mourning is effectively terminated after only seven days. Those who continue to wear mourning garb and withdraw from normal activities beyond the first week consciously set themselves apart from their neighbours. Prior to World War Two, wealthy families of the land-lord–merchant class in San Tin and Ha Tsuen were expected to withdraw for 21 days upon the death of a senior member. I have not encountered any cases in the New Territories that can match the full 49-day mourning period reported for some of China's urban elite (see for example Doolittle, 1865:183ff).

For most villagers, therefore, the completion of the first cycle of seven days (*t'ou ch'i*) marks their re-entry into society. Their liminal state has ended and they are no longer considered a threat to the community (cf. Hertz, 1960). The termination of mourning is accomplished during a dramatic ceremony known as 'putting on the red' (*ch'uan hung*). Led by the same priest who presided over the funeral, this involves the exchange of white clothing for red: white, the colour of death and misfortune, is superseded by red, the colour of life and luck. The ritual commences in the same public arena where the funeral was held. The ceremony concerns only those descendants of the deceased who are contaminated by the 'killing airs' associated with death; others rarely bother to attend. First, a white paper tablet endorsed with the deceased's name is taken from the family altar and placed in a paper sedan chair. When the tablet is moved by the chief mourner those in attendance avert their eyes for the last time. The sedan chair, along with a paper house for the spirit, is then dispatched to the underworld by flame. As the fire burns the priest leads the small procession of mourners (all dressed in full mourning garb) three

James L. Watson

times round the fire in a counter-clockwise direction (during the funeral the assembly moves in a clockwise direction). Cups of wine are offered to the spirit, again in sets of three using the left hand. When the offerings are complete the priest chants to the spirit in what he describes as 'spirit talk' (*shen hua*), a ritual language he learns as part of his training. The chants are designed, in the words of San Tin's priest, 'to settle the spirit' and send it forthwith from the land of the living to the underworld, 'so that it will no longer bother the villagers'. This part of the ritual, executed in a low drone, is probably responsible for the priest's title which is *Nahm Mou Lo*, a colloquial Cantonese term which is impossible to translate but is usually rendered in English as 'chanting fellow'.

With the spirit safely dispatched, the *active* aspect of death pollution ceases to be a threat to those outside the deceased's immediate household. This accomplished, the *passive* aspect of pollution is extinguished in a most dramatic way. At a signal from the priest the mourners strip off their white garments to reveal a layer of new clothing, preferably in bright colours. Sackcloth hoods and hempen shawls are thrown on the fire; white cotton shirts and trousers are carefully waved through the fire three times 'to clean out everything bad'. White tennis shoes, worn as part of the mourning garb, are cleansed in a similar fashion and exchanged for wooden clogs painted bright red. Women produce their jewellery, and , as a precaution, wave it through the fire before wearing it again. Gold jewellery in particular is banned during the mourning period as it is thought to absorb death pollution. Infants undergo a complete change of clothing as well and some, particularly males, are themselves held high over the fire for a brief moment. Mourning 'flowers', knitted from white yarn and worn in women's hair, are burned and replaced with bits of red yarn or ribbon. One set of new, red clogs is dispatched to every household that participated in the funeral. This final act is a public notification that the family is no longer in seclusion. As mourners disperse the priest continues chanting until the last spark of fire dies out. When he removes his own protective red robe, and saunters back to the village teashop, the community phase of mortuary ritual is over.

Precaution and purification

The sequence outlined above does not begin to exhaust the wealth of detail and the multiplicity of symbolism evident at even the simplest of Chinese funerals. De Groot covers the ritual sequence from death to the cessation of mourning in 1425 pages, and apologises to the reader for being too selective (De Groot, 1892–1910). My own account has been selective in the extreme. Death pollution has been emphasised since it is the subject of this paper while other, equally important, features of the ritual have been ignored.

The Cantonese villagers protect themselves against the lingering effects of death pollution in a number of ways. First, there are clear restrictions on the disposition of the corpse. Should a resident be unfortunate enough to die outside the boundaries of his or her own community, the ritual (including those aspects normally confined to the household) must be held on the outskirts of the village. Under no circumstances is a corpse allowed to enter the village gates: 'This would bring bad luck to everyone who lives there', one elder explained. In the past, corpses and funeral processions were also banned from entering many of China's walled cities (see for example Doolittle, 1865:33). The people of San Tin and Ha Tsuen observe other restrictions as well. For instance, ancestral tablets and the images of deities must be shielded from the sight of coffins or corpses. Similarly, the small shrines dedicated to the local 'earth gods' (*t'u ti*) are always screened prior to a funeral. In most villages these shrines are located in the same public arenas used for funerals; the residents of San Tin solved the problem by building corrugated iron shields to cover the shrines. The appearance of these shields is a sure sign that a funeral will take place that day. Villagers also make certain that the doors and windows of their own houses are closed if the procession is to pass nearby.

Other precautions will have become apparent from the account of the ritual. Villagers always use the left hand when touching anything associated with death so that all ritual acts at funerals, including the pouring of wine and the acceptance of white cord, are performed with the left hand. Although villagers would not, or could not, explain why the left hand is preferred ('we always do it this way') many scholars have argued that left in Chinese society is associated with *yin*, while right corresponds to *yang* (see for example Granet, 1973). It is significant that the right hand is used for 'lucky' rituals in the villages under study (i.e. weddings, temple festivals, and sacrifices to gods or lineage ancestors). Often, as a mark of respect, *both* hands are used, but this is not possible if the worshipper has participated in a funeral during the previous seven days. Left and right must never be confused, just as white and red affairs (funerals and weddings) are not to be held on the same day.

The prophylactic qualities of the colour red have been elucidated by Arthur Wolf in an important article on mourning dress in Chinese society (Wolf, 1970). In San Tin and Ha Tsuen, people wear small patches of red to protect themselves when they attend funerals. 'The killing airs (*sat hei*) will not cling to us if we put on a little red', one man explained after I noticed a strip of red cloth pinned to his shirt. This concurs with the view held by Wolf's Taiwanese informants: red, as the colour associated with luck and life, is thought to have prophylactic powers in its own right and thus can be used to neutralise the bad effects of death. This is true in the New Territories as well, with but one proviso: red is effective only against the passive aspect of pollution, that associated with physical decay. Behaviour during the ritual itself makes it clear that red patches have little to do with warding off the unpredictable spirit of the deceased (i.e. the active aspect of death pollution). That can be done only by showing proper respect to the spirit at critical transitions in the ritual.

Fire and water both have purificatory powers but they must be handled with care. Water is used to wash the corpse and to cleanse members of the community when they return from the grave. The greatest possible care is taken in disposing of this spent water once it has been exposed to death pollution. The most dangerous is that used to wash the corpse. It is usually carried far from the village (by corpse handlers) and thrown in a stream that flows directly into the sea. Fire is even more of a problem. As highlighted in the ritual sequence outlined above, sackcloth and other disposable signs of mourning are burned seven days after burial. Items most directly associated with the actual process of death, such as the clothing and bedding of the deceased, may also be burned on the day of burial. Nothing used during the funeral ritual can be kept. Tables, stools, pots, bowls – everything – must be discarded because they are contaminated by the 'killing airs' of death. Again, it is the corpse handlers who dispose of these polluted items. The preferred method of disposal is by flame but there are risks involved. First, villagers pointed out, the 'killing airs' are released and may settle over the village if the wind is not right. Breathing the fumes from such a fire is thought to be a sure way to catch tuberculosis. Second, the smoke of polluted items burned by the corpse handlers could mingle with the ritual paraphernalia (e.g. mock money, charms, and supplies) dispatched by flame to the spirit of the deceased for use in the underworld. According to informants this would contaminate the offerings and render them useless.[3]

Rather than risking a fire the corpse handlers are often instructed to dump the polluted items in a secluded spot outside the village boundaries. The major hamlets of San Tin and Ha Tsuen have special dumping sites reserved specifically for this purpose. Children are warned to stay away from these areas and, whenever adults are forced to walk past, they turn their faces in disgust (some take a deep breath as they approach and hold it as they rush by). In other parts of China the clothing of the deceased is pawned by the funeral specialists (De Groot, 1892:I:68–9) but this is rarely done in the New Territories. Self-respecting villagers would never dream of buying second-hand clothing. The risks of acquiring someone else's contaminated goods are too great.

Inheritance and the distribution of pollution

Certain members of the community are not allowed to participate in funerals. Unless they are direct descendants of the deceased, children under the age of fourteen are excluded. In San Tin, funerals are often held in a plaza directly in front of the main ancestral hall. Until the mid-1970s this hall was used as a kindergarten for village children. On funeral days the school was closed early and the children were sent running home (shading their eyes as they passed the open coffin) just before the water-buying ceremony. It is also considered dangerous for people of certain ages to attend the funeral. These unlucky ages, usually three, are divined in advance by a fortune teller who matches them with the deceased's horoscope. A slip of paper listing the restricted ages is posted near the open coffin and word soon gets around the village. Other restrictions are placed on pregnant women and their husbands. Similarly, households with an infant who is not yet one month old (*man yueh*, 'full month') are not expected to send representatives for fear of carrying the pollution of death with them back home.[4] A neighbour or a kinswoman is usually delegated to stand in for them.

Barring these restrictions every household that has an obligation to attend must send at least one representative to the funeral. The burden of pollution is thus shared with members of the community. Those who participate in the ritual take upon themselves a portion of the 'killing airs' according to their relationship with the deceased. The distribution of contaminated coins to participants is one way of parcelling out the pollution of death. Another is the pouring of wine and the cutting of white cord: one assumes pollution in direct proportion to the number of cups emptied and bits of cord accepted. It will be noted that these distribution mechanisms deal with the passive pollution of death. A large turn-out is thus not only a sign of respect to the deceased but also a way of helping the bereaved cope with the problem of contamination.

James L. Watson

Male mourners (i.e. direct descendants of the deceased) take on pollution in descending order of seniority. The most polluted of all is the chief mourner – the senior son or designated heir. Not surprisingly the chief mourner benefits most from the estate of the deceased (during the ritual he is referred to as *ch'eng chi*, 'heir' or 'inheritor'). Partible inheritance of land and commercial properties, with sons receiving more or less equal shares, is the norm among Cantonese peasants. But this does not apply to houses and domestic goods. In the New Territories region, housing has always been in short supply (see Nelson, 1969) and brothers never live in the same house together after the death of their parents. The senior sons, in descending order, inherit the dwellings of the deceased, with the eldest taking the 'ancestral home' (*tsu wu*) which contains the domestic ancestral tablets. Ordinary peasants rarely own more than one house no matter how many sons they produce. In effect, therefore, a form of *de facto* primogeniture exists with respect to housing in Cantonese villages.

The water-buying ceremony makes this system of inheritance clear. Whoever buys water for the deceased inherits the ancestral home and assumes primary responsibility for the worship of domestic ancestors. Younger brothers, if there are any, must have the inheritor's permission before making copies of the domestic tablets for their own houses. The privilege of inheriting the ancestral home is not automatic; it has to be earned. The essence of the water-buying ceremony is a ritual bathing of the corpse. This task is reserved for the inheritor who, by wiping the face of the deceased with a wet cloth, takes a major portion of the killing airs upon himself. In fact, the ritual bathing is just that, a perfunctory touch on the forehead or cheek. The actual bathing is then accomplished by the corpse handlers who set about their work with professional detachment. When finished, the handlers dress the corpse and make it ready for encoffining.

Although the professionals do the actual labour (and are thereby heavily contaminated), the inheritor is deemed to be the one most affected by this chore. By exposing himself in this way, the inheritor is polluted more seriously than any other mourner. Villagers maintain that one never completely recovers from this exposure to death. The dangers of touching too many corpses are well known. A priest told me that after a male handles seven corpses he is permanently polluted and can never be clean again (this restriction may not apply to women[5]). This is why the priests are always careful never to touch the corpse during the ritual. It also explains why the professional corpse handlers are ostracised so thoroughly. Stories are sometimes told of greedy men who buy water for a whole line of childless agnates, only to contract leprosy in the bargain.

170

The inheritor always plays the role of chief mourner and, as such, he is ritually isolated in other ways as well. For instance, at the funeral he is the only person in the assemblage (save the corpse handlers and the nuns) who does not wear at least one patch of prophylactic red on his mourning garb. Furthermore, the inheritor watches *every* act in the entire proceedings from death to burial. He does not avert his eyes at any time and, thus, risks incurring the wrath of the deceased's spirit more than any other mourner. His younger brothers, sisters, sisters-in-law, wives, and children all avert their eyes at the most critical transition points – and they all wear bits of red to protect themselves as best they can from the passive pollution of death.

Although the designated heir is expected to assume the role of chief mourner, this is not always possible, especially when the inheritor is an emigrant working abroad. In such cases the man's wife, or eldest son, normally stands in for him. Under no circumstances is a married-out daughter of the deceased allowed to buy water, even as a stand-in for her brother. The inheritor, or his representative, buys water for both parents, and sometimes even for his father's secondary wives as well. This is considered a duty owed not necessarily to the women concerned but to their husband, the primary benefactor. Wealthy men, it was pointed out to me, usually have secondary wives which means that the chief mourner must buy extra water to earn his inheritance. People who have no sons, and no property to pass on to a designated heir, face the dire prospect of being buried without the water-buying ceremony. This is an unbearable fate because an unwashed corpse is thought to offend the guardians of hell who condemn the spirit to wander as a ghost. Furthermore, an unwashed corpse (i.e. one without heirs to nurture it) can never make the conversion into an ancestor.

People without heirs try to save enough money to cover their own funeral expenses, with several hundred dollars set aside to compensate any agnate willing to buy water. Destitute villagers are given an abbreviated funeral and are buried at community expense. I witnessed one such funeral for an old woman in San Tin. It was a brief, tension-ridden affair with few people in attendance. The village guard, an indigenous security force, acted as pallbearers but no one was willing to buy water for the deceased. The priest, musician, and two corpse handlers (the minimal ritual set) were paid by the estate of San Tin's central ancestral hall. Members of the community heaved a collective sigh of relief when the guardsmen carried the (very cheap) coffin out to the hills. As no one had stood in to play the role of mourners for the deceased, the seventh day after death passed without the usual cessation of mourning ceremony.

James L. Watson

Most people in San Tin and Ha Tsuen leave at least a house which is reason enough for some member of the community to assume the role of chief mourner. In fact, propertied men who do not have sons of their own can expect to be courted by their non-inheriting nephews or grandnephews. The system of *de facto* primogeniture (with respect to housing) also helps explain why younger sons play such a minor role in the funerals of their own parents. Unlike the inheritor, they wear patches of red to protect themselves and avert their eyes at critical transition points. Younger sons do not even accompany the chief mourner when he buys water for the deceased and – most significantly – they are *not* required to touch the corpse or the coffin. Given the patterns of land ownership in the area under study, these younger sons seldom inherit anything at all from their father's estate, not even a table or a chair (domestic property remains attached to the ancestral home). All legitimate sons inherit an equal share of their father's land but few peasants have much landed property of their own. For centuries the best agricultural land in this region has been tied up in ancestral estates which are owned by corporations of agnates and not by individuals (J. Watson, 1977). It is not surprising, therefore, that younger sons should play such a minor role in the funerary ritual. In real terms they receive very little from the parental estate and, as the ritual makes clear, their obligation to the deceased is slight.

Pollution, fertility and the role of women

By placing so much emphasis on the inheritance of property it might be argued that the approach outlined above ignores other, equally revealing aspects of the ritual. An analysis of inheritance patterns does not, for instance, explain the role of women at funerals. Surviving wives do not attend the funerals of their husbands even though they are supported by the family estate until their own deaths (they do not inherit their husband's property but have rights of maintenance). The trauma of attending one's husband's funeral is thought to be so severe that it is never permitted in San Tin or Ha Tsuen. Neither do husbands participate in the funerals of their wives, but for a different reason: it is considered unfilial, and unlucky, for a wife to leave this life before her husband and, hence, he should not dignify the proceedings by his presence.

Other women do however play a leading role in funerary ritual. Married daughters and daughters-in-law of the deceased must be present if at all possible. They wail and sing laments to appease the spirit until the time of encoffining. Their most important ritual act, however, takes place during the final phase of the funeral ceremony. As noted above, these women are expected to rub their unbound hair against the coffin just prior to its removal from the village. Under normal circumstances a married woman's hair is kept in a tight bun at the back of her head; it is unbound only to be washed. Women do not wash their hair without first consulting an almanac to see if the day is a 'lucky' one. In addition they never wash their hair during menstruation. Hair must be treated carefully because, in the local view, it absorbs unclean essences of all kinds.[6] Thus, by rubbing their hair against the coffin, married women purposely expose themselves to the pollution of death. They do not wash their hair until the cessation of mourning seven days later (similarly men do not wash, or shave, during this liminal period).

The level of contamination to which these women subject themselves is second only to that affecting the chief mourner. When I asked why women rub their hair on the coffin most informants replied that 'daughters should show respect to their parents'. This demonstration of respect is expected of all married-out daughters and daughters-in-law; no distinctions of status are drawn among them. In contrast with male mourners, therefore, women do not play roles that correspond to their material obligation to the deceased. It might be argued that married women 'repay' the dowries they receive from their parents by taking on a share of death pollution, in much the same way that the chief mourner may be said to 'pay' for his inheritance. This explanation is not satisfactory, however, for the simple reason that dowry in the area under study is not a form of pre-mortem inheritance. Parents rarely use their own money to endower daughters. As Rubie Watson (1981) has demonstrated, Cantonese peasants have what amounts to an indirect dowry system (cf. Goody & Tambiah, 1973) whereby the wife-takers actually pay the expenses of the bride's dowry, through the mechanism of a cash brideprice.

There is no reason to assume that both sexes expose themselves to death pollution for the same reason. In fact, women mourners may be engaged in ritual behaviour that has little to do with the actions of their husbands and brothers. Although most informants would not discuss this matter at all, I am convinced that the roles women play at funerals have more to do with fertility and continuity than with the inheritance of property. The actions of daughters-in-law are particularly instructive. As surname exogamy (and, hence, lineage exogamy) is strictly enforced in the New Territories region, these women are all 'outsiders' (*wai lai jen*, lit. = 'those who come from outside'). Outsider women, even aged wives, are never completely trusted in Chinese lineages (see

J. Watson, 1975*a*). Nonetheless, these women are the primary reproducers of the lineage. The ambiguous position of the Cantonese woman is demonstrated by her dual role as daughter and daughter-in-law. She plays a key part in the absorption of pollution at the funerals of her natal parents as well as her husband's parents. As a daughter-in-law she carries a green cloth tucked into her mourning belt throughout the entire proceedings. All daughters-in-law who are still of childbearing age carry identical green cloths. These ritual items are thoroughly purified by waving them through the fire during the cessation of mourning ceremony. The green cloths reappear, sometimes years later, as centre pieces in the back-strap harnesses that Cantonese village women use to carry their infants. The straps of the harnesses are fashioned from the red cloth banners which 'lead' the spirits from the village to the grave. Copper coins[7] employed in the funeral ritual are often used to decorate the harnesses.

By some mysterious transformation that villagers do not even attempt to explain, it appears that the passive aspect of death pollution is essential for the biological reproduction of the agnatic line. Green is the Chinese colour representing spring, growth and fertility. In the construction of the infant harness green combines with red, the colour of life, vitality, and blood. The passive pollution of death, it will be recalled, is associated with the decay of flesh. By exposing themselves to this aspect of pollution daughters-in-law may, in fact, be taking on the fertility of the deceased, embodied in the flesh. The green cloth distinguishes those women who attend the ritual in their capacity as biological reproducers. Married-out daughters do not wear such cloths; to do so would be a confusion of agnatic continuity. It is significant that the green cloth is worn over the abdomen in such a manner that is covers the female reproductive organs. According to my informants, green is an auspicious colour but – unlike red – it absorbs death pollution. Infants later born of these women are not, in any conscious way, thought to be duplicates of the deceased reborn in a new flesh. There is, however, a clear and conscious set of beliefs that point to the continuity between living and dead – especially among males. The ancestral cult is built on these beliefs. Given the logic of the patrilineal ideology and the inherent suspicion of outsiders it is altogether appropriate that daughters-in-law should be expected to expose themselves to the pollution of death as a means of reproducing the lineage. The fact that these women are not themselves members of that lineage, or any other for that matter (R. Watson, 1981), only underlines the ambiguous position of women in Cantonese society.

Daughters and the prestation of pigs

Daughters are another matter. When married women return to their natal villages to participate in their parents' funerals they do not, of course, wear any trace of green on their mourning garb. (The only exceptions might be daughters who remain in their fathers' homes and marry uxorilocally, but no cases of uxorilocal marriage exist in either San Tin or Ha Tsuen.) Daughters attend primarily because they are, after all, offspring of the deceased. According to villagers 'it is natural that they should be here to show respect for their parents'.

There is, however, an important distinction drawn between married and unmarried daughters. Unmarried daughters do *not* rub their hair on the coffin or play a very prominent role in the proceedings. Their actions, in fact, closely parallel those of the deceased's younger sons. No explanation was offered for this obvious distinction except to say that 'it is too dangerous' for unmarried daughters to be near the coffin. Again, in the absence of informant testimony it is difficult to pursue this point except to note the obvious connection between death pollution and fertility. It may be 'too dangerous' for unmarried daughters to expose themselves to the full power of death pollution precisely because they are not yet ready for childbearing. Age is not the critical factor. In fact, at several funerals the women (daughters-in-law) who rubbed their hair on the coffin were younger than the deceased's own unmarried daughters – in all cases the latter stayed well away from the corpse and the coffin.

Married daughters perform one ritual act that sets them apart from the other women mourners. They bring a (raw) pig's head and tail to the funeral of each parent. This offering – head and tail – is presented at many ritual occasions and it symbolises, in the words of my informants, 'a good beginning and a good end'. At funerals the auspicious connotations relate to the life of the deceased, a good ending in this case implying that the spirit will be transformed into a benevolent ancestor. The pig's head and tail are placed on the 'spirit table' (*shen t'ai*) immediately in front of the coffin and are not removed until the proceedings are over. All offerings placed on this table are, according to the priests, for the benefit of the deceased's spirit. On the evening of burial the mourners assemble in the deceased's home where they consume the head and tail in a specially prepared meal. Only direct descendants of the deceased, and daughters-in-law, may eat the sacrificial pig – this excludes the husband or wives of the deceased should they survive. In one sense the meal is a communion with the dead. It is believed, for instance, that the spirit has already consumed

James L. Watson

the 'essence' (*cheng ch'i*) of the offering and, by eating the residue, the living are somehow assisting the spirit. The meal must be totally consumed; every scrap of pig's meat must disappear before the mourners can leave (it would be a 'bad ending' not to finish everything). The symbolic implications of this meal are not lost on the more sophisticated participants. Just as the pig's flesh is consumed, so too must the ancestor's own flesh disappear in order to attain a 'good ending'.

It is highly significant that *raw* pigs are used for the funeral prestation. A complex code – hingeing on whether the pigs are raw, roasted, or boiled – underlies the offerings made in the Cantonese ancestral cult. This topic will be explored in detail elsewhere. Suffice it to note here that raw offerings are neutral and do not convey contamination. Had the pig's head and tail been *roasted*, as is the case for offerings made at weddings and at certain lineage ceremonies (see below), the meat would have absorbed the 'killing airs' of death. No one, not even the chief mourner would dare eat such a meal. As soon as a raw offering is cooked, however, it is susceptible to contamination and could be affected by the residual pollution that permeates the home of the deceased. This, according to my informants, is the reason why the post-funeral meal is not shared by those outside the immediate circle of mourners.

In order to understand the funeral prestation one must look, first, at the position of daughters in the Chinese kinship system and, second, at the rules of pig sacrifice in Cantonese society. Daughters, although highly valued and loved by their parents, are raised only to be sent out in marriage. They become, as we have seen, outsiders responsible for the reproduction of other lineages. Parents refer to their unmarried daughters affectionately as 'my excess baggage' (i.e. someone to be raised but not kept in the family, unlike a son). When asking about the daughter of a friend it is considered polite to refer to her as 'your precious gold' (*ch'ien chin*, lit. = 'thousand gold'), a reference to her value not only as a filial child but also as a potential bride. At marriage, daughters are transformed into wives through the exchange of marriage payments, the largest being an impressive brideprice. Daughters are essential for the creation of affinal ties that extend beyond their father's own lineage.

Looked at from one perspective the prestation of a pig's head and tail could be construed as the repayment owed to the deceased by affines. The debt, in this case, is for providing women who became daughters-in-law. If one analyses the ritual repertoire associated with the prestation of pigs in Cantonese society the relation between wife givers and wife takers becomes evident. Pigs are always presented by supplicants, usually in payment of a debt. In most cases, the object of a pig prestation is a god or direct lineal ancestor. The funeral offering is thus special for it is made to the spirit of a person who is not yet a god (see Wolf, 1974) and is outside the debtor's own lineage (i.e. neither god nor ancestor). It would appear that, by sending a pig's head and tail, the wife takers are acknowledging their ritual inferiority *vis-à-vis* the wife giver (i.e. the deceased). This is not entirely correct, however, because at an earlier stage in the cycle of prestations the relationship between affines was reversed. As part of the marriage exchange the wife givers always send a (roast) pig's head and tail to the wife takers. This exchange parallels the system of indirect dowry characteristic of Cantonese peasants: the pig involved is, in fact, provided by the wife takers who end up receiving the head and tail – just as they pay a brideprice which is spent largely on dowry. The appearance of a pig's head and tail at the funeral (often many years later) thereby strikes a balance between givers and takers. The prestation pays off the last debt owed to the deceased by affines. One might argue that the pig's head and tail among other things symbolise a 'good beginning and a good end' to the relationship between affines. When this final debt is paid, all ties to affines are terminated and the deceased becomes totally dependent on male descendants (or patrilineal heirs) for sustenance in the afterlife. Affinity ends at death.

It should be emphasised that only *one* pig's head and tail are presented irrespective of the number of married daughters involved. In contrast to the rules that dictate the ritual behaviour of male mourners, therefore, no distinctions are drawn among daughters. They all pay an equal share of the cost of the offering and they all perform the same acts (unmarried daughters, of course, are not involved). Male affines rarely attend funerals in San Tin or Ha Tsuen and, should they appear, they do not bring pigs. For reasons too complex to outline here, affinal ties among Cantonese peasants are normally kept alive by women, not men (see R. Watson, 1981). Given the structure of affinal relations, therefore, it is logical that women, in this case daughters of the deceased, should be employed as the agents for this final prestation. It would be altogether too humiliating for a male affine to present a pig's head and tail in person.

The collective nature of the funeral offering deserves further consideration. Daughters rarely marry into the same lineage and their husbands (or fathers-in-law) may even be enemies. The fact that only one pig's head and tail are used is thus an important key to the ritual: it is not particular sets of affines who are represented by the offering but the *idea* of affinity itself. The emic view of pig prestations fits this interpretation. When daughters make an offering at the funerals of their parents, villagers take it as a public statement that the deceased has had a full and complete life, which includes balanced relationships with affines. Daughters thus play a key role in determining whether a person has had 'a good beginning and a good end'. This is one reason why Cantonese villagers feel it is so important to have children of both sexes. As one elderly woman put it to me 'you can't leave this life properly without a daughter to bring the pig's head and tail'.

Conclusions

I would like to conclude on two general points, one concerning the role of women and the other the nature of death pollution in China. First, women: if the interpretations of the mortuary ritual presented above are accepted as adequate, the role of women at funerals highlights the ultimate androcentrism of traditional Cantonese society. Women are responsible not only for the continuity of the agnatic line but also for striking a proper balance between affines. Men subject themselves to death pollution *only* when they are required to do so, usually as inheritors of the deceased's domestic property. Women, on the other hand, are expected to take on pollution irrespective of any material obligations owed to the deceased.

The ritual actions of a Cantonese married woman reflect her dual role as daughter and daughter-in-law. In one role, that of daughter-in-law, her exposure to the corpse is ultimately related to biological reproduction and fertility as embodied in the flesh of the deceased. In her other role as daughter, she takes on a portion of the pollution of death as a representative of her husband's family – the deceased's affines. In both cases she exposes herself to pollution for the benefit of others, primarily men.

In Bloch's terms, therefore, Cantonese women are indeed 'left holding the corpse' (see chapter 8) but their ritual subordination does not end here. They do not even survive, as individual entities, beyond the first three or four generations after death. *Women do not become ancestors* (at least in the context of the larger lineages). Their personal names never appear in lineage records and, unless they marry, their existence is not even noted in written genealogies. Women are not commemorated by individual tablets in ancestral halls and they disappear from the domestic altar after three or four generations. The nameless and, hence, ancestorless qualities of the Cantonese woman are highlighted by the fact that she only appears in these formal contexts (genealogies, tablets, etc.) under the surname of her father – an outsider (on names see R. Watson, n.d.) Furthermore, in the Cantonese conception a woman's bones are thought to be the products of an alien lineage, deriving (like her name) from her father. This is why it is inconceivable, from my informants' point of view, to expect benefits from a tomb that contains only the bones of a woman.

Women, it should be noted, are subjected to the same double burial procedures as men and their bone urns are entombed along with their husbands, but they do not become the object of ancestral rites. There is a puzzle here: why should women's bones, as the products of another lineage, be preserved at all? According to (male) elders, women – as mothers – deserve to be treated with respect for helping to create the line of descent. The exhumation and preservation of women's bones does not, however, imply that they are involved in the transmission of 'wind and water' to the living. As in life, women in the tomb exist as nebulous appendages of their husbands; they have no identity of their own and their personal names are forgotten. The male ancestor's bone urn is buried in the centre of the tomb (where the geomantic forces are concentrated) while his wives' urns are placed on either side. Male and female bones are never mixed. In this sense, therefore, the exogamous Cantonese are very different from the endogamous Merina; the latter make no distinctions between predecessors' bones in their collective tombs (Bloch, 1971).

The people of San Tin and Ha Tsuen maintain that human flesh, in the absence of life, represents a particularly dangerous combination of *yin* (female) forces. Bones, when charged with auspicious 'wind and water' are primarily *yang* – the male element (on similar dichotomies in other societies see Lévi-Strauss, 1969:373–5; Huntington and Metcalf, 1979:100ff). Women, as demonstrated above, deal exclusively with the *yin* remains of the corpse (i.e. the rotting flesh), thereby performing an essential service for their husbands' lineages. Men avoid the corpse whenever possible but commune freely and enthusiastically with the *yang* remains. The ancestral rites are performed by men for men, in the total absence of women.

The realm of the ancestors is thus pure (flesh-free) and exclusively male (*yang*). In order to maintain this pure realm, however, males must reproduce themselves through the flesh of women they take from alien lineages. After death a prospective ancestor must be cleansed of every particle of flesh he inherits from his mother. Women, as the very embodiment of *yin*, are transient beings. They do not survive beyond the living memory (which itself is dependent on the flesh) of their immediate descendants. Men, on the other hand, not only gain a kind

James L. Watson

of immortality for themselves but they also attain continuity with their ancestors – both at the expense of women.

The second issue that concerns me in this concluding section is the general problem of pollution: what exactly *is* death pollution? Chinese mortuary customs are, by their nature, so complex and contradictory that it may never be possible to arrive at a satisfactory answer. In the present essay I have found it useful to distinguish between two aspects of death pollution: active, as represented by the release of the spirit upon death, and passive which derives from the rotting flesh. Does the notion of active pollution among the Cantonese correspond to the release of sin, as Parry (1980) indicates is the case in Hindu society? This seems unlikely because sin, as such, is not a highly developed concept in traditional Chinese culture (see Eberhard, 1967). I would suggest that the active aspect of Cantonese death pollution is more directly related to the release of a disembodied spirit which, by definition, is 'out of place' and thereby dangerous. A spirit that no longer inhabits a living body and has not yet been settled in some way is disrupting the natural order of the cosmos.[8] This condition is described by many informants as *luan*, a Chinese term which means 'chaos' or 'disorder'. *Luan* is a central theme in the Confucian classics that deal with social relations and political affairs; the spectre of disorder is often cited as a reason for maintaining the status quo.

The spirit of the deceased must be controlled like any other entity in the cosmos. In the view of my informants a disembodied spirit loses its strength, or 'essence' (*cheng ch'i*) over time. It is most active, and unpredictable, during the first seven days after death and then gradually settles. There is thus a shift from terrible, awe-inspiring power during the early phase of mortuary ritual to total dependence on the part of the spirit by the time the final entombment takes place, years after death. The seven aversion points[9] in the ritual are a recognition of the power of the active spirit. Fear of the corpse and respect for the spirit are taught at a very early age (men usually speak in terms of respect while women admit to a deep fear, *p'a*, of the deceased). Children learn from their parents and grandparents to dread the appearance of a coffin or anything associated with death (see also Anderson, 1970:181ff).

Fear of the corpse is, however, confined to the initial phase of mortuary ritual. It corresponds, I would argue, to the settling of the spirit and the concurrent disintegration of the flesh. The spirit continues to be powerful and unpredictable as long as the flesh exists; its 'essence' weakens as the flesh gradually disappears. The fear and dread evident at Cantonese funerals contrasts sharply with the

180

matter-of-fact, instrumental attitudes exhibited by descendants later in the mortuary sequence. The bones, once they are free of flesh, are treated in a cool, calm manner as they are manipulated for worldly benefits. As noted above, in order to be effective, the bones must be cleaned of every minute scrap of flesh. The people of San Tin and Ha Tsuen usually employ exhumation specialists to undertake this final chore.[10] These men, who rank somewhat higher in status than corpse handlers, polish the bones and arrange them in ceramic pots (*chin t'a*, 'golden pagodas') for final reburial. Once the bones have been so treated they become, in the words of my informants, 'neutralised' or 'digested' (*hsiao hua*) and ready to transmit geomantic influences to the living.

The transmission of 'wind and water' (*feng shui*) is accomplished through a pig sacrifice ritual held annually at the grave of the ancestor. The good influences of the environment flow through the bones into a series of roasted pigs which are displayed in front of the tomb. These pigs are then carried back to the village where they are divided among the living (male) descendants. Note that *roasted* pigs are used in this particular ritual and not *raw* pigs as at the funeral. Roasted offerings, it will be recalled, absorb essences while raw offerings are unaffected. Note also that *flesh*, in this case pig's meat, is essential to tap the beneficence offered by the ancestor's bones. The bits of sacrificial pig meat, once exposed to the bones, are thought to be influenced in some way by the ancestor. The offerings must not come into contact with any other spiritual essence or contaminating substance, and they are consumed in the privacy of descendants' homes.

In order to be effective, therefore, the bones must be free of the ancestor's *own* flesh but they cannot function without activating the flesh of sacrificial animals. The bones can safely transmit geomantic influences because they are neutral and no longer carry the passive pollution of the human corpse. It would be considered the most revolting of sacrileges to eat bits of roast pork which have been exposed to the decaying flesh of a predecessor.

Passive pollution is the most revealing aspect of Chinese funerary ritual. It is, in my informants' conception, the immediate consequence of disorder, namely uncontrolled death. The proper products of death are bones, not rotting flesh. It is not death as such that is objectionable but, rather, disorderly decay. Like the disembodied spirit, the lifeless corpse is out of place; it is an offence to the proper order of the cosmos. Living males and settled ancestors are, equally, members of the lineage. They maintain relationships of exchange and share in property (ancestral estates). But a newly-dead corpse, in the flesh, is not

James L. Watson

yet a proper ancestor and, if not settled, may cease to be a member of the lineage. The unbroken line of descent can be recognised only when a reciprocal relationship develops between living and dead – and this, of course, depends on establishing the ancestor in his final, flesh-free tomb.

The decomposing flesh of a human is the ultimate form of disorder (*luan*). The people of San Tin and Ha Tsuen believe that it interferes with the smooth transition from a proper state of life to a proper state of death. The object of funerary ritual is, in their view, to pass safely through the initial, polluting phase of decomposition to the point where the bones can be manipulated. What is interesting about the passive pollution of death in Cantonese society is that is has to be managed. It cannot just be left to pollute the cosmos, either in the world of the living or in the realm of the ancestors. Death pollution has to be taken on, or incorporated, into the flesh of the living. It is essential for biological reproduction. Ritual actions of women at funerals indicate that passive pollution is directly related to the release of the deceased's life 'essence' or fertility. This must be managed and transferred to the next generation.

The fact that death pollution has to be absorbed in some way by the living implies that the decomposition of a person's flesh releases the accumulated disorder caused by all the previous deaths to which that person, and his or her predecessors, have been exposed. The passive pollution of the flesh must be taken on by men who inherit the worldly goods of the deceased and by women who are responsible for reproducing the line of descent. Only in this way can the proper order of the cosmos be maintained.

NOTES

The field research upon which this essay is based was carried out in 1969–70 and 1977–8. I would like to thank the following institutions for their financial support: The School of Oriental and African Studies (University of London), the Social Science Research Council (UK), the Joint Committee on Contemporary China (American SSRC), and the Foreign Area Fellowship Program (USA). I am indebted to Maurice Bloch, Lionel Caplan, Mark Hobart, Jonathan Parry, Andrew Strathern, Judith Strauch, Rubie Watson, and to other members of the University of London's Intercollegiate Anthropology Seminar for their comments on this paper.

1 In one case a founding ancestor of the Teng lineage migrated to the Hong Kong region from central China in the fourteenth century. He brought with him the bone urns of his grandparents and greatgrandparents which he 'planted' in auspicious locations. Descendants believe this action is largely

responsible for the economic success of their lineage (see R. Watson, 1982:757).

2 A 'proper' funeral follows the ritual sequence outlined in this paper. It assists the spirit to pass through hell but does not ensure elevation to ancestral status (this depends on economic factors). Slaves (*hsi min*) were buried 'improperly', without coffins or elaborate ritual (J. Watson, 1980:317), as were vagabonds and strangers. There is always a danger that improperly buried spirits might return as wandering ghosts and, hence, many lineages sponsor large-scale expiation rituals every ten years which are, in effect, collective funerals (this, at least, is how most villagers perceive the rituals).

3 This raises the intriguing point that the spirit of the deceased is adversely affected by the decay of its own earthly remains.

4 Households with newborn are affected by pollution of another kind. Among Cantonese, birth pollution is referred to as *tu* ('poison') and its effects are categorised along with illnesses that involve incubation, purging, or eruption – such as smallpox and measles (Topley, 1974:234). In the villages under study the term *sat hei* ('killing airs') is never used in the context of birth. The pollution of death is of a different order and is much more dangerous than birth pollution. Villagers in Taiwan also make a clear distinction between the two types of pollution (Ahern, 1975:195ff).

5 Older women sometimes make a practice of assisting their neighbours during funerals and may even help bathe the corpse (particularly if the professional corpse handlers are delayed). It is notable that such women are always well beyond childbearing age and are – invariably – widows. The same women are also responsible for making certain that the specialists, including the priest, perform their tasks properly. As a consequence, older women are usually the community's experts on funerary ritual. Men, by contrast, often know very little about this domain of ritual and concentrate on later phases of the mortuary sequence. Women who take on this role are treated with great respect – even awe – by other villagers. In one sense, therefore, women may gain status by controlled contact with death while men can only lose. According to a local priest, a man's male essence (*yang*) is thought to be depleted every time he touches a corpse while women, as the embodiment of *yin*, are not so affected.

6 The relationship between hair and pollution is, of course, the subject of much discussion in anthropological circles (see for example Leach, 1958; Hallpike, 1969; Hershman, 1974). The Chinese data are particularly interesting on this matter. Ideally Cantonese women leave their hair unwashed for 100 days after birth (Topley, 1974:237; on birth pollution see note 4 above). Raw pigs used during the funeral must have their bristles removed prior to the ritual – otherwise the prestation would absorb death pollution. There is also an obvious connection between animal hair and danger. In San Tin, for instance, domestic cats are physically restrained (tied to doors) until the coffin leaves the village. This custom is no doubt related to the symbolic equation between cats and tigers. Some domestic cats are thought to have inherited the magical hair of tigers and, should such an animal leap over the coffin, it is feared that the corpse would be transformed into a terrible monster (see De Groot, 1892:I:43–4).

7 Henry Dore, in his encyclopaedic survey of Chinese mortuary customs,

James L. Watson

notes (1914:I:47–8) that in some circles a copper coin is placed in the mouth of the corpse. The eldest son then keeps this coin and wears it around his neck (on a red string). Dore offers no explanation. In San Tin and Ha Tsuen coins are thought to absorb and distribute the pollution of death.

8 After death, Chinese Buddhist monks are sometimes preserved from decay and kept on display, as evidence of their spiritual power (see for example Stevens, 1976). Although the flesh remains on these corpses they are not polluting in the usual sense because the spirit is thought to inhabit the remains (cf. Pina-Cabral, 1980). Buddhist mummies do not, therefore, disrupt the proper order of the cosmos. These 'flesh bodies', as they are called, cannot become ancestors because their bones are unusable and they are devoid of kin (men who become monks are normally expelled from their lineages of birth).

9 The seven aversion points are: 1) the moment of death, 2) moving the corpse from house to coffin, 3) fixing the coffin lid, 4) lifting the coffin onto the carrying frame, 5) lowering the coffin into the grave, 6) burning a red lantern at the grave after interment, and 7) transferring the temporary tablet from the domestic altar to a paper sedan chair, seven days after burial. Points 1 and 6 are not discussed in this paper. The red lantern leads the spirit to the grave; its destruction by fire is said to deprive the spirit of a means of returning to the village.

10 In Taiwan this task is usually performed by the descendants themselves (Thompson, 1981). Ahern (1973:204ff) describes this process in her study of Taiwanese mortuary rites and notes that the flesh must decay naturally. As one of her informants put it: 'cutting off the flesh would be just like killing the ancestor' (Ahern, 1973:205). Ahern argues that the flesh represents the ancestors' control over the living, manifested in the bequeathal of property (cf. Goody, 1962), whereas the retention of bones symbolises the residual authority of the ancestors (Ahern, 1973:209).

Chinese terms

Chinese terms are in Mandarin, standard Wade–Giles romanisation, except for sat hei and Nahm Mou Lo which are in colloquial Cantonese, Yale romanisation. The numbers in the following glossary correspond to those in *Mathews' Chinese–English Dictionary*, 1963, Harvard University Press: an tsang 26, 6702; cheng ch'i 362, 554; ch'eng chi 386, 452; ch'ien chin 906, 1057; chin t'a 1057, 5978; ch'uan hung 1442, 2383; feng shui 1890, 5922; hsiao hua 2607a, 2211; hsi min 2467, 4508; lao jen hui 3833, 3097, 2345; luan 4220; mai shui 1890, 5922; man yüeh 4326, 7696; Nahm Mou Lo 4620, 7180, 3833+radical 9; p'a 4856; pai shih 4975, 5787; sat hei (sha ch'i) 5615, 554; shen hua 5716, 2215; shen t'ai 5716, 6016; shu pai hsiung ti 5881, 4977, 2807, 6201; t'ou ch'i 6489, 579; tsu wu 6815, 7212; tu 6509; t'u ti 6532, 6198; wai lai jen 7001, 3768, 3097; yang 7265; yin 7444.

REFERENCES

Ahern, Emily M. 1973. *The cult of the dead in a Chinese village*. Stanford: Stanford University Press.

184

1975. 'The power and pollution of Chinese women', in *Women in Chinese society*. eds M. Wolf & R. Witke. pp.193–214. Stanford: Stanford University Press.

Anderson, Eugene N., Jr. 1970. *The floating world of Castle Peak Bay*. Anthropological Studies 4. Washington: American Anthropological Association.

Blake, C. Fred 1978. 'Death and abuse in marriage laments: the curse of Chinese brides', *Asian Folklore Studies*, **37**, 13–33.

Bloch, Maurice 1971. *Placing the dead: tombs, ancestral villages, and kinship organization in Madagascar*. London: Seminar Press.

Chen Ta 1939. *Emigrant communities in South China*. Shanghai: Kelly & Walsh.

Das, Veena 1977. *Structure and cognition: aspects of Hindu caste and ritual*. Delhi: Oxford University Press.

De Groot, J.J.M. 1892–1910. *The religious system of China*. 6 vols. Leiden: Brill.

Doolittle, Justus 1865. *Social life of the Chinese*. London: Sampson Low & Sons.

Dore, Henry 1914. *Researches into Chinese superstitions. vol. 1*. Shanghai: T'usewei Printing Press.

Dumont, Louis & Pocock, David 1959. 'Pure and impure', *Contributions to Indian Sociology*, **3**, 9–39.

Eberhard, Wolfram 1967. *Guilt and sin in Traditional China*. Berkeley: University of California Press.

Freedman, Maurice 1966. *Chinese lineage and society: Fukien and Kwangtung*. London: Athlone.

1969. 'Geomancy', *Proceedings of the Royal Anthropological Institute for 1968*, pp.5–15.

Gallin, Bernard 1966. *Hsin Hsing, Taiwan: a Chinese village in change*. Berkeley: University of California Press.

Goody, Jack 1962. *Death, property and the ancestors: a study of the mortuary customs of the LoDagaa of West Africa*. Cambridge: Cambridge University Press.

Goody, Jack & Tambiah, S.J. 1973. *Bridewealth and dowry*. Cambridge: Cambridge University Press.

Granet, Marcel 1973. 'Right and left in China', in *Right and left; essays on dual symbolic classification*. ed. R. Needham. pp.43–58. Chicago: University of Chicago Press.

Hallpike, C.R. 1969. 'Social hair', *Man*, **4**, 254–64.

Hershman, P. 1974. 'Hair, sex, and dirt', *Man*, **9**, 274–98.

Hertz, R. 1960. *Death and the right hand*. (trans. R. & C. Needham) Chicago: Free Press.

Huntington, Richard & Metcalf, Peter 1979. *Celebrations of death: the anthropology of mortuary ritual*. Cambridge: Cambridge University Press.

Leach, Edmund R. 1958. 'Magical hair', *Journal of the Royal Anthropological Institute*, **77**, 147–64.

Lévi-Strauss, Claude. 1969. *The elementary structures of kinship*. (trans. and ed. R. Needham) Boston: Beacon Press.

Needham, Rodney 1967. 'Percussion and transition', *Man*, **2**, 606–14.

Nelson, Howard 1969. 'The Chinese descent system and the occupancy level of village houses', *Journal of the Hong Kong Branch of the Royal Asiatic Society*, **9**, 113–23.

James L. Watson

Parry, Jonathan 1980. 'Ghosts, greed and sin: the occupational identity of the Benares funeral priests', *Man*, **15**, 88–111.
  1981. 'Death and cosmogony in Kashi', *Contributions to Indian Sociology*, 15:337–65.
Pasternak, Burton 1972. *Kinship and community in two Chinese villages*. Stanford: Stanford University Press.
  1973. 'Chinese tale-telling tombs', *Ethnology*, **12**, 259–73.
Pina-Cabral, João de 1980. 'Cults of death in Northwestern Portugal', *Journal of the Anthropological Society of Oxford*, **11**, 1–14.
Potter, Jack M. 1970. 'Wind, water, bones and souls: the religious world of the Cantonese peasant', *Journal of Oriental Studies* (Hong Kong), **8**, 139–53.
Stevens, Keith 1976. 'Chinese preserved monks', *Journal of the Hong Kong Branch of the Royal Asiatic Society*, **16**, 292–7.
Thompson, Stuart 1981. 'Field report on Ch'ing Han Village, Yun Lin Hsian, Taiwan', School of Oriental and African Studies (London), Department of Anthropology.
Topley, Marjorie 1952. 'Chinese rites for the repose of the soul, with special reference to Cantonese custom', *Journal of the Malayan Branch of the Royal Asiatic Society*, **25**, 149–60.
  1974. 'Cosmic antagonisms: a mother–child syndrome', in *Religion and ritual in Chinese society*. ed. A.P. Wolf. pp.233–49. Stanford: Stanford University Press.
Watson, James L. 1975a. 'Agnates and outsiders: adoption in a Chinese lineage', *Man*, **10**, 293–306.
  1975b. *Emigration and the Chinese lineage*. Berkeley: University of California Press.
  1977. 'Hereditary tenancy and corporate landlordism in traditional China', *Modern Asian Studies*, **11**, 161–82.
  1980. 'Transactions in people: the Chinese market in slaves, servants, and heirs', in *Asian and African systems of slavery*. ed. J.L. Watson. pp.223–50. Oxford: Basil Blackwell.
Watson, Rubie S. 1981. 'Class differences and affinal relations in south China', *Man*, **16**, 593–615.
  1982. 'The creation of a Chinese lineage: the Teng of Ha Tsuen, 1669–1751', *Modern Asian Studies*, **16**, 69–100.
  n.d. 'Milk names, marriage names, and nicknames: the person in Chinese society', paper presented at the Intercollegiate Anthropology Seminar, University of London, June 1981.
Wilson. B.D. 1961. 'Chinese burial customs in Hong Kong', *Journal of the Hong Kong Branch of the Royal Asiatic Society*, **1**, 115–23.
Wolf, Arthur P. 1970. 'Chinese kinship and mourning dress', in *Family and kinship in Chinese society*. ed. Maurice Freedman. pp. 189–207. Stanford: Stanford University Press.
  1974. 'Gods, ghosts, and ancestors', in *Religion and ritual in Chinese society*, ed. A.P. Wolf. pp.131–82. Stanford: Stanford University Press.
Wong Yo-yui. 1939. 'The filial mourning head-dress society in the villages of Chang-I, Shantung', in *Agrarian China*. (comp. by Institute of Pacific Relations) pp.204–7. London: George Allen & Unwin.

7 Social dimensions of death in four African hunting and gathering societies

JAMES WOODBURN

In this chapter I discuss beliefs and practices associated with death in four African hunting and gathering societies – the Hadza of Northern Tanzania, the net-hunting Mbuti Pygmies of Zaire, the Baka Pygmies of Cameroon and the !Kung Bushmen of Botswana and Namibia.[1] Hunters and gatherers form a tiny minority of sub-Saharan African societies and their total population is substantially less than 1% of the whole sub-Saharan population. All of these societies are hunting and gathering in a world of agriculturalists and pastoralists and although each has enough space to be able to retreat for periods of the year from contact with these neighbouring farmers, all are profoundly aware of the similarities and differences between their custom and the custom of their neighbours and of the fact that certain of their customary practices – not least those associated with death – are regarded by their neighbours as curious, even abhorrent. Two of these societies, the two Pygmy ones, are forest-dwelling and two, the Hadza and the !Kung Bushmen, live on the dry open savanna, the !Kung habitat being rather drier than that of the Hadza. These societies are not merely geographically widely separated but are culturally and linguistically quite distinct: if they share any historical connections they are certainly extremely distant ones.

I should start by stressing that members of all these societies are constantly dealing in death, in the death of the game animals they hunt. Death is for them a way of life. Killing animals is a real focus for the daily life of men: every man has constantly at hand the weapons needed for killing, and most men frequently do kill at least small animals. For pastoralists, or for agricultural peoples who keep domestic animals, killing animals is a special activity which stands in marked contrast to the daily care and attention devoted to them; but for hunters and gatherers death is the routine focus for their interaction with animals, and dead animals are a focus for their interaction with each other. Animal death and the procedures leading up to and following it appear, at least in some of these societies, to be ideologically

James Woodburn

elaborated although the ethnographic evidence remains fragmentary. There are a whole series of prohibitions and injunctions associated with hunting (especially the hunting of large game), with the dismemberment of the carcass and the sharing of the meat. Fulfilment of these injunctions and prohibitions brings good fortune and breach of them is believed to have the most serious consequences.

Among the Hadza these injunctions and prohibitions centre on the relationship between the sexes. The whole process of hunting big game (male productivity) is symbolically linked with the whole process of female reproduction (female productivity). Activities in one process are mystically dangerous for activities in the other. A man whose wife is menstruating cannot hunt big game because the poison of his arrows is believed to lose its efficacy. If his wife is pregnant he cannot walk on the tracks of a wounded game animal because this will cause it to recover from its wounds. Reciprocally, if a man whose wife is pregnant laughs at or mocks the dead but not yet dismembered carcass of a game animal, the unborn baby will be born with defects which resemble the characteristics of the dead animal (Woodburn, 1974). For the Hadza at least, while animal death is ideologically elaborated and intimately linked with human reproduction and fertility, human death is not. It is treated in a simpler and more straightforward way and the tenuous links that can be established with human fertility are neither developed nor established as part of a wider system of beliefs. At the end of this paper I discuss some possible reasons for this lack of elaboration.

Hadza death beliefs and practices

The Hadza as individuals fear death and display their fear but human death, unlike animal death, is hedged around with remarkably few procedures, prescriptions, taboos or rituals. Beliefs, too, are rather simple, unstructured and straightforward. There is no real corpus of doctrine or of formal practice.

I should say at once that in some respects my knowledge is limited. During the entire period of nearly four years that I have spent living among the Hadza no one, apart from one child who died two days after birth, ever died in a nomadic camp in which I was at the time living, nor was I ever informed of a death at a nearby camp in time to be able to witness the procedures followed.[2] My knowledge of what actually happens when somebody dies is based not on observation but on a mixture of accounts, often somewhat contradictory, about what does and does not happen. The Hadza are not keen to talk about what happens at death partly because it is an obviously distasteful subject but, even more important, because they know it is a subject about which outsiders are sensitive and which can lead to the Hadza being treated with scorn and labelled as primitive.

Immediate procedures when a death occurs

When a Hadza dies in camp with other Hadza present, as most do, he or she will usually be buried soon after death. The burial is likely to be near the surface and the Hadza may take advantage of an old anteater hole or other site which will ease the labour of digging. They usually have no metal digging tools and, although the wooden digging sticks used for digging roots are adequate for the task, it would be quite a long process to dig a deep grave. Men do the digging, except in the case of an infant who would usually be buried by the women. But in the case of the infant (a two-day-old) who died in a camp in which I was living, the child was buried unceremoniously by a man at dawn in the hut of its parents: he told me that he did the burying because the women were afraid. Usually most of the men in the camp, especially the older men, will dig the grave and inter the corpse but there is absolutely no rule specifying or excluding particular kin or affines. Those who are not helping will stay some distance away. Most Hadza are buried lying on the left side facing a high mountain, Mt Hanang (called Diroda in Hadza) but some lie on the right side facing Mt Oldeani (called Sandzako in Hadza)[3] and a few others face the sunset. Some informants suggested that this last direction is used for people who are not pure Hadza but are of part-Isanzu descent.

The surface of the grave may sometimes be trodden down after water has been poured on it, in order to make a hard surface so that disturbance by hyaenas is less likely. The treading of the grave, when it is carried out, seems usually to be done by the men and to be treated as an entirely straightforward, practical matter. The women bring containers of water which are poured out over the surface of the grave. The men mix the water with the clay soil and tread it down to form a flat surface which will soon dry hard in the sun.[4] Sometimes people are not buried at all but the framework and grass thatch of a temporary hut are simply pulled down on top of the corpse. Even when someone is buried, a hut may be pulled down or the grave covered with branches, again with the idea of deterring disturbance by hyaenas and other scavengers.

At the time of death and during the burial the women cry and wail. People may come from neighbouring camps to join in the lamentation. The men say that it is the women who feel the death most and it is they who do most of the crying and wailing. Only the closest male

James Woodburn

associates of the dead person join in and then only in a restrained fashion.

The Hadza link death and burial with their major religious celebration, the sacred *epeme* dance performed in pitch darkness each month. It usually continues for two or three nights in succession in every camp in which there are enough participants and enough head-dresses, leg-bells and dance-rattles. At this celebration the initiated men dance, one by one, a solemn dance while the women sing an accompaniment of special *epeme* songs. The dance stresses kinship and joint parentage and seeks to reconcile the opposed interests of men and women which are so manifest in many other contexts. Failure to hold the dance is believed to be dangerous. Performing the dance is believed to maintain and promote general wellbeing, above all good health and successful hunting.

The dancer is supposed to be not himself but *epeme*, a powerful sacred being important in other contexts as well. The women and children must not see who it is who is putting on the *epeme* costume or who is dancing in it. Usually each dancer dances two or three times, often interspersed with dances by others. Every time he dances as *epeme*, he is dancing for someone. In the first dance, he usually dances for himself. In subsequent dances he dances for someone else, most commonly one of his children – either an actual child or one of a number of objects owned by his wife which stands for a child, such as a specially decorated gourd in which fat is kept (*a'untenakwete*) or a decorated stone or clay 'doll' (*han!anakwete*). He may also dance for other close kin or affines. Unmarried men often dance for their brothers. Or men may dance for other people's surrogate children. I remember, for example, one man dancing for the decorated gourd 'son' of his mother-in-law, that is for a surrogate brother-in-law. After every individual dance a dialogue is held between the *epeme* dancer, who uses a special ritual whistling language used only in this context, and the women who call out their affectionate greetings using the kinship term applicable to the 'person' for whom that particular dance has been held.

The dead are linked to *epeme* in two ways. Firstly, objects associated with *epeme* are often laid out on the grave – in particular, the ostrich-plume dance head-dress (*kembako*) which, more than any other object, stands for *epeme*. Objects which represent surrogate children in the *epeme* context – especially the decorated fat gourd (*a'untenakwete*) – will be broken on the grave. I was told that it is particularly appropriate if the dead person's mother's *a'untenakwete* – which can be said to represent the dead person's sibling or even the dead person

190

himself – is broken on the grave. But, of course, often the mother will be dead or living elsewhere and then some other *a'untenakwete*, probably one belonging to the man's wife and standing for his own child, will be broken. I was also told that to break a gourd on the grave is especially relevant if the dead person is a parent. Everybody abandons the camp the same day or the next day and just before departure the ostrich-plume head-dress and any other unbroken *epeme* objects will be collected up from the grave.

Epeme is also relevant in a second way. At some point the dead person will be commemorated by being danced for at an *epeme* dance. Some people told me that this might happen quite soon, within days or weeks of the death, but the more usual opinion was that it would normally happen months later, after several *epeme* dances had been held since the person's death. The evidence suggests that the dead person is simply being commemorated and not that he or she (or any sort of spiritual counterpart) is believed to be present at the commemoration. The Hadza told me that the person is simply being remembered with affection and that the purpose of the commemoration is not to placate the ghost or to ward off any danger, because the dead are not dangerous for the living. Apparently the *epeme* dance at which the dead person is mentioned is not seen as special or as significantly different from other *epeme* dances. The living will be danced for in the usual way at the same dance.

The Hadza say that it is good if an ordinary *epeme* dance can be held within a few days or weeks of a person's death but that this is not in any sense obligatory. The point is simply that the *epeme* dance is believed to establish and maintain a state of wellbeing and good order and that a short while after a death is seen as a suitable time for seeking such a state of affairs. However, since the dance is, in the ordinary way, held every month and can only be held at the time of the month when there is a period of total darkness without moonlight, there is not much room for manoeuvre over the timing of the dance which may well not be affected by the death.

All these procedures may sound rather elaborate in the light of what I stated earlier; I am frankly not sure how much of this really is usually done. It certainly is not likely to be done in the case of an infant. In the case of the two-day-old child who died, there was no wailing, no breaking of gourds and the parents slept a night on top of the grave before building a new hut the next day. Camp was not abandoned. For anyone other than an infant, camp would, I think, always be abandoned. Interestingly, the mother of the infant wore large quantities of decorative beads for some days after the death: I was told that these were nothing to do with the death but were to mark the fact that she had given birth to her first-born child. It seemed curious to me that she continued to wear these festive beads even after the child had died. I do not want to make too much of one instance, which may or may not be typical, but it is, I think, consistent with Hadza values that mourning did not affect matters.

These procedures are for people who die in camp when other Hadza are present. But a minority of Hadza die elsewhere and for them, there are no such procedures. Seriously ill people are sometimes abandoned when Hadza move camp in the course of their frequent nomadic moves which take place on average every two or three weeks. People who cannot walk are not likely to be carried for long. They will be left with food and water and with their possessions either to die on their own or, if they are lucky, to recover enough to be able to make their own way somehow to the next camp. Others may meet with fatal accidents on their own in the bush of which the most frequent are snake-bite (a real risk especially when hunting hyrax) or falling from a tree when seeking honey (pegs are driven into the tree and these sometimes break). In cases like these there is no question of mortuary ritual in the absence of a body, which will have been taken by hyaenas and other scavengers soon after death.

Grave sites are not marked and are not visited. There is some fear of pollution from handling a corpse and one of the rare occasions on which people wash their hands is after participating in a burial. I once came upon some human bones protruding from an eroded bush pathway and the Hadza kept well clear and would not let me remove them (I thought, and still think, that there was a remote possibility that they might be the fossil bones of some early hominid!). Death pollution beliefs however, are, unlike menstrual pollution beliefs, not elaborated or made much of.

As far as I have been able to establish the Hadza have no concept of good and bad deaths. Suicide is regarded as very strange but is not marked out as specially abhorrent or dangerous. Many of the younger people know of no cases of suicide but the older people talk of a woman who became depressed after the death of her husband and eventually took poison. People assured me that no special procedures would be used after death by suicide.

Cause of death

Unlike their pastoral and agricultural neighbours, the Hadza are not concerned to establish the cause of death. They believe in witchcraft and sorcery but they do not believe that other Hadza (except those who are very closely associated with members of neighbouring pastoral and agricultural tribes) are capable of practising them.[5] They do believe that some people die as a result of the witchcraft and sorcery of outsiders, but most people are held to die 'naturally' or as a result of either deliberately or inadvertently eating sacred *epeme* meat outside the proper context. The cause is, however, for the Hadza a matter for speculation but not for decision or action.

Consequences of death (after the immediate procedures)

Human death is believed to have a brief damaging effect on hunting success. During a visit to the Hadza in 1981, after this chapter was first written, I discovered to my surprise that the Hadza have a remarkably similar belief to the Baka (see below, p.196) about one consequence of human death. Two men who had seen an impala from a look-out point where they and I were sitting, ran to hunt it. Both shot at it from close range, both missed and the animal got away. They speculated that a woman whom they knew to be very ill at another camp had died. A death which is not yet known to people is believed to deflect men's hunting arrows so that they miss the game animals at which they are directed. Once known, the death has no effect on hunting but while it remains unknown it can affect hunting for several days.[6]

There is no clear belief in an afterlife. The Hadza sometimes talk of a dead person having gone to Diroda or jumped over Sandzako, the mountains facing which they are buried, but these expressions may be no more than euphemisms for saying that someone has died. Other Hadza are quite explicit that when one dies, one rots and that is that.

After the burial, there is no ban on the use of the dead person's name or on the use of his possessions, no special clothing or decoration or other formal mourning procedures for the survivors. The head hair of the widow or widower, of the children who live in the same hut and of other very close associates may be shaved off, especially, I was once told, if the dead person used to search their hair for head lice, but this is not obligatory. The widow or widower may remarry without formality as soon as she or he chooses to do so.

The property of the dead man or woman is shared out widely among those who happen to be present at the time. As the Hadza say, 'Everybody cries, everybody gets something'.

Relations with outsiders

The much more elaborate death beliefs and practices of their pastoral and agricultural neighbours impinge on the Hadza in various ways:

James Woodburn

a) There has for many years been some general pressure from outsiders on the Hadza to behave more respectably – e.g. to bury their dead 'properly' and to give proper attention to the need for divination after a death. The Hadza are cautious when discussing these topics with outsiders for fear of making themselves seem foolish or 'primitive'.

b) A very small minority of Hadza with close connections with the Isanzu, a neighbouring Bantu-speaking people, believe themselves to be possessed, following a severe illness, by *alungube* (the Hadza form of the Isanzu word for 'spirits of the dead'). Men possessed by *alungube* occasionally run naked into the night and are believed to be guided by these spirits to select particular pieces of plant or wood or stone as medicines. Sometimes they may believe themselves to be possessed by specific named ancestors who have to be placated by gifts of honey mixed with baobab pulp at an *epeme* dance. I was told that all this is a comparatively recent importation and that in the past Hadza were not possessed by *alungube*.

c) Another small minority of Hadza assist members of a different neighbouring tribe, the Iraqw, by removing their death pollution. An Iraqw widower or widow has to have sexual relations with and have his or her head shaved by a person of another tribe to get rid of death pollution. Some Hadza men are willing to perform this service. Hadza women are said to be more reluctant. The Hadza men involved are uneasy that they might become ill as a result but appear not to be seriously concerned. I have, however, heard this cited as the cause of the eventual death of one old man whom I knew well and who had earlier readily admitted to me his occasional participation. In payment, the Hadza are given clothing which belonged to the dead person and often money as well. The Iraqw do not appear to mind if the Hadza help themselves to the many possessions of the dead man which are abandoned as polluted.

Baka Pygmy death beliefs and practices

For the information on the Baka I am greatly indebted to Robert Dodd, who has recently returned from carrying out field research among them and who has compiled some notes for me to use. I shall give this material largely in his own words but shortened and slightly altered to fit the requirements of this paper.

A life after death?

The Baka view of death, and of life after death, has been complicated in recent years by external influences which have partly been assimilated by these hunters and gatherers. Such influences have come from the Bantu villagers, who have taught the Baka to inter their dead, and from the missionaries, who have preached about a life after death and who have misinterpreted a Baka category – *molili* – in order to demonstrate that the Baka have a traditional concept of *soul*. When someone dies, his *molili* – the light in his eye or his shadow, perhaps best translated as his 'vitality' or his 'essence' – leaves his body. Traditionally oriented Baka say it just goes away and for ever. *Soul* is not an appropriate translation.

At one level, death in a Baka camp is a personal tragedy. Close kin, especially women, weep and wail and word is sent to out-living kin and affines who will visit the camp of the deceased. If they arrive in time, they will view the corpse and offer comfort and solace to the bereaved widow, widower or parents. At another level, however, the occurrence of a death in a camp has little importance. For, in spite of the missionaries' insistence, and of the stated beliefs of some Baka in certain areas that the soul of a dead person goes to reside in the 'Big Village' (*ngbé gba*), the Baka do not traditionally believe in a life after death; nor do they have any concept of ancestors, ghosts or human spirits. When a person dies, there is an immediate period of personal grief and a sense of great loss, and then life continues as before.

Traditionally there is no search for the cause of death among the Baka. They believe that they can be killed by the witchcraft of the villagers (one Baka told me that *all* death was caused by witchcraft) but there are no accusations and no other action is taken.

Until the recent past, the only mortuary act performed by the Baka was the pulling down of the hut over a corpse; the local group then quit the camp and never returned to that particular part of the forest. When questioned on what happened to an individual when he is dead, conservative or 'traditional' Baka, like those with whom most of the research was done, reported that, 'When you're dead, you're dead and that's the end of you'.

Death in a village camp

Today, if a death occurs in a village camp, that is, in a camp built alongside a village of Bantu cultivators, the body is interred at the edge of the encampment near to the forest and this usually takes place on the same day as the death. The burial arrangements are supervised by the Bantu villagers, one of whom sometimes actually helps the Baka, generally the deceased's sons-in-law, to dig the grave. In spite of the difficult and often antagonistic relationships that exists between the Baka and the Bantu, a funeral is one of the few occasions when the villagers show genuine concern and sympathy for the hunter–gatherers. At one funeral I attended, a villager supervised the digging of the grave and when he was satisfied that the hole was deep enough and everything was 'decent', withdrew to his own house saying that he would leave these poor people to bury their brother and to continue their grief in private.

This man had earlier explained that the Baka until recently had left their dead to be eaten by wild animals in the forest. This he found a disturbing and primitive way of dealing with death and it was for this reason, he said, that he and his fellow villagers always helped the Baka to do things 'properly'. 'They need to have a good, deep grave', he explained, 'so that the corpse can rot in peace'.

Following the villager practice, a body is interred with no coffin. It is laid on an open bamboo bier and completely covered with a cloth. A piece of woven

195

roof thatch is placed at an angle to cover the face in the grave to prevent direct contact with the soil.

After the villager had gone, the Baka lowered the body into the hole and close kin were led weeping to the graveside for one last look. The soil was then replaced to a level of about 18 inches. Two men then jumped down into the grave and stamped down the soil, probably breaking the protective thatch in the process. The villager would, no doubt, have been upset to see this apparently disrespectful treatment of a corpse. Such treatment, though, seems consistent with the Baka's traditional view that when you're dead, that's the end of you; a dead body is nothing and has to be disposed of quickly and life has to continue. The grave was then filled up to ground level. Baka village camp graves are unmarked and after a few weeks the forest grows over the area and soon people forget exactly where they are.

Death in a forest camp

I was never present when a death occurred in the forest but the Baka assured me that even there they dug 'very deep' graves for their dead. Exactly how they managed to do this without having spades or other digging tools was not explained and I suspect they were giving me the answer they thought I wanted to have.

Death in a camp has an adverse effect on hunting for a while. Poor hunting is caused by 'bad luck' and this can be brought on by a wide range of events – a death, a marital row the night before a hunt, the harbouring of bad feelings towards another person, pregnancy, and so on.

If a group of Baka is hunting in the forest and someone of their clan dies in their camp, then the hunt will be unsuccessful. 'Bad luck' will remain with the hunters for as long as the identity of the deceased is not known to them. If they return to the camp and receive the information that so-and-so has died, then the effects of the 'bad luck' will be immediately removed and hunting will be good. There is no ritual here but luck is self-regulating once the knowledge has been obtained. If the dead person is of a *different* clan from the hunters even though he is resident in the same camp, hunting luck will *not* be adversely affected.

An interesting comparison with these beliefs can be made when one looks at the reverse of the death process – pregnancy. The Baka believe that a pregnant woman can be a cause of 'bad luck'. When hunting is bad, the hunters ask around to see if a woman is pregnant and she has not announced the fact to the camp. For, when the announcement has been made, hunting will be good once more. The announcement of a new pregnancy is made by the husband and wife in a joint ritual.

Mbuti Pygmy death beliefs and practices

In this section I draw my material directly from Colin Turnbull's impressive ethnography on the net-hunting Mbuti in his book *Wayward Servants* (Turnbull, 1965). His data on mortuary practices in this and other sources is considerably richer than my short account would suggest. I start by describing what happens when death occurs in forest camps and deal later with the rather more elaborate procedures which are adopted when the Mbuti are living in or near a village of one of the neighbouring agricultural peoples.

For the Mbuti a death or an impending death involves the person's nuclear family and a few other people who have been particularly close to the dead or dying person during their lives. The whole band community is drawn into the procedures for bringing the activities of the community back to normal after the death (Turnbull, 1965:142, 262–3). Personal grief is freely expressed by close relatives, 'by young and old together and may at times become apparently uncontrollable. In the same way that the Mbuti are given to excessive bursts of laughter, often developing into near hysteria, so when they weep they do so with what amounts almost to violence.' A close relative arriving at the camp of a dying person 'will burst into tears and wailing loudly will enter the hut and throw himself on the ground at the bedside of the dying person'. Sometimes the relative may seek to express grief by wounding himself or herself though other people would intervene if there were any danger of serious injury.

The rest of the adults in the band will sit around outside their huts, watching the wailers run in and out of the sick person's hut, and while they themselves are likely to be serious and upset they are also likely to make jokes at any excess of zeal on the part of any mourner. Young children continue playing as though nothing were going on; youths sit morosely by themselves, or wander off into the forest on foraging expeditions. (Turnbull, 1965:142–3)

As soon as the dying person dies there is a renewed burst of wailing and then the camp begins to quieten down. Burial takes place the same day, if enough daylight is left, or as early as possible the following day (p.143). In the forest members of the nuclear family of the person who has died are responsible for disposing of the body. They may be aided by others but help is not generally needed (pp.144, 262). They 'scratch a shallow hole in the floor of the hut and bury the deceased person there, pulling the hut down over the grave'. 'During burial . . . there is likely to be a final outburst of wailing from the relatives, particularly female, and some may try to throw themselves into the grave' (p.143). Both at this time and more generally, women are more active at wailing than men (Putnam, 1950:341; Turnbull, 1965:146).

As soon as the burial is over the camp is abandoned, 'nothing being left to indicate the grave site, nothing being buried with the body except maybe a few very personal belongings such as bark cloth, bracelet or necklace. All other property is divided before the camp is abandoned' (Turnbull, 1965:143). When a very small child dies, people do not always abandon the camp or even the hut in which the child lived (pp.143–4).

After the burial and the move to a new site, the band elders seek to restore 'quiet' and to bring the situation back to normal as soon as possible. 'Only the genuine sobbing of the immediate family is permitted and this may be heard coming from their huts at any time of the day or night, never in public' (p.143). 'While personal grief is recognised and allowed, it is still resented and every effort is made to minimise it by those not so directly concerned' (p.144).

The death of an adult is likely to be followed by a major festival, the *molimo*, within a few days after arrival at the new camp (p.263). A child's death is not usually marked in this way (p.144). The *molimo* is not held after every adult death, not even after the death of every great hunter. It is particularly appropriate that it should be held if at the time of the death there is a combination of poor hunting, ill humour and general sickness. A death 'at a time of good hunting and general contentment may pass unmarked except by the usual summary burial and change of camp, all expression of grief being confined to the immediate family concerned' (p.261). The stated purpose of the *molimo* is to 'awaken' and 'rejoice' the forest which must have been sleeping when matters were going badly (p.262). It is not concerned at all with the fate of the individual who has died (p.145).

The *molimo* . . . calls for vigorous hunting during the daytime, and equally vigorous singing and dancing at night. It involves the entire band except the children and through its very emphasis on life it reinforces band solidarity. Through the sheer pleasure found in *molimo* activities personal grief is lessened, and through the symbolic nature of some of the songs and dances the despair that death could otherwise awaken is averted. Death is acknowledged, in the *molimo* fire dance, as inevitable and as being unconnected with any unnatural force. (p.144)

'The sexual act is represented in the *molimo* dances . . . and there is very evidently expressed concern with the regeneration of life' (p.280). The *molimo* affirms 'a belief in life and in the continuity of life, and in the continuity of the band despite the fact of death' (p.145).

Death is treated by the Mbuti as entirely natural (p.146). Outsider diviners in the villages may name an Mbuti as responsible for causing another Mbuti's death by witchcraft but when this happens 'there was not the slightest thought that the "witch" actually had anything to do with the death' (p.75). There is no publicly expressed concern for or fear of the dead; on the contrary, the pressure is to forget them as soon as possible. People are reluctant to mention them by name, or even to talk about them, but there is no rigid prohibition (Turnbull, 1965:184, footnote). They avoid speculating about whether there is a life after death and 'their response to villagers, missionaries or any who claim a knowledge of [the] afterlife is to say, "How do you know? Have you died and been there?"' (p.247).

For much of the time the Mbuti are living in or near the villages of neighbouring agricultural peoples who have very different death beliefs and practices. If a death occurs there, the Mbuti leave the funeral arrangements in the hands of the villagers (p.143). The Mbuti attitude to villager death ritual, as to other villager rituals, is to accept the externals but none of the implications (p.74). In the village the entire band is mobilised to take part in the burial procession. The eldest son acts as chief mourner. Youths who are not necessarily connected with the deceased in any way other than by band membership dig the grave under villager supervision. They don't take this very seriously and may laugh and joke even when the body is being lowered into the grave (p.143). The villagers may insist on burying the body with cloths and sleeping mats but the Mbuti are particularly reluctant to allow anything of value to be buried with a body and they do their best to retrieve such valuables at the last moment without being seen (p.145).

Similarly head-shaving seems to be of little significance to the Mbuti, though they frequently do shave when a member of the band dies. But, unlike the villagers, they are not consistent in the practice, and they leave their hair lying around where it has fallen to the ground, whereas the villagers are scrupulously careful to collect their own hair cuttings, which they take off into the forest or to a stream, and secretly hide (p.145).

Villagers expect the Mbuti to continue mourning over a period and in a village camp sporadic formal wailing breaks out about three times each day for about two or three days. The villagers like the wailing to be loud and enthusiastic but Mbuti elders object strongly, especially if the mourner is not a close relative, and seek to restore 'quiet' to the camp as soon as possible (p.143).

!Kung Bushman death beliefs and practices

In spite of having four excellent books on the !Kung, all published within the past five years (Lee & DeVore, 1976; Marshall, 1976; Howell, 1979; Lee, 1979), I have found data on only some of the aspects of the subject with which we are concerned here.

Unlike the other societies so far discussed the !Kung have clearly formulated beliefs about an afterlife and there is quite a lot of data on this which I will come to shortly. I have found very little information about the immediate procedures when death occurs. Marshall states : 'Burial ... has no effect upon the status in the afterlife – whether a person is buried properly bound in a deep round grave or scratched into a shallow trench or not buried at all and eaten by beasts' (Marshall, 1962:243). In a brief list of rites in Marshall's book (1976:178–9) there is no mention of death ritual, so the assumption must be that the procedures at death are relatively mundane and simple.

It is clear from Yellen (1976) that a camp site is abandoned after a death: 'A single dry-season camp may be occupied for as long as six months. It would be abandoned for a site nearby, generally less than 100 m away, *only if a death occurs in the camp* or if it becomes extremely rank or bug ridden' (Yellen, 1976:65, my emphasis). The evidence suggests that inheritance is unimportant:

There is not much property to inherit. Land and the resources of food and water are owned by the band, not privately by individuals. A considerable amount of an individual's personal property is destroyed at the time of his death. This is not done to provide implements for the spirits in the afterlife. The !Kung believe that the spirits of the dead have their own heavenly objects and need nothing from earth. It is done because no member of the family wants to use the common objects of the dead, which too vividly remind them of their loss. Only the more rare and important possessions are kept, such as assegais and fine ornaments. These are inherited by the eldest son. Failing a son, the spouse or a daughter or sibling or, failing these, some other close relative who was present would take the things. Whoever took them would be expected to give some of them to other relatives. (Marshall, 1965:260)

Every !Kung is believed to have within him a special substance called *n!ow* which is produced in the person by his or her mother's uterine fluid when it flows on the ground at the time of the person's birth. So do certain large game animals. The infant's *n!ow* affects the weather (positively or negatively) at the time of his birth. At death the weather is said to be affected in the same way by the *n!ow* (Marshall, 1957:236).

Marshall (1976:379) writes, 'The !Kung fear death, but no more acutely or consciously, I suppose, than does most of mankind'. They don't express their fear openly. It can be seen, Marshall suggests, both in their preoccupation with hunger and starvation even when food is not lacking and in their preoccupation with the protection of their health (of which more will be said in a moment).

Apart from suicide, no distinction is made between a good death and a bad death (Marshall, 1962:243). Marshall doesn't specify how suicides are treated.

Causes of death

Death is caused by the great god, ≠Gao!na, life giver and death giver, who sends good or evil according to his will or to his whim, and not according to man's deserts. He sends death via the lesser god, //Gauwa, and more particularly by means of his messengers, the undifferentiated spirits of the dead, the //gauwasi. When they are told to kill, they do so. 'When a person dies, //gauwasi come soon to take his spirit' (Marshall, 1962:242). Any of them may come – either ancestors of the dead person or non-related spirits. 'The !Kung fear them, pray to them to invoke their mercy or sympathy, exhort them in anger' (p.241). They also hurl sexual and other insults at them (Marshall, 1969:376). They have power to provide good or evil but people fear them and expect evil (p.350). They have some (but apparently not very much) independence of action (p.350). But 'they want nothing from men and there is no point in offering them things' (Marshall, 1962:243). 'The concept of having special relations with their own ancestors or of worshipping ancestors is lacking' (p.241).

The !Kung hold frequent medicine dances at night, the aim of which is to protect people from sickness and to ward off death brought by the //gauwasi (Marshall, 1969:439). Those who do the warding-off are trance dancers – the majority of the adult men. The trance dancers have the ability to see and to drive away the spirits of the dead (Lee, 1968). People must come to the dance. If the spirits of the dead see a person sitting alone at his own fire apart from the dancing group, they might kill him (Marshall, 1969:350). The medicine dance is held usually when the moon is full (p.356), after a successful hunt or when visitors arrive or are about to depart. Sometimes they hold it when there is sickness in camp though this is not a frequent reason.

When the curings fail and death occurs, the !Kung do not blame the trance dancers directly. They believe that his *n/um* (medicine) is weak or that it has stopped working altogether, and, in the last analysis, that the great god is determined to take the person and will not allow him to be cured. To this they must be resigned. (Marshall, 1969:379)

So death here is not a product of the victim's own action or of the actions of other !Kung. It comes from outside the social body. Lee cites (1968:52) an exceptional, isolated case, however, in which the belief in the power of spirits of the dead was transmuted into the equivalent of a witchcraft accusation. Two old men had been quarrelling over a period of years. One became ill and accused the other saying, 'He has spoken ill of me. His ancestors have overheard these words and now they come to bother me. Why can't he control his ancestors?' The accused man then had to come to the victim's bedside and to ask his offending ancestors to go away. In a quite different context a !Kung who had on his own initiative become a settled farmer was suspected by other !Kung, to whom he was not as generous as they would have wished, of having 'learned techniques of witchcraft from black medicine men' (Lee, 1976:413).

James Woodburn

Consequences of death

Much has already been said. Perhaps it should be mentioned that a !Kung avoids referring to dead people by name, regardless of whether or not he accorded them reserved behaviour in life. Avoiding their names shows respect for the dead but it also saves the speaker from danger. The dead man's spirit might overhear his name being uttered and show displeasure by sending sickness (Marshall, 1976:245).

There is no indication that I have found of any stress on mourning or any specification of a period during which a widow or widower may not remarry.

The implications of the data

Perhaps I should first make a very general comment about the nature of the data. Human death is relatively invisible in these societies in comparison with societies whose members live in much larger communities and at much higher population densities. This means that inevitably anthropologists will, at best, have only been able to observe a small number of instances and must rely heavily on informants' statements whose accuracy may be affected by the sensitivity of the topic. Caution in handling the data is necessary and I hope I have been sufficiently cautious.

My argument is that in these four instances, there are fundamental similarities in the form and in the meaning of the set of beliefs and actions connected with human death which require explanation. There are also differences and distinctions, in my view relatively minor, which require comment but which are largely beyond the scope of this paper. I shall say only a little here about these differences.

The similarities are these:
1) The actual procedures for treatment of and disposal of the body are relatively simple and mundane. They go beyond, but not very far beyond, the directly practical requirements for getting rid of a rotting corpse. The general rule that camp is rapidly abandoned after a death in all four instances is not to be seen as an indication of some strong formal belief in pollution (though there *are* pollution beliefs), or as arising from some moral obligation to the dead man or his spirit. Movement is, in all these societies, very easily accomplished and takes place quite casually for the most trivial of reasons: it is quite unlike the movement of people with substantial investment in dwellings. Movement to leave a corpse behind would be obviously practically desirable and could be expected to occur anyway for practical reasons in highly

nomadic hunting and gathering societies. In a society in which to move is almost as simple as to stay where you are, what would be surprising and, indicative of something more ideological, would be an explicit emphasis on staying put, on staying in one place.

Having said this, however, I do not wish to suggest that the 'practical' explanation is sufficient: in all of these societies there is an apparently explicit *rule* of moving camp after death. The Hadza say the site has become 'hot' and they talk about the pollution of death. The important point is that the rule does not make demands on people which go much beyond the practicalities of the situation.

Although I haven't found much evidence, there seems to be minimal emphasis on preparing the corpse – wrapping, annointing, binding, decorating, etc. Procedures for preparation and disposal of the corpse can be said to involve very little provision of time, labour or material goods by the mourners.

2) The various tasks and responsibilities connected with the burial or disposal of the corpse and with other procedures which follow death are apparently not in general allocated to specific kinsmen and affines. Allocation is informal except in the village context when Baka sons-in-law dig the grave and Mbuti eldest sons act as chief mourners. There is some division of labour by sex, with women expected to take a more active part in public lamentation and men expected to do most of the work of grave digging and grave filling.

3) There is no search for the cause of death. No divination or other standardised procedures are used for diagnosing why the person died. People repudiate the idea that death is caused by the supernatural actions of other members of their own society – that is by the witchcraft or sorcery of their fellow hunter-gatherers. It is seen as simply 'natural', or as a result of an unpredictable decision by God, or of the mysterious powers (poison, witchcraft, sorcery) of outsiders, or as a result of the victim's own greed or carelessness (e.g. in eating *epeme* meat). The cause is a matter for speculation not for action or decision. There is no attempt to reach an agreement on the cause.

4) There is no clearly defined distinction between a good and a bad death involving different procedures and different consequences for the dead man and for the mourners.

5) There may or may not be a belief in an afterlife.[7] If there is, the afterlife is unaffected by the individual's behaviour in this life, by the actions of the mourners at the time of the mortuary ritual or by subsequent offerings.

6) After the practicalities and immediate ceremony, if any, at death, ordinary life goes on. There may even be an immediate assertion of

normality as is expressed in the Mbuti *molimo* ceremony. There are minimal rules for mourners or other survivors. The site of death and the remains may be avoided but if they are not the danger does not seem to be very serious. The clothing and possessions of the dead person are buried with him or are quickly and rather casually distributed. There may be some restriction on uttering the name of the dead person, but there is no rule about it and no serious consequence flows from using the name (except perhaps in the !Kung case). There is no clear marking out of the widow or widower and no rule restricting the timing of remarriage or whom they may remarry (apart, that is, from the restrictions which apply equally to first marriages).

7) There are no chiefs, shamans or other specialists whose special task it is to administer or control death rituals.

8) Death procedures are only peripherally connected with ideas of fertility of human beings or of plants and animals or of the natural world more generally. Among the Hadza, objects (ritual children) which may be said to symbolise parenthood, and especially the reproductive capacity of mothers, are broken on the grave (see p.190 above). I have no Hadza explanation of why such objects are broken but there seems no reason to believe that the act does anything more than to state the obvious point that the dead person is finished both as child and as parent.

Among the Mbuti, after a death the natural and social world is regenerated through ritual including explicit sexual imagery. However this ritual is not obligatory and is held only when other matters are going badly – when hunting is unsuccessful, when people are ill-humoured and sick (see p.198 above). Among the Baka a pregnancy and a death (and among the Hadza only a death) briefly affect hunting success until they are publicly acknowledged (see p.193 and p.196 above): once acknowledged, disorder is converted into order and hunting is again effective. Among the !Kung an individual's birth and death, his beginning and his end, have a strictly transient effect on the weather (see p.200 above). All these are themes that might provide a starting-point for elaboration into a set of systematic beliefs about fertility and regeneration in death but the evidence does not, I think, support the idea that such a set of systematic beliefs has already developed in any of these four societies.

Conclusions

The material can be summed up by saying that beliefs and practices associated with death are in all four of these societies relatively simple and straightforward and would apparently be even simpler were it not for the desire to avoid humiliation by their pastoral and agricultural neighbours who find it difficult to accept the apparently casual practices of the hunter-gatherers. In sub-Saharan Africa, in general, beliefs and practices associated with death are rather variable but the set of similarities that I have outlined above do stand out as very unusual even in comparison with the Nuer, long famed for the simplicity of their death procedures (Evans-Pritchard, 1956:144–76). Other Africans do not (or did not) *all* practise ancestor worship though probably most do (or did); not all believe (or believed) that death is usually a consequence of witchcraft/sorcery by a member of their own tribe though almost certainly most do (or did); not all use elaborate burial ceremonies – some, like the Masai, apparently leave bodies out for the hyaenas – though probably most do bury and do use elaborate procedures either at burial or during later mortuary ceremonies. What I would be very surprised to find in any pastoral or agricultural African group is the particular combination of factors which I have described above.

Are these factors, then, a direct product of nomadic hunting and gathering? Clearly they are not, because in other parts of the world nomadic or semi-nomadic hunters and gatherers often have relatively elaborate mortuary beliefs and practices (see for example E.H. Man, 1932:73–9 and A.R. Radcliffe-Brown, 1948:106–14, 285–329 on the Andamanese; A.P. Elkin, 1956:295–320, W. Lloyd Warner, 1958: 412–50, M.J. Meggitt, 1962:317–30 and T.G.H. Strehlow, 1964:739–40 on the Australian Aborigines; J. Teit, 1900:327–36, 357–60 on the Thompson Indians of British Columbia). There are also many nomadic hunters and gatherers in other parts of the world with death beliefs and practices as simple as those of these four African societies.

In general terms it can be said that hunters and gatherers with relatively simple death beliefs and practices are those with what I have defined elsewhere as immediate-return rather than delayed-return economies, social organisation and values (Woodburn, 1978; 1979; 1980; and in press). Without going into detail here, an immediate-return system is one in which activity oriented directly to the present (rather than to the past or the future) is stressed, in which people use their labour to obtain food and other resources which are consumed on the day they are obtained or casually over the days that follow, in which there is a minimum of investment in long-lasting artefacts or in long-enduring debts, obligations or other binding commitments to specific kinsmen, affines, contractual partners or to members of bounded corporate groups, however these are recruited. The emphasis is on joint participation in and sharing with an *ad hoc* local community, undifferentiated except by age and sex, and more generally on *ad hoc* pragmatism rather than on planning or continuity.

The only thorough-going immediate-return systems are those of certain hunting and gathering societies, but an immediate-return style is found in some specific, restricted contexts in other societies. The vast majority of human societies – including many hunting and gathering societies – have delayed-return systems.

I think the points that emerge are really rather straightforward. The death beliefs and practices of these four societies are ones which stress personal, temporary grief and the temporary shared grief of the wider food-sharing community undifferentiated except by age and sex. There is no emphasis at all on dependence between specific kin or affines, nor on their moral responsibilities to each other. Questions of succession and inheritance (and of successors and heirs) scarcely arise since there is no office of household head (if by household head we mean someone with a measure of real control over assets and personnel) nor any other office of much significance, nor any property of much value, to be transmitted from one generation to the next. When someone dies, he is not *replaced* socially by someone else in the sense that he or she is in delayed-return systems.[8]

Within delayed-return systems elaborate mortuary ritual and formal mourning are most stressed when an office-holder, particularly an important office-holder, dies and least stressed when a small child who holds no office and no property dies. For such a child, mortuary ritual and mourning may be set aside altogether and the corpse disposed of in an entirely practical, non-ritualised manner (see for example Evans-Pritchard, 1956:156). It seems obvious that, other things being equal, where death involves major social readjustments and the risk of conflict and disorder, death beliefs and practices will be more elaborate and more ritualised than where such adjustments involve no reallocation of authority or of assets but are largely a matter of personal feelings. What is obvious within societies also applies between societies. In those immediate-return societies in which individuals are to a large extent self-provisioning, in which they do not depend on intergenerational transmission (either *inter vivos* or on the death of the person of senior generation) for access to crucial property or status, there is unlikely to be much ideological development of the fact that persons of senior generation beget those of junior generation and are both displaced and replaced by them.

In these systems the dead are not dispossessed in the interests of the living who derive no significant benefit from any death. And just as the living are not believed to have the capacity or power to damage others by witchcraft or by cursing them in these systems in which individuals are so self-dependent and so free from vulnerability to the malice or incompetence of their associates, so too they are not fearful of the capacity of the dead, whom they have not dispossessed, to damage them.[9] They have few formal obligations or commitments to the living and few, too, to the dead and accordingly few opportunities to wrong the living or the dead.

The fact that any strong expression of the idea of replacement would be out of place here means that an obvious part of the basis for the association between death and fertility is lacking. People need no successors to hold their offices, or heirs to manage their property, and the propagation of the next generation is not a matter of the same anxious concern that it so obviously is when heirs and successors are necessary. At the same time part of the force of the analogy between birth and death – the fact that one comes into the world and goes out of it without commitments and without property – is seriously weakened if one also has few commitments and little property during life.

More generally the idea of social continuity is not one which is stressed in immediate-return systems which are in so many respects strongly oriented to present activity. Economic activity is focused on immediate production and immediate consumption, and social activity in general is not burdened by substantial long-term concern, commitment or planning. Consistent with this, the focus in death beliefs and practices is largely on immediate practicalities – the disposal of the corpse, the expression of personal grief and the grief of the wider community – rather than in provision for social replacement, reproduction and long-term continuity.

Of these four societies, the one in which mutuality – the sense of mutual attachment, the obligation to participate and to share on an egalitarian basis – is most emphasised is !Kung society. And among the !Kung there are some significant long-term obligations in the system of *hxaro* exchanges (Wiessner, 1977). Interestingly, among the !Kung alone, the spirits of the dead – not specific ancestors but the undifferentiated spirits of the dead – are believed to constitute a serious danger, bringing illness to people and having to be kept constantly at bay by the trance dancers of the medicine dance. I suppose it could be argued that, just as the dead are more likely to be considered to be dangerous when death robs them of their riches and of their positions of power, so here where the dead have more to lose than in other immediate-return systems, they are not seen as neutral, irrelevant or even non-existent, but as dangerous. But there is an

James Woodburn

important difference: among the !Kung, just as among other immediate-return systems, the living have nothing to gain from a person's death. So the implied resentment of the dead has less to feed on.

More to the point, I do not think that the type of explanatory framework I have developed can explain differences of this sort adequately. I am not arguing for a tight one-to-one correlation between society and ideology, between the specific characteristics of immediate-return systems and the specific characteristics of death beliefs and practices. All I am suggesting is that an immediate-return system does not provide fertile ground for the ideological elaboration of death beliefs and practices in general, nor for a link between death and fertility in particular.

NOTES

1 I would like to thank Alan Barnard and Robert Dodd who provided me with helpfully detailed and thought-provoking comment on this paper which I would have liked to have used more effectively. I am additionally indebted to Robert Dodd for preparing ethnographic notes on the death beliefs and practices of the Baka Pygmies which have been of great value in compiling this paper.
2 This may appear surprising but really it is not: the crude death rate from the one African hunting and gathering society on which we have good demographic data, the !Kung Bushmen, is sixteen per thousand years lived (Howell, 1976:141). Probably the figure is not very different for the Hadza. If all deaths occurred in camp, then in a camp of average size one would expect on average one death about every two years.
3 Both mountains are well outside the area in which the Hadza live but both are visible on a clear day from many parts of the area.
4 I was given one account of how women may tread the grave using the dance step usually reserved for men and used only at the sacred monthly *epeme* dance (see below) and of how they may sing certain sacred *epeme* songs, one of which is as follows: 'He (using an honorific term applied to a dead man) has gone to sleep in the dust; he has got his back dirty through lying in the dust'. During my most recent visit to the Hadza in 1981, men whom I consulted denied that women could ever tread the grave using the *epeme* step or that they would sing *epeme* songs in this context.
5 I here describe the 'traditional' situation as it existed during the main period of my field research in the late 1950s. In the government settlement schemes of today, witchcraft fears are rampant and people fear both non-Hadza and now, increasingly, other Hadza, who are said to have learnt witchcraft from non-Hadza and to be using it against their fellow Hadza. This change in belief has happened during a period in which there has been a great deal of genuine ill-health and many deaths in the settlements and in which it has become more difficult for Hadza to move away from those with whom they

208

are in conflict without sacrificing vital interests. Moreover in settlement conditions non-Hadza diviners ready to explain misfortune in terms of witchcraft are far more accessible and influential than they were in the past.

6 Unlike the situation among the Baka (see p.196), an unrevealed Hadza pregnancy has no effect on Hadza hunting additional to or separate from the effect of pregnancy in general on hunting (see p.188).

7 Apparently there are very few societies in the world in which people don't believe in an afterlife. At any rate Frazer in his vast compendium *The belief in immortality and the worship of the dead* states: 'The question whether our conscious personality survives after death has been answered by almost all races of men in the affirmative. On this point sceptical or agnostic peoples are nearly, if not wholly, unknown.' (Frazer, 1968:133).

8 A dead wife or a dead husband may later be replaced by a new spouse. But in these societies marriage involves fewer property commitments and other obligations to the spouse or to affines than in most delayed-return systems. The emphasis is on the personal relationship between spouses rather than on alliance between two bodies of kinsmen. In this situation, social constraints on remarriage after the death of a spouse (or after divorce) are minimal. The widower or widow is not polluted and is not restrained, except by personal feelings, from remarrying whenever he or she chooses.

9 What I say here may not apply to the !Kung. I discuss this issue at the end of this paper.

REFERENCES

Elkin, A.P. 1956. *The Australian Aborigines: how to understand them.* Sydney: Angus & Robertson.

Evans-Pritchard, E.E. 1956. *Nuer religion.* Oxford: Clarendon Press.

Frazer, J.G. 1968. (First published, 1913–24) *The belief in immortality and the worship of the dead.* 3 Volumes. London: Dawsons of Pall Mall.

Howell, N. 1976. 'The population of the Dobe area !Kung', in *Kalahari hunter–gatherers: studies of the !Kung San and their neighbors.* ed. R.B. Lee & I. DeVore. Harvard University Press.

1979. *Demography of the Dobe !Kung.* New York: Academic Press.

Lee, R.B. 1968. 'The sociology of !Kung Bushman trance performances', in *Trance and possession states.* ed. R. Prince. Montreal: Bucke Memorial Society.

1976. '!Kung spacial organization: an ecological and historical perspective', in *Kalahari hunter–gatherers: studies of the !Kung San and their neighbors.* ed. R.B. Lee & I. DeVore. Harvard University Press.

1979. *The !Kung San: men, women and work in a foraging society.* Cambridge: Cambridge University Press.

Lee, R.B. & DeVore, I. (eds) 1976. *Kalahari hunter–gatherers: studies of the !Kung San and their neighbors.* Harvard University Press.

Man, E.H. 1932. (First published, 1885) *On the aboriginal inhabitants of the Andaman Islands.* London: Royal Anthropological Institute.

Marshall, L. 1957. 'N!ow', *Africa*, **27**(3), 232–40.

1962. '!Kung Bushman religious beliefs', *Africa*, **32**(3), 221–52.

209

James Woodburn

1965. 'The !Kung Bushmen of the Kalahari Desert', in *Peoples of Africa*. ed. J.L. Gibbs, Jr. New York: Holt, Rinehart & Winston.

1969. 'The medicine dance of the !Kung Bushmen'. *Africa*, **39**, 347–81.

1976. *The !Kung of Nyae Nyae*. Harvard University Press.

Meggitt, M.J. 1962. *Desert people: a study of the Walbiri Aborigines of Central Australia*. Sydney: Angus & Robertson.

Putnam, P. 1950. 'The Pygmies of the Ituri Forest', in *A reader in general anthropology*. ed. C.S. Coon. London: Jonathan Cape.

Radcliffe-Brown, A.R. 1948. *The Andaman Islanders*. Glencoe, Illinois: The Free Press.

Strehlow, T.G.H. 1964. 'Personal monototemism in a polytotemic community', in *Festschrift für Ad.E. Jensen*. ed. E. Haberland, M. Schuster & H. Straube. Munich: Renner.

Teit, J.A. 1900. 'The Thompson Indians'. *Memoirs of the American Museum of Natural History*, **2**.

Turnbull, C.M. 1965. *Wayward servants: the two worlds of the African Pygmies*. London: Eyre & Spottiswoode.

Warner, W. Lloyd 1958. *A black civilization: a study of an Australian tribe*. New York: Harper & Brothers.

Wiessner, P.W. 1977. 'Hxaro: a regional system of reciprocity for reducing risk among the !Kung San'. Unpublished Ph.D. Thesis, University of Michigan.

Woodburn, J.C. 1974. 'The interpretation of Hadza and other menstrual taboos'. Unpublished paper.

1978. 'Sex roles and the division of labour in hunting and gathering societies'. Unpublished paper delivered at the 1st International Conference on Hunting and Gathering Societies, Paris, June 1978.

1979. 'Minimal politics: the political organisation of the Hadza of North Tanzania', in *Politics in leadership: a comparative perspective*. eds W.A. Shack & P.S. Cohen. Oxford: Clarendon Press.

1980. 'Hunters and gatherers today and reconstruction of the past', in *Soviet and western anthropology*. ed. E. Gellner. London: Duckworth.

(in press) 'Egalitarian societies'. Malinowski memorial lecture, May 5th 1981.

Yellen, J.E. 1976. 'Settlement patterns of the !Kung: an archaeological perspective', in *Kalahari hunter–gatherers: studies of the !Kung San and their neighbors*. eds R.B. Lee & I. DeVore. Harvard University Press.

8 Death, women and power

MAURICE BLOCH

This chapter attempts to generalise about the different practices relating to death in different cultures and different societies, and in particular to suggest explanations for differences in funerary practices such as whether there are important or unimportant rituals, whether corpses are thought of as polluting or not and whether bodies are destroyed or preserved. Striking cross-cultural recurrences such as the association of mourning and women will also be examined. This, however, is done here in terms of questions raised by a re-examination of data on the Merina of Madagascar presented elsewhere (Bloch, 1971).

The Merina are a people who live in central Madagascar and who number over a million. They were traditionally divided into localised kin-groups which we may call demes. These were groups of people who traditionally lived in clearly-defined geographical areas focused on a few river valleys which had been turned into irrigated rice fields. For the Merina the association between the people of the deme and the land of the deme is, and should be, eternal. Indeed, the notion of ancestral land, that is land belonging to the deme, is totally merged with the notion of ancestors. The ancestors had lived and were buried in the ancestral land; the land, in the form of terraces, had been made by the ancestors. This merging is so complete that it is quite usual for Merina to say who their ancestors were by giving the name of a village. People are thought of as descendants of the land as much as they are thought of as descendants of their ancestors. The deme members are often referred to in the euphuistic metaphors of formal oratory as 'hairs growing out of the head' which is the ancestral land. Furthermore, the ancestors and the ancestral land are also merged with the living. This is because the living members of the deme should in their ideal moral representation be nothing else but continuators of the ancestors, the present incarnation of the continuing entity that is the deme (Bloch, 1974).

This of course is an idea which is only developed in highly formal contexts; but in these contexts the triple merging is expressed as an ideal which is to be striven for in spite of, and against, the divisive present and its alternative sources of identity and power. The ideal should be striven for because if it is achieved then the blessing of the ancestral land and of the ancestors will be passed on to the living, as a result of the identity of generations the power of the past will effortlessly fill the present and the living representations of the deme.

The notion of blessing is central to traditional Merina religion whether pre-Christian or Christian. The Malagasy word I translate as blessing is *tsodrano* and it means literally: 'the blowing on of water'. This phrase refers to the notion that the ancestor, God, or whoever does the blessing, is thought to transmit it by blowing water from his mouth.

What a blessing gives to the blessed can be summed up by the English word 'fertility' understood in a very wide sense. Fertility in this sense includes, as the Merina make explicit in the speeches which accompany blessing and which list in turn these different benefits, the gift of many children both male and female (seven of each), the gift of crops, the gift of wealth, and the gift of strength. It is the power of total enablement to total achievement. Without blessing, a person is impotent in all senses of the word.

The *tsodrano*, or blessing, should then be passed down from the ancestors and the ancestral land to the living. However, the very old and people in the social position of elders are as caretakers and transmitters of the fertility of the deme, the right intermediaries of blessing. Such people become this by literally blowing water, which has been associated with the ancestors and ancestral land either by invocation or physical contact, on to their descendants. In this way the blessing coming from the past is transmitted, and at the same time legitimates the position of the elders.

The power of blessing is intimately linked with another central aspect of Merina thought, the avoidance of dispersal and division of the deme. Since ideally the deme merges the ancestral land and the ancestors, the living as heirs of both must retain both in order to ensure the continuation of the deme. Dispersal of the assets of the deme, whether people or land, is the worst betrayal that living deme members can commit. This horror of dispersal manifests itself in three linked ways: the enjoinment of endogamy on the living, the stress on the regrouping of inherited land, and on the regrouping of the corpses of the dead.

Merina demes were ideally endogamous and the reason given for this endogamy was the regrouping of inherited land. Although Merina inheritance rules are quite complex and variable, in normal circumstances all children of a woman or a man inherit some land irrespective of their sex. The marrying of close kin is therefore seen as a device for avoiding the potential dispersal of rights to ancestral land to outsiders through the process of diverging inheritance. The Merina phrase for such endogamous marriages means literally 'inheritance not going away'.

This simultaneous regrouping of people and of ancestral land by endogamy is paralleled by the regrouping of the dead in the ancestral tombs of the deme. Tombs are for the Merina a central symbol. Merina tombs are massive megalithic structures half underground, half overground. In each ancestral area there are a large number of tombs but the fact that they are all in the same ancestral land means that the divisive aspect represented by this multiplicity is ignored in the general way tombs are thought of. All the tombs in ancestral areas are thought of as sharing the same elements and said to be 'related' or even 'one'. Each tomb can contain an almost unlimited number of corpses and so is a symbol of community. The presence of the tombs of a certain deme in an area is what makes this area the ancestral land of that deme. This is because the tombs contain the remains of the collective ancestors placed in the earth or land (*tany*). The tombs are therefore the medium of the merging of ancestors, deme and land. In the same way as the land must be regrouped, so the corpses of the dead must be regrouped in the tomb so that the common substance of the deme, whether land or corpses, is not scattered. This communal aspect of tombs is underlined by the fact that when a new tomb is built a number of corpses of deme members from other tombs must be brought in before an individual can be placed there. One can never be alone in a tomb.

Regrouping is the most sacred, most imperative duty of the living and it alone ensures the continuing strength of the blessing passed on within the deme, because the power of life in blessing depends on the non-dispersal of the land/ancestor substance of the deme.

Tombs, ancestral land, ancestors, indivision, blessing, are to the Merina so many aspects of the same thing: the good. However, in reality we find that the symbolical construction of the good actually depends on an equally constructed antithesis, the image of division.

The main element in this antithetical symbolic construction is one representation of women. Women for the Merina are not always symbolically associated with division. Since demes are in theory endogamous, women are not outsiders to the deme; as children and parents (*anaka, raiamandreny*, two terms which do not specify

213

Maurice Bloch

gender) they are as much the heirs of and the recipients of ancestral blessing as the men; like them, they should be buried in the tomb. There is, however, another representation of women which occurs in different contexts and focuses more on their role as wives and mothers. Among the Merina, individual lines of filiation are often represented as being in opposition to the undivided, undifferentiated descent of the deme as a whole. The stress on individuating divisive lines is often represented in Madagascar as characteristic of women as mothers, as opposed to fathers, who are represented as being more concerned with the common good. Similarly, as wives, women are often associated with division in that their tie to their husband leads to division within the sibling group of their partner. This view of women as dividers of the deme is expressed in ritual where the individual house stands for the domestic group isolated from, and in opposition to, the undivided deme. In such rituals the house is represented as women's territory, as the place of individual and individuating birth and death. By contrast in the male initiation ceremony, circumcision is represented as birth by the group represented by men, and the circumcised child is taken out of the house in a ritual sequence which is analogically linked to entry into that supreme symbol of unity and regrouping, the tomb. Women in their aspect as individuating mothers, houses and heat (the symbol of biological birth) are made to stand in opposition to the undifferentiated deme, the tomb, blessing and ancestral fertility, all associated with cold (Bloch, 1974). It is against this background that we can understand the funerary ceremonies of the Merina (Bloch, 1971:ch.5).

The first funerary ceremony is individual burial and takes place when somebody dies. The dead person is usually buried in a single grave somewhere on a hillside without any particular sepulchre and near the locality where the death took place, irrespective of whether this be part of the ancestral land of the dead or not. This is burial outside the tomb. Physical death and individual burial of this sort is marked by two central emotions. The first is sorrow – at death people weep and should be sad: visitors before and after the death come to weep with the bereaved. Indeed, the behaviour of the mourners is often dramatic in its intensity. It is quite clear that this socially-organised sorrow usually matches emotions which to those concerned appear as internal and uninstitutionally triggered. The Merina do not make the opposition which is common in European cultures between genuine individual feelings and artificial institutionalised expressions of feeling. For them the two are complementary.

For the Merina the outward manifestation of sorrow is mourning. Mourning consists in an attack on oneself. This takes a variety of forms ranging from expression on the part of the mourners of wanting to die, to attempts at mild self-mutilation. Mourning consists in voluntarily making oneself look unattractive. Women mourners do not plait their hair but leave it tousled, they wear old clothes, they sit on dung heaps to receive visits of condolence. Mourning is therefore self-punishment implying that the death is to a certain extent the mourner's fault for which a woman atones by these self-deprecating practices.

One aspect of these self-deprecating practices consists in almost revelling in the second element of individual funerals: pollution. The Merina continually stress their horror of decomposition. This is particularly linked to the idea of wetness. So long as the corpse is still wet and decomposition is therefore still taking place it is supremely polluting and any contact however indirect requires ritual cleaning. After a death the house in which the corpse has been has to be washed, as well as everything that is in it. Fires are put on thresholds of the houses of people returning from funerals so that the contamination they bring back does not re-enter. People returning from funerals should wash themselves thoroughly. Tools which have been used for digging the grave should be thrown away. The list of such examples is long but the message that death and decomposition pollute is unambiguous. One manifestation of the self-deprecation of mourning is a willing taking on of this pollution. For example, the close mourners are expected to throw themselves on to the corpse before burial as an extreme form of self devaluation.

The first point of all this we should examine is that both sorrow and pollution are, in Madagascar as in so many cultures, principally focused on women. It is women who should weep both individually and as a group. It is women who take on mourning for death. This they do – as we have seen – sitting on a pile of rubbish outside the home of the deceased, their hair undone, their clothes loose about them. It is they who receive the condolences of others and weep with the female visitors. It is women also who are associated with the pollution of death. It is they who must wash the corpse and then wash themselves and all the things in the house, and it is mainly they who ritually take on pollution by throwing themselves on the corpse. Individual burial is, therefore, a time of sadness, of pollution and of women.

The second funerary ritual of the Merina, the *famadihana*, involves exhumation of the totally decomposed and by now 'dry' corpse from its individual grave and placing it in the communal family tomb in the ancestral land of the deceased. This involves the careful recovery of the bones of the deceased and also equally important the powdered remains of the flesh which are suggestively called earth. Because the

215

Maurice Bloch

Merina often actually reside a long way away from their own ancestral land, and because they are buried immediately after their death in the locality where they have died this often involves a long journey in order to return the corpse to its own ancestral land. On such journeys the notion of joyous return is dominant and is often celebrated with music and dancing. As a whole the second burial contrasts in this way with individual burial and this contrast is continually stressed. The *famadihana* is a time of joy as opposed to sadness and above all it is a time of *tsodrano*, of blessing, of fertility, of children, of crops, of wealth, etc. It is a time of blessing because regrouping and returning the dead, and especially the entry of the corpse into the land ensures and demonstrates the canalisation, affirmation and victory of the un-divided deme. It is regrouping *par excellence*. All who participate in the *famadihana*, whether by taking part, or contributing towards the expense, therefore receive blessing and fertility.

Only a brief outline of this complex ritual can be given here. Whether the corpse has come from far or near, it usually spends one or several nights in the house of mourners near the tomb. There it is watched over by women. Once the actual day has come the central part of the *famadihana* begins with a short journey at midday, from the house where the exhumed body has been kept, to the tomb. The time is very important as the corpse should enter the tomb at the time of the maximum glory of the day, the time of strength and clarity. This notion is so important that clocks marking the Merina midday (3 o'clock) are often painted on the tomb. The body is carried to the tomb on the shoulders of women who are quite literally *driven* forward by the men. Going anywhere near the tomb without proper authority, and above all having any contact with dead bodies, is an extremely frightening thing for the Merina. The procession to the tomb emphasises this by the men's first *forcing* the women to shoulder their burden, then *forcing* the women to go, then *forcing* them to dance at pre-arranged stages on the journey. The atmosphere all along, and particularly at these halts, is inevitably extremely tense and there is no reason to doubt what people say: that the women at least, if not the men as well, are terrified by this contact with the dead and with the tomb. On arrival at the tomb, however, it is the men, not the women, who actually enter it and take out those bodies which are to be exhumed. Once these have been taken out of the tomb they are thrust on to the shoulders of women to accompany the new corpses which have been brought. Then the women, bearing the corpses, are once again driven round the tomb several times. In all these actions the men are continually encouraging and even coercing them in acts which are clearly distasteful.

216

The central part of the ceremony occurs when men, standing on top of the tomb, make long speeches asking for blessings, *tsodrano*, saying how happy the dead are at being regrouped and declaring who has presented the various shrouds in which the corpses will be wrapped before they are returned to the tomb. During this time the women sit with the corpses on their laps around the tomb. After the speech-making the women are made once again to dance with the corpses, but by then the atmosphere takes on a bacchanalian turn, the fear seems to vanish into somewhat hysterical joy. They start to throw corpses, which have by now been wrapped in many layers of new shrouds, up and down, very often crunching them up as the bones are very brittle and will ultimately disintegrate into the dust from the decayed flesh. Finally the corpses are replaced in the tomb by the men.

It seems to me that there are two questions which immediately arise in relation to this somewhat strange ritual. One can easily understand within the general logic of Merina ideology why returning the corpse to the familial tomb should be occasion for joy and blessing, but it is less easy to see the reason for either the assault on the corpses or for the equally clear, though less direct, assault on women and their emotions.

The answer to the first question concerning the assault on the corpses has been discussed in *Placing the dead* (Bloch, 1971) where I pointed out that the tomb and the descent group are thought of as undifferentiated. This means that individual corpses stand in their individuality against the 'ground-up togetherness' of the tomb, and need to be reduced physically to 'togetherness' to be true, blessing-giving ancestors. The symbolic complex that is denied by this attack is individuality and, inevitably associated with it, specific filiation. Individuality, as we have seen, is also symbolically associated with women in that individual kinship lines are seen as being perpetuated by exclusive and particularistic emotions which are believed to be felt and maintained by women. It is marked by attachment to individual houses which as 'birth places' are also the realm of women.

In this light the assault on women can be represented as an assault on another aspect of the negated totality. Women, like the individual corpses, have to be vanquished before blessing through entry and regrouping in the tomb and the ancestral land can be achieved. The Merina funerary rituals first dramatise an association of women with sorrow, mourning, decomposition and then by an assault on them transcend sorrow, mourning and decomposition. What is being acted out in the *famadihana* is that blessing in unity is achieved through victory over individuals, women, and death itself (in its polluting and

Maurice Bloch

sad aspects) so that these negative elements can be replaced by something else: the life-giving entry into the tomb. This is achieved by breaking through, vanquishing this world of women, of sorrow, of death and division.

The different role of men and women in the *famadihana* shows well how this victory is dramatised. It is only men who enter the tomb, who stand on it, and speak from it on behalf of the community (men and women). It is mainly men and old women who transmit *tsodrano*. On the other hand, it is only young women, mothers and sexually-active women who are forced to come into contact with the corpse and who, by their defeat, transform the corpse into a non-individual, non-biological life-giving force.

Two general points can be made at this stage. The first is that the kind of analysis suggested here would fit in with the generally received anthropological wisdom that death is a challenge to the social order, in this case represented by the tombs, and that funerary practices are ways of transcending individual death to maintain the continuity of that order. I would, however, like to reverse this argument by pointing out that this symbolical order – the eternal non-individualist deme, continuing undivided in its merged representation of people and land – has no material referent. Actually this *image* is created by and in rituals, of which the *famadihana* is one of the most important. When we look at this ritual we can see that in fact the deme in its ideal construction is achieved by acting out a complex dialectical argument. The ideal image is constructed by stressing a phantasmagoric ritually-constructed antithesis – the world of women, pollution, sorrow and individuality. Then, once created dramatically this world is vanquished by the right order of midday, the triumph of the regrouping in the tomb. In other words order is created by the ritual and it is created very largely through dramatic antithetical negative symbolism. What is striking is that the positive is left vague and unelaborated while the negative is much more specifically and concretely represented. We can say that the positive is created by the negative. In this light we can understand what at first is a puzzle: why should a ritual which acts out victory over death so revel in stressing decomposition, pollution and division as the *famadihana* clearly does? The answer is that in order to deny that aspect of things emphatically and thereby 'create' the victory, the enemy must be first set up in order to be knocked down.

Women as agents of death and division therefore have the central role, not only the negative role but also the creative role, since the creation of symbolic order is dependent on negation. Death as disruption, rather than being a problem for the social order, as

218

anthropologists have tended to think of it, is in fact an opportunity for dramatically creating it. More specifically one could here reverse Durkheim's famous insight that it is society which creates the individual and not vice versa, by saying that, in this case at least, it is society which creates the anti-individual and hence creates the illusion of the group and that it does this on the basis of the devaluation of a particular symbolic representation of women.

The third general point is that the order that is achieved and represented through the ritual drama is a non-temporary order of the eternal deme, eternally merged with its lands for ever and ever, and that this apparent permanence is created by the denial of the main discontinuous processes in the social group, i.e. death. More specifically this is achieved by equating and collapsing death with birth. Much of the symbolism of the *famadihana* is a symbolism of birth. Although I was never told directly that entry into the tomb is a kind of birth, several observers have reported this type of statement both for the Merina and for nearby people, and it is implied by much of Merina symbolism. The analysis of the Merina circumcision ceremony confirms this point.

The circumcision ceremony is another major Merina ritual. Like the *famadihana* the circumcision ceremony is seen principally as passing on *tsodrano*. Circumcision is made to stand symbolically in opposition to biological birth, which is defined in the ritual as polluting, as associated with women and individual houses. Throughout the night preceding circumcision, women act out and emphasise their association with biological birth and with the pollution this implies by, for example, putting dirt on their head, one of the most polluting acts for the Merina. However, the dark night of women, of biological birth, of pollution, of the individual house, is acted out only the better to transcend it. At dawn, the boy who is to be circumcised is taken away from the women, who are dancing a mime which emphasises their pollution since it involves them throwing dirt on their head. He is then taken out of the house, to be circumcised, 'cleaned', as the Merina often say, on the threshold. From the threshold the child is then passed to the united men who stand together in the light of morning outside the house, fitting symbols of indivision. The circumcision becomes an alternative and cleansing birth totally different from the divisive polluting, individuating birth which must always take place inside the house.

The same kind of pattern is therefore acted out in the circumcision ceremony as is dramatised in the funerary ceremony. Individual biological birth, like individual biological death, is elaborately represented as associated with women, only to be vanquished so that group unity is asserted by deme entry in the one case, and tomb entry in the other. However, the link up between circumcision and funerary ritual is even closer. Much of the symbolism of the circumcision ceremony, as indeed much of the symbolism of initiation ceremonies throughout the world, refers to the death and tomb. Throughout the circumcision ceremony the notion of cold, which is a symbol associated with the tomb, is stressed in numerous ways. Cold is symbolically opposed to heat which is linked to houses, biological birth, women and disorder. Similarly, in some parts of Madagascar the officiants of the circumcision ceremony actually wear bits of shrouds tied round their waists during the ritual. Most striking of all, the circumcision on the threshold exactly parallels the ritual of the washing of the corpse on the threshold as it is being taken out on the journey which will end in the tomb.

The circumcision ceremony, the socio-moral birth, as opposed to the defiling biological birth, is thus equated in a number of ways to the social death, entry into the tomb, which like social birth is the source of fertility since it is the source of blessing, *tsodrano*. The circumcision ritual declares that social birth is the same as social death, while the *famadihana* declares social death is the same as social birth. Birth and death in their deme aspect are the same. This symbolical collapse of apparent opposites then becomes one of the main elements in the construction of the eternal deme. Indeed, the very notion of the permanent association of undivided people with undivided land, unaffected by time requires this collapse. One can say, therefore, that in Merina ideology the concept of birth and death are systematically collapsed in these rituals and made one by opposing them to an antithesis acted out by women, biological birth and biological death. In the ideological construction nothing is born, nothing dies and therefore nothing is transformed or legitimately transformable.

The points we have considered above can be further demonstrated by referring to the third important ritual of the Merina, the royal bath. Like the circumcision ritual this can only be referred to sketchily but we do already possess a number of analyses of this great ritual (Razafimino, 1924; Molet, 1956; Bloch, 1977).

The ritual of the royal bath occurred every year marking the renewal of the year, of people, and crops. The ritual was, therefore, an occasion on which *tsodrano* was to be transferred, but unlike the rituals of *famadihana* and circumcision, this took place at the level of the state, and not at the level of the deme. In this case the agent of blessing was the monarch, but, as for the other rituals, he was acting as the medium of the ancestors and the ancestral land of the kingdom. The central part of the ritual which gave it its name consisted of the King's taking a bath in pure water in which had been mixed 'earth' obtained from the royal tombs of the royal ancestors. After the bath the king sprayed this water on to his subjects by way of blessing. The elements of blessing and of continuity are therefore identical to those found in the *famadihana* and the circumcision ceremony. As for those rituals, the blessing requires contact with the ancestors on the part of the legitimate head of the group and then the spraying on of water.

The parallel, however, goes much further and two of the main commentators on the ceremony of the royal bath, Razafimino and Molet, have noted the similarity between this ritual and funerary rituals. This is most clear if we take into account the practices preceding the actual day of the bath. On the day before the bath all families in the kingdom had to mourn their dead who had died in the previous year. This mourning took exactly the same form as the mourning at an individual death and was therefore carried out by women. This day of mourning was followed by a night usually referred to as the 'bad night'. During this night estranged husbands could force their wives to spend a night with them. Similarly the night could take on the aspect of what has been described as a sexual orgy, in that men could sexually assault any woman they could lay their hands on, irrespective of the normal rules regulating sexual intercourse. From the accounts we possess it is clear that the central and common element of these practices was rape, i.e. a fundamental assault on women (Callet, 1908:167–8). Then after that bad night, the dawn of the new year came with the royal blessing of the royal bath water scattered on to the subjects.

The ceremony of the royal bath acts out the same logic as the circumcision and *famadihana* ritual. The gift of blessing, of fertility, of renewal of *tsodrano* is achieved by the victory over death, individuality and division, and this victory is won in the successful battle against women. The mourning of the first day focuses on death, decomposition, sorrow, the individual dead and women. The intervening night acts out an assault on the representatives of this antithetical world. The day of the bath is the victory over death, the beginning of the new agricultural year, the blessing of fertility and reproduction. The diagram below shows the common pattern of the three rituals.

However, two other important elements in these rituals come more sharply into focus when we include consideration of the royal bath. Molet's analysis of the ritual of the royal bath is problematical in a

221

Maurice Bloch

Violence		Tsodrano
Night		Day
		Group Death/Birth
		Fertility
Individual Death and Burial		Famadihana
————————————▶	Women	————————————▶
Birth		Circumcision
————————————▶	Women	————————————▶
Individual Death and Mourning		Royal Bath (Fandroana)
————————————▶	Women	————————————▶

number of ways, but what has made it particularly controversial is his assertion that the royal bath, like other Malagasy rituals such as the *famadihana*, had its origin in the practice of necrophagy for the purposes of retaining within the living the substance of the dead of the group. In fact the evidence given by Molet for this bold historical hypothesis is extremely weak. Nonetheless it is quite clear that the symbolical logic we have considered fits in well with the theme of the retention and re-use of life substance in that in a very literal sense the royal bath implies the intimate contact of the living monarch with decayed material from his predecessors. The traditional sources used by Molet seem to imply something like necrophagy in the language they use to talk of this material connection, though this is perhaps simply metaphorical. I believe this is as far as the evidence will go, but that such an interpretation was possible shows us the nature of some of the ideas at work in Merina symbolism and how the notion of the re-creation of life out of death lies at the core of the royal bath ritual.

The second element highlighted by consideration of the ceremony of the royal bath is the political side of Merina funerary rituals. The legitimising aspect of the central participation by the monarch in a ritual of fertility, blessing and renewal is evident. In the royal bath the King places himself as the medium through which the power necessary for the continuation of life has to flow. Furthermore, the association of the King with the eternal order of recurring seasons places his authority outside the vagaries of historical change and beyond the possible challenges of rivals.

222

Permanence and fertility are the two keys to the ritual representation of the monarch but this is also true of the ritual representation of the elders in the parallel rituals of circumcision and above all *famadihana*. As we saw, there also the elders are the necessary medium of eternal *tsodrano*. The legitimacy of their position therefore depends on the created image of the eternal regrouped deme: this mixture of individual ancestors and land, and furthermore the creation of this phantasm itself depends on the emphasis on the decomposition of the body, the pollution of natural birth, the guilt of sorrow and the attribution of all this to women. In this way Merina legitimate authority, whether that of kings or of elders, constructs itself on the reinterpretation and transformation of birth, and above all, of death.

The second part of this chapter moves away from the Merina case to see how far some of the elements identified above can be recognised in other systems.

Rural Merina social organisation is in some aspects dominated by the type of authority characterised by Weber as 'traditional'. Weber meant by this the type of authority which is represented as being a part of an eternal order grounded in nature and/or divinity. This order therefore appears as unchallengeable and so too is the authority which it implies. In such a system, where power is represented as traditional authority, power-holders are legitimised insofar as they appear, not as the makers of their own superiority, but as caretakers of a well-organised world. It is not as individuals that people have legitimate positions in society but because of their positions in the eternal order which they temporarily incarnate. In such systems, therefore, individuality is an obstacle and a challenge to power and it has to be elaborately negated.

I would like to suggest that in social systems like that of the Merina, whose ideological representation implies an unchanging permanent organisation, a kind of victory over individuals has always to be achieved and that this manifests itself in the negation of biological death and biological birth. This victory is what we have seen so fully acted out in the Merina rituals discussed above, although the particular cultural stress on the community of the deme is probably a much more specific manifestation. This victory is necessary because both birth and death imply discontinuity and individuality, things which of their nature are a challenge to the permanent representation of a society based on traditional authority where people are mere caretakers of eternal positions.

I would suggest, therefore, that in all societies where authority is linked to an ideal, unchanging order the funerary rituals have in one way or another to overcome the individuality of a particular corpse and in particular the fact of its individual death which also implies the fact of its individual birth. This is because both death and birth negate the notion of eternal unchangingness. Furthermore, this negation of individuality and of death seems, in nearly all cases, to be acted out by linking it closely with the horror of the pollution of decomposition of the body. In the representation of the funerary ritual individuality is what decomposes and is what has to be thrown out so that the ideological order can be created as an emotional force by first stressing pollution and then getting rid of it. In arguing that pollution and horror of decomposition is used in this ideological way, I am not of course denying that there might be something biological in human repulsion at bodily decomposition, but I am saying that ideology builds on and elaborates the natural in order to reinterpret it. This explains why funerary rituals are not simply ways of coping with decomposition but often rather seem to be occasions for revelling in it.

It follows therefore that in those societies focused on traditional authority there will, as Hertz had noted, always be a double aspect to funerals. One side will focus on pollution and on sorrow, something which in the end has to be removed and another side will always assert the continuity of something else, a reassertion of the vanquishing and victorious order where authority has its legitimate place. This reassertion is what necessitates the negation of the processes of death (and therefore of birth) and the reaffirmation of the eternal order where birth and death are overcome by representing them as the same thing and where therefore everything is fixed for ever and ever.

At first sight those societies which – like the Merina – make this distinction fully by practising some kind of double funeral are relatively few, but in fact this duplication can occur in many different forms. For example, the Indonesian, Melanesian and Chinese opposition between flesh and bones and the different treatment which these should receive seems to be an example of this same ideological bifurcation which leads to the same result. The flesh, the female part, is polluting and has in these cases to be totally dispersed before the bones, the male part, can release their power of fertility and blessing to the next generation. This is the explanation of the temporary burials of Borneo, on platforms away from the earth, on which the flesh of the body must first decay before the bones can be buried so that the social order can reproduce itself. This is also the explanation of the common New Guinea practice of cleaning the bones of one's ancestors of any remains of flesh before these can be used to canalise fertility and the power of the clan.

The division between the polluting element and the life-giving element may, however, take on a less material form. In West Africa for instance we find the distinction noted by Fortes (and one which can be made for many other parts of Africa) between the ancestral soul and the individual destiny (Fortes, 1959). This distinction and the different treatment accorded to the two elements in many ways parallels the distinction between flesh and bones discussed above. The individual destiny is matrilaterally inherited, capricious and dangerous. It has first to be placated and finally got rid of before the ancestors, who represent the structure of the external unchanging order of authority can be properly installed in their shrines and bless their descendants.

This double element is also present in the Christian and Hindu traditions in the distinctions between body and soul. In these religions the body is dirty and decaying while the soul is eternal. In much Christian iconography of the late Middle Ages decomposition of the body is often emphasised so that the purity and incorruption of the liberated soul can emerge all the more strongly by contrast. The body is not explicitly thought of as particularly feminine, but since it is considered particularly biological this links it with a female element in much of the ideology of Christian civilisations (Bloch & Bloch, 1980). Hindu practices insist on the total destruction of the body and at first sight this seems totally different from the careful conservation of the body among the Merina. But on closer inspection this contrast turns out to be superficial. For the Hindus the body has to be totally destroyed, burnt, flushed down rivers, broken up, but this is in order that the soul (the other side of our opposition) may be more easily freed. This contrast parallels the Merina distinction between the body in its first state when it is individually buried and polluting, and its second state when buried in the tomb it is pure and regenerative. In all these funerary systems we find therefore in one form or another the double aspect we noted for the Merina. On the one hand we have an aspect of the dead which is separated in order to rejuvenate the permanent social order and on the other we have the individuating polluting aspect of the corpse, which is emphasised and expelled only the better to clarify and create its opposite.

Not only is the double element discussed above revealed in a great many systems but the symbolic definition and representation of the two sides also often resembles each other in unrelated cultures.

We have already noted how the devalued side, the side of decomposition, is so often acted out by being associated with women while the other side – the eternal order of traditional authority which shines pure and creative against this contrasting background – is

225

associated either with men or with the group as an undifferentiated entity. This contrast is not in any way universal but the inequality between men and women offers a potential symbolical way of expressing the ideologically unacceptable, which is also the means for the symbolic creation of the ideologically sanctioned.

If the polluting aspect of the corpse is often associated with women it is even more common for women to be the channel for the expulsion of the polluting element through mourning. Mourning in the Merina case involves the mourners taking on to themselves the pollution and sorrow of death, as though the mourners had to atone for the death of their kinsmen. By taking on defilement the mourners clean the corpse and liberate it for its re-creation as a life-giving entity. Such elements seem to be central in all types of mourning, but so is the recurrence of the major and dominant role of women in mourning practices all over the world which if not universal is surprisingly common.

It is surely no accident that in nearly all the cultures we know, it is principally women who are expected to weep, whether this be the organised weeping that we find in such places as Iran, or the disorganised individual weeping of Britain or France. Similarly it is again and again the case that it is women who wear mourning in its varying manifestations. The iconography of the crucifixion gives us another example of this with the standard placing of the women at the foot of the cross. Such poems as Kingsley's: 'For men must work and women must weep; and the sooner it's over, the sooner to sleep' again emphasise the same idea. Perhaps most striking of all is the way in which it is women who carry death around with them with their black dresses in the whole Mediterranean area. Again and again women are *given* death while the social order is reaffirmed elsewhere. Thus although European Christian cultures do not make the same connection between flesh and female substance that we find in China or Indonesia, in all those cultures nonetheless it falls to women to take on and take away the sorrow and pollution of death.

If the negative side in funerary ceremonies seems to show the same features again and again, it is not surprising that we also find recurrence on the positive side. This is especially so in the, at first surprising, fact that funerary ceremonies are often linked with fertility and that participation in them is repeatedly seen to lead to increased fertility. This is fertility in the wide sense of the power to reproduce, whether people, plants or animals, or even more generally the 'community' in its symbolic form. The fertility or 'life' which is reaffirmed in funerary practices is above all legitimate fertility often contrasted, as it is for the Merina, with illegitimate individual polluting sexuality.

Ethnographic examples of the notion of fertility, linked with funerary practices have been amassed by Frazer and perhaps some of the most explicit examples are to be found in some of the West African ethnographies on people such as the Mossi, Sara, Dogon and the Lodagaa.

These are all cases which can be explained in the perspective hinted at above where I argued, after Weber and Marx, that what characterises traditional authority is that it is power legitimated as being a matter of caretaking of an eternal and unchanging order: an illusory order which as we saw in the Merina example is created in part at rituals such as funerary rituals.

We also find a great similarity in the way the timeless order is created in funerary and initiation rituals. Again, as with the Merina this order is created by collapsing birth and death and by representing them as the same thing. This is because without the contrast between birth and death, existence becomes simply the product of canalising and retaining creativity within rightful channels. Merging birth and death in the funerary ceremonies is what creates a picture of fertility which transcends the biology of mere dirty mortality and birth. Funerary rituals act out, therefore, not only the victory over death but the victory over the physical, biological nature of man as a whole. Birth and death and often sexuality are declared to be a low illusion, located in the world of women, and true life, fertility, is therefore elsewhere. This is why funerary rituals are an occasion for fertility. This is fertility dispensed by authority, whether it be that of the elders or of the priests, while in the meantime women are left holding the corpse.

Most generally, therefore, funerary practices are central ideological practices in that they are based on the type of three-stage argument which characterises ideology: 1) they take over certain pre-cultural biological and psychological phenomena in order to *re*present them, in this case death, sorrow, pollution; 2) this *representation* then incorporates these phenomena so that they appear homogeneous with legitimate authority, the main manifestation of which is fertility; 3) authority is verified by appearing natural because on the one hand it incorporates the evident processes of biology and on the other it corresponds to deeply felt emotions. Ideology feeds on the horror of death by first emphasising it then replacing it by itself. This process is often carried out at the expense of the humiliation and the attribution of guilt and pollution to women.

In the last part of this paper I want to move away from systems which parallel the Merina example and the ideal type which I have been

227

constructing from it, to clearly different funerary practices and see how far these different systems can be considered as transformations from the example with which I started.

The first variant is really hardly a variant at all and I shall exemplify it by the Greek Homeric system as we find it in the Iliad. One of the features which is striking in the Iliad is that so much of the book is taken up by fighting over corpses, an example of which is the famous episode of the fighting over the corpse of Hector. The central notion which underlies this grisly episode is the ancient Greek value of the perfect youthful body (Humphreys, 1981; Vernant, 1981). The ideal is to die young, in the prime of life, and then for the body to be immediately cremated so that disfiguration and decay do not occur. The image of the uncorrupted youth continues and maintains the undiminished life of the ideal society. The perfect body in itself is the source of the timelessness of the second side of the funeral, in that it represents an unchangingly vigorous martial order of society composed forever of incorruptible heroes. It is interesting in this respect that what defines a 'hero' in this system is his half-divine (immortal) and half-human (mortal) ancestry. Death without corruption removes the mortal half and gets as close as possible to creating an Immortal who belongs in this world (as opposed to the gods who really belong elsewhere). The Homeric funerary practice follows the Malagasy pattern in that the first part involves the mourning and washing of the corpse by women, while the second part involves the eternal fixing of the memory of the uncorrupted body of the hero by cremation, and the association of this perfect strong body with that of its successors by means of the funerary games which follow. In this light it is not difficult to understand why the Trojans want the body of Hector. Without the body they are unable to ensure that it will continue uncorrupted in memory for ever, as they wish their state will remain. Without the corpse, the women can mourn but the regeneration cannot occur.

If it is clear why the Trojans want the corpse of Hector, it is at first less clear why the Greeks are so keen to take it away from them. The reason for this seems to lie in an aspect of all the systems considered so far. In these systems the funerary practices negate individual life and death, and replace it by a notion of continual life, of which individuals are only temporary recipients, and which is taken away from them during the funeral in order that the vitality may be recycled within the group. One might call this a limited good view of life. In such a system, by stopping one's enemies from performing the funerary rituals one diminishes their power. It is to do this that the Greeks want to disfigure Hector's corpse and give it to the dogs. We have therefore in this example our first transformation of the Merina case, a modification which can be called 'negative predation'.

The second transformation is similar and can be labelled 'positive predation'. In these cases it is not a matter of depriving your enemies of their substance by denying them their corpses and the possibility of a funeral. It is rather a matter of taking over their corpses and allocating to yourself the vitality which they hold. This notion is the basis of head-hunting, of which the Jivaro (Harner, 1962) and the Iban offer excellent examples (though in somewhat different ways). With head-hunting the killer takes the substance of his enemies in order to increase himself by this notional means. A slight modification of this pattern is also found in many societies in the Philippines and in New Guinea where the very act of killing gives to the killer the power of his victim. This leads to those elaborate exchanges of corpses or feuds which have been discussed by several ethnographers of the region but especially by de Coppet for Maliata (de Coppet, 1973). Negative predation and positive predation are little more than extensions of the central notions examined so far, that funerals are a matter of recovering a generative power; this being done by canalising away the polluting side of death.

The other two variants we may consider by way of conclusion are radically different. The examples examined above imply a 'limited good notion of fertility of life'. This limited good is transferred by transforming death into life-death in the funerary ritual. This is clearly not always the case. Some funerary rituals only consist of the first of the two sides we have distinguished, the polluting and sad aspect of the funeral; the second half, the ideological creation of timelessness and fertility, is largely absent. The funerary practices of Europe seem to me to fall very largely into that category and this is true also of such people as the Nuer of the Sudan. This difference can probably be explained in terms of the different way in which the source of creativity and continuity is represented in these societies. The societies we have examined so far represent the source of fertility in people. Power is legitimate as it is the canalisation of the fertility of predecessors. In European and Nuer ideology, creativity is attributed to an extra human god in the case of the Nuer, and God and/or capital in western societies. Creativity and legitimate power is in those cases a matter of mediating between these mystical sources of power and ordinary men. In these systems therefore there is no need to transform the corpse into a source of continuing fertility. Authority legitimises itself by associating itself with the dispensation and organisation of these other

Maurice Bloch

reproductive mechanisms which are usually reaffirmed after a death but not as part of the funeral. Death in these cases is still polluting and an occasion for sorrow; it has to be negated as much as in Merina ideology since its occurrence implies discontinuity, but because continuity is reaffirmed elsewhere, we do not have the positive element of creating fertility out of the corpse which is acted out in *famadihana*.

Finally there are those societies which seem almost to ignore the dead, abandon them and do nothing much about them. Examples of such societies are the Siriono and the Hadza (discussed in this volume) where there is no authority except of men over women and where there is therefore no symbolic representation of permanent structures. This means that in those societies, discontinuity and individuality is no threat but only an irrelevance. In these cases there is practically no reason for elaborate funerary rituals. When someone dies one leaves the corpse with as little fuss as possible and then moves on.

ACKNOWLEDGEMENTS

I would like to thank the Anthropology Department of Gothenberg University and especially Professor G. Aijmer for comments on an earlier draft and Dr S. Humphreys and J.P. Vernant similarly. I am grateful to Mrs. H. Jarrett for drawing my attention to the poem by Kingsley.

REFERENCES

Bloch, J. & Bloch, M. 1980. 'Women and the dialectics of nature in 18th century French thought', in *Nature, culture and gender*. eds C. MacCormack & M. Strathern. Cambridge: Cambridge University Press.
Bloch, M. 1971. *Placing the dead*. London & New York: Seminar Press.
   1974. 'Property and the end of affinity', in *Marxist analyses and social anthropology*. ed. M. Bloch. London: Malaby Press.
   1977. 'The disconnection between rank and power as a process. The evolution of states in central Madagascar', in *The evolution of social systems*. eds J. Friedman & M. Rowlands. London: Duckworth.
Callet, R.P. 1908. *Tantaran ny Andriana eto Madagascar* Tananarive (first edition of this version 1878).
de Coppet, D. 1973. 'Premier troc, double illusion', *L'Homme*, **13**, 10–22.
Fortes, M. 1959. *Oedipus and Job in West African religion*. Cambridge: Cambridge University Press.
Harner, M. 1962. 'Jivaro souls', *American Anthropologist*, **64**, 258–72.
Humphreys, S. 1981. 'Death and time', in *Mortality and immortality*. eds S.C. Humphries & H. King. London: Academic Press.
Molet, L. 1956. *Le bain royal à Madagascar*. Tananarive.
Razafimino 1924. *La signification du Fandroana*. Tananarive.
Vernant, J.P. 1981. 'Death with two faces', in *Mortality and immortality*. eds S.C. Humphreys & H. King. London: Academic Press.

Index

Index